D1431664

LITERATURE OF THE
ITALIAN RENAISSANCE

THE MACMILLAN COMPANY
NEW YORK · BOSTON · CHICAGO · DALLAS
ATLANTA · SAN FRANCISCO

MACMILLAN & CO., Limited
LONDON · BOMBAY · CALCUTTA
MELBOURNE

THE MACMILLAN COMPANY
OF CANADA, Limited
TORONTO

LITERATURE
OF THE
ITALIAN RENAISSANCE

By Jefferson Butler Fletcher

NEW YORK
THE MACMILLAN COMPANY
1934

TO MY WIFE

PREFACE

I HAVE digested into this book lectures given to graduate students at Harvard and Columbia during a considerable number of years. The major interest of the majority of these students was in English. My intention, accordingly, was to give them a background of continental literature. The rest of my course dealt with the literatures of Renaissance France and Spain.

Obviously, then, this book makes no pretence of being a thorough literary history of the Italian Renaissance, nor even a formally organized text-book. It offers no especially novel points of view, except such as may come from the individual responses of the writer. The justification of the book, if any, is in the fact that the lectures it embodies have seemed to be stimulating to a number of student generations. And since the material cannot in the nature of things be given much longer as lectures, I have thought it might serve of some use printed.

I am under manifold obligation to many writers, but they are those that any student of the period must know. It seems needless therefore to list them. My special thanks, however, are due to my friend and colleague, Professor William Witherle Lawrence, for valuable criticisms and suggestions.

The translations in the book, unless otherwise attributed, are by the author.

CONTENTS

LITERATURE OF THE
ITALIAN RENAISSANCE

I

RENAISSANCE

RENAISSANCE is the name given to the period of European history following the Middle Ages. At least, this European Renaissance began in Italy. At least, its birth-century was the fourteenth, during which the great triumvirate of Dante, Petrarch and Boccaccio abruptly wrested from France the literary and cultural leadership of Europe. The sixteenth century saw the climax and close of this Italian hegemony. Torquato Tasso, the last great literary figure of the Renaissance in Italy, died in 1595. The climax of the period was reached in the first third of the century, the generation of Ariosto.

The influence of the Italian Renaissance passed over the rest of Europe like a wave. The literary crest of this wave came in France in the middle third of the sixteenth century, or generation of Ronsard,—in England in the last third of the century, or generation of Spenser,—in Spain in the first third of the seventeenth century, or generation of Lope de Vega. In Germany, the violence of the Reformation stifled literary creation, even though intellectually the Reformation itself expressed the individualistic emancipation of the Renaissance. In *belles lettres* sixteenth century Germany has only naïve Hans Sachs and fantastic Johann Fischart to show. Even Holland is richer in Cats, Vondel, Hooft and Huygens. Of these at least Vondel has significance for us in his influence upon Milton. Portugal reflects the Renaissance in Camoens and the

Pastoralists. There were literary stirrings elsewhere,—in Poland for instance.

No doubt the major common factor everywhere was imitation of the Classics. But the rest of Europe chose its classics at Italian dictation, and read them through the coloured glasses of Italian criticism. Renaissance Italian literature, moreover, came to be regarded as a third classic on a parity almost with the masterpieces of Greece and Rome.

The key to the period, accordingly is in Italy.

I

"The Revival of Learning"

Magnus ab integro saeclorum nascitur ordo;
Jam redit et Virgo, redeunt Saturnia regna;
Jam nova progenies, caelo demittitur alto.

("The great line of the centuries begins anew. Now the Virgin returns, the reign of Saturn returns; now a new generation descends from heaven on high.") Italians of the early Renaissance appropriated Virgil's prophecy for themselves. They looked confidently to the rebirth—the renaissance—of a Golden Age, the dawning of a new and better day. Dante translates Virgil's words after his own fashion:

"A new age impends;
Justice returns, and the first time of men;
And a new progeny from heaven descends."

Dante thought that Virgil unwittingly prophesied the birth of Christ. He also, I think, used Virgil's words to predict the return of that Justice which Christ sanctioned and sanctified,— the justice of Caesar, of imperial Rome. Dante—as indeed also Virgil—believed in what since has been called "cyclical

[2]

regeneration," the notion that in some sense history repeats itself in cycles; and he believed that a second Augustan age of Rome was presently to be inaugurated, present usurpation of temporal power by the Roman Church being abolished. Then would return the "first time of men," the time of Innocence in Eden, of Innocence repurchased by Christ's Passion. More sanguinely still, Petrarch addresses the Roman populace of his day as the veritable *"Populus Romanus,* Conqueror of the Nations"—as if imperial Rome were already reborn, or had never died. A generation later, the archaeologist Ciriac of Ancona spent his fortune and himself searching the world through for vestiges,—manuscripts, inscriptions, coins and medals, fragments of marbles and plans of monuments,—of antique Rome. When asked why, he replied: "I go to awake the dead." To jump a century—and a frontier—François Rabelais wrote to a friend: "Out of this thick Gothic night our eyes are opened to the glorious torch of the sun."

No doubt, this self-gratulatory enthusiasm was largely mistaken. Certainly, Dante's and Petrarch's vision of a revived Augustan Empire of Rome and at Rome proved to be a vain dream. The Empire was about to die; the separate sovereign nations of Europe were about to take form.

Grossly unfair, also, is Rabelais' description of the Middle Ages as "a thick Gothic night," *epaisse nuit gothique.* Not long since Professor Grandgent of Harvard delivered an address entitled *The Dark Ages,* slily revealing as he progressed that he meant our own time as in many respects intellectually and spiritually the benighted one. We still use the adjective *medieval* to describe something out-of-date or even barbarous. Our newspapers, for instance, speak of the Nazi terror as "medieval." I am not sure that the Middle Ages were crueller than other periods. They certainly were not stupid or ignorant. Whatever the defects of medieval

[3]

education, it produced a fineness of reasoning, an athleticism of thought, which is today rare. Much that we live by started in the Middle Ages,—our capitalistic system itself, for instance, which first took shape in the medieval Italian communes. There is a certain unfairness in accrediting to the Renaissance a revival of learning, meaning classical learning—as if the Middle Ages were unread in the classics. On the contrary, in all departments of secular knowledge the medieval mind deferred, even slavishly and no doubt uncritically, to Graeco-Roman authority. Medieval theology itself is a synthesis of Scriptural revelation and Greek reasoning. Plato dominates one wing of Catholic opinion, deriving from St. Augustine. Aristotle dominates the other wing, represented by St. Thomas Aquinas. As for faith in the revival of the world-dominion of Rome, that faith has been called "the great illusion" of the Middle Ages. It by no means began with Dante and Petrarch.

Some recent historians, accordingly, deprecate the name Renaissance as carrying an altogether too *cataclysmic* conception of historical development. We should remember that the spokesmen of the so-called Renaissance lived in pre-evolutionary days. We reject their faith in the possibility of abruptly breaking with the past, of treating it as if it had not been, and so of starting afresh. We see too plainly that the past lives on into the present—to thwart us. So, believing that the term Renaissance implies a false philosophy of history, the author of a recent important work on European literature in the fifteenth and sixteenth centuries altogether bans the name, leaving the period, so to speak, anonymous. Yet the same author has written an even more important work on *The Medieval Mind*.

Now surely the European Mind of, say, 1550 deserves a name just as much as the one, say, of 1250. If we will not call the later mentality Renaissance, what shall we call it?

Practically speaking, it is extraordinarily difficult to alter a time-honoured nomenclature. We might continue to use the word Renaissance for convenience, even while grateful for the warnings of its possibly misleading implications. Time indeed corrupts all names.

Moreover, without adventuring into the deeps of philosophy of history or of evolutionary theory (which may admit cataclysms), I may suggest—as a literary chronicler merely —that the idea or ideal of *renaissance*, of rebirth, did produce what may justly be called a cataclysm in the development of a literature.

Consider the literary situation in Italy at about the beginning of the fifteenth century. There is an *Italian* literature sprung as if indeed full-grown from the head of Minerva. Before Dante, Petrarch and Boccaccio,—whose lines overlap, —there was hardly even an Italian literary language; after them, there has been nothing written in Italian of equal collective merit. And then, immediately and suddenly, Italy appears ready to throw this whole magnificent achievement into the discard. At the very beginning of the fifteenth century, in a Latin dialogue, these contemptuous words are put into the mouth of Niccolò Niccoli, a distinguished literary personage of the same Florence that produced the three Masters. An indiscreet interlocutor has dared to make appeal to these last. Niccoli retorts angrily: "What Dantes? what Petrarchs? what Boccaccios? Think you I judge by vulgar opinion? or that I approve or disapprove with the multitude?" I leave Dante, he says, to "butchers and bakers and suchlike folk, for by his choice of language he seems to have wished to be their intimate."

This astonishing attitude was not the whim of an eccentric individual. It was the position taken by the whole higher intelligence of Italy for upwards of seventy-five years more. It was not altogether ingratitude, for all three Masters had insisted upon the unapproachable superiority of Latin. Boccaccio had made the flat declaration that "things in the vulgar tongue cannot make a man of letters," *le cose volgare non possono fare un uomo letterato*. So ruled the father of Italian prose. And the singer of Madonna Laura habitually deprecated his Italian verses, his *rime*, and imputed his *laurel* and his hope of enduring fame to his Latin poetry, and secondarily to his prose Latinity. Niccoli's words were indeed an offence against the Dante who had defended Italian, the *vulgaris eloquentia* that might be, that he himself was creating. But then Dante too had acknowledged the present incomparable superiority of the classical languages made fine art—"grammars" as distinguished from mere spoken idioms—by the supreme poets of antiquity; and he had prescribed imitation of them. Besides, Dante's own Latin was medieval, and crabbedly scholastic. The new school saw nothing of the vigour and finesse, of the liveness, of medieval Latin, international speech of learning that had been shaping since Augustine. Now the one permissible medium not only of learning, but of any enduring work of literature, of cultivated converse itself, was to be the Latin of ancient Rome. The parity of Greek was recognized only later, and then as a purely literary medium.

It is not difficult to date the foundation of this new school, or to name its founder and first headmaster. One has only to compare Petrarch's Latinity with Dante's. In Petrarch's Latin ancient Rome speaks again. In language at least, he by himself inaugurated a real renaissance, embodied an actual rebirth, of classical antiquity. Speaking like antique Romans is not quite indeed being reborn into their life. Still, to renounce one's own language for that of another people is a long step towards naturalization among that people. So Machiavelli recognized when he advised a new prince first of all and above all to impose his own language upon his alien subjects. And such has been imperialistic policy ever since. Everywhere also, a prime requirement for naturalization has been ability to speak the language.

Petrarch's life-aim was to satisfy that prime requirement for citizenship in ancient Rome revived,—to satisfy it himself, and to induce his compatriots to satisfy it also. So might he and they reënter into their birthright. Dante ever testifies to his pride—even excessive pride (*Par.* xvi, 1 ff.)—in his Roman blood. If he accepted a German like Henry of Luxembourg as legitimate successor to Caesar,—one whom his fellow-Florentines scorned as "a petty German prince,"—it was because he held the crowning and anointing of Henry at Rome to be a mystical naturalization.

Patriotic hope of actual restoration of the *imperium Romanum* hardly persisted beyond the fourteenth century. Symonds thinks it died with Rienzi. The patriotic motive of the classical revival in Italy was perforce modified. In 1444, seventy years after Petrarch's death, the representative humanist Lorenzo Valla pithily sums the new aspiration. He admits with Dante that Italy is no longer "mistress of provinces," that Rome has lost her world-dominion, but, he declares, "Wherever the Roman language is spoken, there is the Roman empire," *Ubicumque est parlata lingua Romana, ibi est imperium Romanum*. These significant words are set in the preface to a thesaurus of Latin phrases, *Elegantiae latinae linguae*.

This title became indeed the text governing for the most part intellectual activity in fifteenth century Italy. The common objective was to become adept in the "elegances of Latin speech." For that reason Valla's thesaurus had enormous vogue, was as "useful," as Erasmus was later to declare, "as the fingers of one's hand." Elegant Latinity, *eloquentia*,— the two terms amount to the same thing,—became the acid test for all literary expression, oral or written. It covered as many sins as charity. One of the most highly praised poems of the century celebrated sodomy; another syphilis; both were full of Latin elegances. University professors threw disgusting verbal filth at one another—to show the range of their Latin vocabularies. Poggio Bracciolini justified his indecent *Facetiae* on the same ground. Indeed, the fairest way of taking the bulk of fifteenth century humanist writings is as exercises in Latin composition. Theme and content were of altogether secondary importance. Moreover, his mind fixed upon antiquity, the humanist affected scorn for mere contemporary happenings. Dante and Petrarch were intensely concerned with the live issues of their day; Poggio Bracciolini remarks passingly upon the inevitable ruin of his divided country, but shrugs the matter aside as beneath his interest. "I shall follow letters," he says; *Ego sequar litteras.*

Such an attitude,—and it was fairly typical,—hardly suggests any patriotic motive whatever, whether political or cultural. The possession of elegant Latinity, of *eloquentia*, became a valuable asset. It was the making of professors, ambassadors, even popes. Tommaso Parentucelli spoke so eloquently—that is, in such elegant Latin—at the funeral of Pope Eugenius IV that he was elected to succeed him as Nicholas V; and the fittingly principal achievement of this scholarly Vicar of God was the foundation of the Vatican Library. Nicholas was followed by another polished Latinist, who was also author of a widely popular society romance better in style than in morals. Aeneas Silvius Piccolomini assumed the title of Pius II less, it is said, as a reminder to Christian piety than of Virgil's *Pius* Aeneas. Caustic Gregory

Heimburg said of Pius II: "Great is eloquence; subtract it from this pope, and nothing remains."

Latin eloquence was an asset to the individual; the so eloquent individual was an asset to the state. Pius II had in his earlier days written to an English friend, the Bishop of Chichester and Keeper of the Privy Seal: "Persevere, therefore, friend Adam. Hold fast and increase the eloquence you possess; consider it the most honorable thing possible to excel your fellows in that in which men excel other living creatures. Great is eloquence; nothing so much rules the world. Political action is the result of persuasion; his opinion prevails with the people who best knows how to persuade them." The Duke of Milan, enemy of Florence, testified that the eloquence of her Chancellor, Colluccio Salutato, had damaged him more than a thousand horsemen.

Particularly to the fifteenth century despot was an eloquent tongue or pen useful to have in his service. Many if not most of these new princes were also *new* socially—successful politicians like the Medici in Florence, or victorious soldiers of fortune, *condottieri*, like the Gonzagas of Milan. Not a few—like the powerful Ferrante of Naples—bore on their arms the bar sinister. As poet laureate, historiographer, envoy, advocate, a trained master of eloquence might whitewash tyranny and transmute brutality and treachery into seeming heroism and statesmanship. Even an ancient ruling house like that of Este at Ferrara showed itself eager to immortalize itself and to add lustre to its court by works of eloquence. Successful humanists became fully aware of their own value. Francesco Filelfo recommends his services to the Sultan, saying: "I am one of those who, celebrating with eloquence illustrious deeds, make immortal them that by nature are mortal."

The humanist's most immediate and widest opportunity for livelihood and influence was by instruction in his new art of eloquence itself. As private tutor, schoolmaster, professor, he became the educational director first of Italy and then of Europe. He formulated the curriculum and methods of the classical, or liberal, education which prevailed with little change until almost our own day. The original stress in the humanist curriculum upon good Latinity, *eloquentia,* is in some degree still maintained at Oxford in the time given to Latin composition.

The two outstanding classical professors of the century were Guarino of Verona for the first half, Poliziano for the second. Both drew mature students also from without Italy. To Guarino's final lecture hall at Ferrara came the Englishmen William Grey, later Bishop of Ely, the poor wandering student John Free, the later Dean of Wells, John Gunthorpe, Robert Flemming, and the brilliant and cultured if tyrannical and cordially hated Earl of Worcester, John Tiptoft. About Poliziano gathered such men as Grocyn, Linacre, Latimer and the German Reuchlin. Guarino was more the pure grammarian; Poliziano, poet as well, taught *eloquentia* by example as well as by precept, preluding his lectures by original poems in the language and style of the authors under discussion. Meanwhile, the idea of the English public school, —to be given definitive shape by Dean Colet at the beginning of the sixteenth century,—was anticipated in principle three-quarters of a century earlier by Vittorino da Feltre in his *Casa Gioiosa,* or "House of Joy," outside Mantua. There living with his boys, he instilled the Greek ideal of the sound mind in the sound body, and succeeded in making study of the classics a pleasure as well as a discipline. He received others besides sons of the rich and aristocratic, insisting only upon character and intelligence. Vittorino's influence indeed evidenced a true renaissance of the spirit,—the spirit rather of Athens than of Rome.

Indeed, as all hope of a political revival of Rome died

away, and it was realized that the descendants of the Romans must, as Valla said, look only to an empire of language, of culture, Greek assumed increasing importance. For after all, Rome owed to Greece the best in her culture, and especially in her literature and art. For Dante Virgil was "most-high poet," *poeta altissimo,* but Homer was "sovereign poet," *poeta sovrano,* and Virgil's only begetter. But Dante's admiration for Homer was wholly by hearsay. He knew no Greek; and of translation in any real sense there was none, only crude paraphrases of the story of Troy. Petrarch and Boccaccio were little better off. They doubtless had more critical knowledge about Homer, but they could not read him. Petrarch did indeed induce a certain Byzantine Greek to undertake a Latin translation of the *Iliad,* but he was disgusted with the result. Only a generation later, a Francesco Filelfo could declare himself—let us hope somewhat in the spirit of jest—the superior of Virgil as an orator, and of Cicero as a poet, and of both as eloquent in Greek as well as in Latin.

A considerable impulse was given to the study of Greek by the conclave at Ferrara and Florence in 1438–9 of representatives of the Greek and Roman Churches. Hope of healing the schism between East and West failed, but the coming of the Greeks to Italy was not fruitless. Among them came some notable Greek scholars,—one indeed remaining to become a cardinal of the Roman Church, Bessarion. Not only did he—and others—disseminate interest in Greek language and literature, but also as Neo-Platonists inspired Cosmo de'Medici to found the Platonic Academy of Florence from which the literary Platonism of the Renaissance derived. Much stress has been laid upon the influence and teaching of Greek exiles from Constantinople after its capture by the Turks in 1453, but few of these men counted for much.

Although the Middle Ages possessed a by no means meagre

library of classical authors, the questing zeal of the fifteenth century humanists added materially, recovering among many long-lost texts some destined to be of prime importance in the directing and forming of later European thought and taste,—such as, for instance, Aristotle's *Poetics,* Plautus's comedies, Quintilian on oratory, Vitruvius on architecture. Even more important than these accretions, however, was the development of a juster historical and aesthetic perspective in the reading of ancient authors. Developing also was a method of textual criticism anticipating not only that of modern philology, but of modern science as well. A startling early triumph was Valla's decisive proof by linguistic tests that the deed of the so-called Donation of Constantine— warrant of the major temporal dominion of the Papacy— was a forgery of a much later period.

Self-dedicated as the humanists may have been to *eloquentia,* two generations of intelligent men could not absorb themselves in pagan writings to whatever formal end without these also materially affecting their mental and moral outlook. Inevitably these *litterae humaniores* became unchristian, even antichristian, propaganda, expressing as they did beautifully and persuasively pagan ideas and ideals. The most eminent of fifteenth century humanists, Lorenzo Valla, was also the most antichristian in the tendency of his teaching. At the least, "humaner letters" became in effect letters turning men's attention from things divine to things human. Humanism, begun as a literary gospel, developed into a gospel of life, presenting the perfectibility of humanity itself as the supreme end and highest good. Paganism penetrated into the very Church. A succession of such Popes as Nicholas V, Pius II, Sixtus IV, Alexander VI, Julius II, Leo X, Clement VII —themselves humanists or at least alumni of *litterae humaniores* rather than of *litterae divinae,* connoisseurs of the fine arts and polished men of the world—could not fail to infect the whole ecclesiastical hierarchy under them. Under Leo X Rome seemed to have returned to the days of Augustus. Once more God was called Jove; the saints were rebaptized as gods and goddesses; heaven was transformed into Olympus; the pontifex assumed the title of *Divus* and *Optimus Maximus;* cardinals were hailed as senators; a bull was burned in the Coliseum at the death of the Pope to placate the powers of evil. One cardinal of the Church, Bembo, advises another, Sadoleto, to "avoid the Epistles of St. Paul, lest his barbarous style should spoil your taste."

In spite of lip-service to Christian ethics,—or at least to austere Stoic doctrine,—the real moral philosopher of the humanists was Epicurus. Valla again—in a highly significant essay, which I shall discuss in its place—frankly declares pleasure to be the highest good. He means pleasure of the senses, and holds beauty to be the highest enjoyment of the highest sense, which is sight. Later the Neo-Platonist Marsilio Ficino was to elevate this gospel of sensible Beauty into one of intellectual Beauty; and Ficino's chief apostle to the laity was to be Pietro Bembo, who died a cardinal of the Church. Quite in the spirit of Valla, however, Bembo's superior, Leo X is said to have exclaimed upon hearing of his elevation to the seat of St. Peter: "Let us enjoy the Papacy now that God has given it to us."

II

The Italian Revival

Boycott upon Italian as a literary medium was not altogether absolute—even among professed humanists. Indeed, the most variously gifted of them all, Leo Battista Alberti, defended and praised it. Alberti was one of the three truly universal men of the Renaissance, the other two being Leonardo da Vinci and Michelangelo Buonarroti. Painter, sculptor, architect, he also wrote notably upon these arts. He was a distinguished mathematician and physicist, incidentally a famous athlete. As humanist, among many Latin works he wrote a comedy that experts mistook for a lost original. He also, however, wrote much in Italian, especially an essay *On the Family,* which is still good reading, and holds its own among the numerous conduct-books of the next century. Furthermore, Alberti planned a systematic campaign for the rehabilitation of the vernacular. There was to be a yearly contest, in which the best poem was to be awarded a laurel wreath. One is reminded of the German *Meistersänger* and of the *Puys* in southern France. One such *certame coronario* was held in the Duomo of Florence in the year 1441, but no prize was awarded, and the experiment was not repeated. Not until the next generation was humanistic disdain for the vulgar tongue effectively challenged.

Writing in Italian indeed, was a man whose challenge might have been serious enough if only his writings had seen the light in his day. Unfortunately, the extensive manuscripts of Leonardo da Vinci are being published for the first time now. Consequently, their amazing range of interest and felicitous style were without influence in his time.

Little or nothing else of lasting significance in Italian was produced during the first three-quarters of the fifteenth century. The only real exception would be anonymous folksong, and the charming imitation of it by the Venetian humanist Leonardo Giustinian.

The Florentine vernacular indeed showed the greatest vitality, even if nothing notable was produced in it during these times. After all, it was the medium—in the raw—of Dante, Petrarch, Boccaccio. Also, the continuingly vigorous and individualistic life of the Florentines called for a self-expression for which no dead language however *eloquent* was adequate. These sturdy and downright burghers had naturally little taste for the ornate artificiality and remoteness of the *eloquentia* of the humanists, even if they understood it. Sooner or later Florence was bound to break the absurd ban upon her "noble vernacular," her *eloquentia vulgaris*. In Lorenzo the Magnificent she had the fortune to find a champion of the Tuscan speech of twofold power,—power to defend and voice it as critic and poet, and power to make his purpose prevail as patron and virtual prince. Also, he vitalized the cause of an Italian revival by a profession of patriotic faith, promising a literary achievement to Florence proportionate to her "prosperous success" as a nation.

Thus in Lorenzo a new national spirit is asserted. At the same time, he still, like Dante, admits the superiority of classical Latin, and urges the ennoblement of Italian by imitation of it. In his own poetry he set example of such imitation,—an example even more effectively followed by his dependent and friend, Angelo Poliziano.

But even while preaching and practising imitation of the classics, Lorenzo was too much of a realist, too much of a Florentine burgher, to imitate slavishly or by rule. Rather—to use Du Bellay's and Sidney's figure—he, and still more Poliziano, devoured the classics whole and made them wholly his; then wrote as his spirit, so fed and informed, moved him. At times indeed, he threw off his humanist gown to compose in the tunic of Florentine realism, and in the idiom unadorned also of the Tuscan peasant. In this realistic vein he was emulated and surpassed by another intimate and dependent, the humourist Luigi Pulci.

As instigator and director of the Italian revival, Lorenzo has imposed his name upon his generation. The last third of the fifteenth century is called the Laurentian age. Thanks predominantly to his genius, Florence then led in politics, literature, art. Yet, as it happened, there were stirrings both north and south, in Ferrara and in Naples.

In the gay and pleasure-loving Ferrarese court, revival of Italian literary art was hardly inspired by any patriotic ardour. It was rather, on the whole, a response to feminine demand for entertainment. Dante had long ago explained the origin of vernacular love-poetry as a condescension to unlearned ladies. By the end of the fifteenth century indeed, ladies of the court of Ferrara were by no means unlearned. Most of them had been tutored by humanists, and knew some Latin, and perhaps a little Greek; still, they would probably enjoy more easily plays, poems, romances in the mother-tongue. Highly educated Duchess Isabella d'Este herself writes to Venice for books of chivalry and romance, "especially," she says, "about the paladins of France." Many writers, local or imported, were already catering to the court taste, but one of them, Count Matteo Maria Boiardo by an enduring master-piece, the *Orlando Innamorato*. The title betrays its gallant motivation: the unconquerable paladin of France must at last bow in surrender—to a fair woman.

The share of Naples in the Italian revival was in a sense accidental. Her one significant contribution was the pastoral romance *Arcadia* by Jacopo Sannazaro. Sannazaro was a prominent humanist and Latin poet, pupil and friend of a still greater Latin scholar and poet, Pontano, who wrote, however, nothing in the vernacular. If at the turning of the century, Sannazaro published the Italian *Arcadia*, a work of his youth, it was—to take his word for it—because, while he was living as an exile in France, the manuscript of the piece had been purloined, and piratically printed in an edition full of errors. He might, he declares, have been willing to let his base offspring die, but if it apparently was to live, he would at least do justice by it. But he would have been unpleasantly amazed to learn that this Cinderella of his begetting was destined to outlive the grave and serious works of his maturity written, as he believed, in imperishable Latin.

III

The Full Renaissance

Italian literature, renascent in the age of Lorenzo, attained full maturity in the generation following, and then went into a decline broken by intermittent bursts of vitality. Lorenzo de'Medici was in principle right when he associated the possible triumph of Italian language and letters with the "prosperous success" of the Italian state. He was thinking of Florence, but the fate of Florence was linked with that of Italy. By the end of the first third of the sixteenth century the precise opposite of any prosperous success had happened. Florence, all Italy, had become politically enslaved. By irony of fortune, the Pope Clement VII who finally sold Florence was the bastard of Giuliano, Lorenzo's murdered brother, and saved and brought up by Lorenzo himself.

The fulminations of Dante and Petrarch against local divisions and jealousies were abundantly justified by the events of the fifteenth century. Most of the city-states had hardened into despotisms subject to the irresponsible caprice and selfishness of the political gamesters and soldiers of adventure, their masters. No doubt Lorenzo de'Medici himself was a political "boss" and a despot, but though his methods may have been unscrupulous, his vision was clear as to the perils of disunion and discord. With consummate address, he maintained during his lifetime a truce between the five chief Italian powers—Florence, Milan, Rome, Venice, Naples—on the basis of a

[17]

balance of power. It was a triumph of personal courage and diplomacy. At his death in 1492 the fragile structure of peace collapsed. Italy illustrated once again the fable of the bundle of faggots. The frivolous invasion of Charles VIII of France in 1494 showed up her helplessly disunited state. Her conquest was thereafter delayed, not by any effective resistance of hers, but by the fact that both France and Spain wanted her, and had first to settle with each other. For a while the desperate game of the militant Pope Julius II of playing off one invader against the other postponed the catastrophe; but Julius's successor, indolent and pleasure-loving Leo X, was no match for Francis I or Charles V. The end came in 1527. Francis disposed of, Charles's forces under the Constable of Bourbon took and sacked Rome. It was not only the destruction of a city; it was the final pricking of the bubble of imperial greatness for the Italians—final, until perhaps our own day. The patriotic urge which started and sustained the Renaissance in Italy ceased abruptly. Florence indeed held out three years longer, only, as I have said, to be betrayed by Clement VII, nephew of the great Lorenzo himself. Thereafter Medici dukes rule over Florence, but more and more must take their orders from Madrid or Vienna. Italy ceases to be even potentially a nation and becomes in Metternich's sneering phrase "a geographical expression."

Machiavelli, Castiglione, Ariosto—the three outstanding writers of the full Renaissance react diversely to the tragic conditions of their country. None more clearly than Machiavelli foresaw the impending catastrophe, but as the famous last chapter of the *Prince* proves, he did not altogether lose hope. Another new prince like Caesar Borgia, with fortune as well as ability, *virtù*, might weld the *patria* into iron resistance, and save it. It was to that justifying end that the "strong medicines" of so-called "Machiavellism" were to be administered. Castiglione reflects another Italy—not the political ruin but the social pattern, "the glass of fashion and the mould of form" for all Europe. In the serene and gracious world of his *Courtier* there is no hint of domestic dissension or of foreign peril. The palace at Urbino is an ivory house of dream where stately yet gallant gentlemen discuss with refined yet witty ladies matters light and grave touching good society. The Courtier's highest function is to advise his Prince, but what counsel would be his in these troublous times is not told. He is by definition high-minded, but his morality is the code of honour among gentlemen, and his religion the love of beauty in ladies. Castiglione's ideal is a modernized knight-errantry, elegantly noble but disdainfully aloof from vulgar actuality. Ariosto gave entertainment for the courtly society that Castiglione depicts. But Ariosto was not merely the court entertainer. Sincere patriot also, he foresaw what Machiavelli foresaw—but without hope. His *Orlando Furioso* is a poetic tale of faerie and illusion, but it also reflects the poet's deeper mood of disillusionment and tragic irony. Also, Ariosto was personally out of tune with the frivolous and sycophantic court-life itself.

Forlorn hope, bland unconcern, ironic humour—such are the respective moods towards their country's plight of these three "master-craftsmen of the mother-tongue." Most other writers of the period, even before 1530 and nearly all thereafter, seem like Castiglione to ignore what is going on. The historian Guicciardini coldly explains the disastrous situation, and cynically advises his compatriots to forget it and look to their private interests—as he was doing. A nobler stoicism finds expression in a few poems by Michelangelo, military engineer of Florence in her last stand; but the majority by choice or by discretion follow Guicciardini's advice. Their attitude is Poggio's *Ego sequar litteras.* High priest of this academic class is Pietro Bembo, Cardinal and elegant man of the world, humanist, purist, platonist and Petrarchist, sentimental poet and witty if indecent playwright. In his following *belles lettres* become formally polite letters. His audience is a polite one, which he aims to make politer still. The Florentine Neo-Platonic gospel of beauty is to be the refining influence—with ladies of fashion dispensing it. The hymnal of its ritual of gallantry and good form will be of Petrarchan sonnets tempered to the proprieties of the drawing-room. For Bembo the Tuscan of Petrarch and Boccaccio is not merely a noble vernacular, it is a sacred one, which to alter or depart from would be profanation. Words or phrases not used by the two Masters are vulgar, and cannot make a man of letters. Boccaccio, who had said as much of *all* "things in the vulgar tongue," would have been amused to find his own vulgar things a consecrated exception.

IV

Decline of the Renaissance

Ascription of causes is always risky, and it may be that other factors were cumulatively as responsible for the decline of Italian literature after 1530 as the loss of national independence, but at least the two were coincident. Machiavelli died in 1527, year of the sack of Rome. Castiglione lived on until 1529, but the *Book of the Courtier,* on which his fame rests, had been written over twenty years before. Ariosto died in 1533, but forty of the forty-six cantos of his masterpiece had been published as early as 1516. After 1530, only one poet and one prose work rise significantly above the mediocre level—Torquato Tasso and Benvenuto Cellini's autobiography.

Tasso's masterpiece is indeed the exception that proves the rule. Its title implies a mood of heroic patriotism, the new and larger patriotism of Christendom against the invading Turk. Tasso appealed to a real enthusiasm born of desperate peril. But once the peril allayed with the victory of Lepanto, Italians were already too weakened in moral fibre to retain or even to appreciate an heroic mood. Nor had Tasso an heroic temper. Ariosto, for all his surface levity, had more. Tasso's poetic virtue is in the sentimentally idyllic and preciously decorative. He is at his best in the porcelain daintiness of his pastoral *Aminta*. What lives in his epic—or rather romance—of the first crusade is the prowess, not of Christian warriors, but of the subtle siren Armida. If there is an heroic figure, it is that of the beautiful pagan amazon Clorinda, a heroine out of the medieval romances of adventure. And she is most appealing in the pathos of her death—at the hands unwittingly of her lover. Pathos again and tenderness are the appeal of Erminia, model of Spenser's Pastorella and of Shakespeare's Perdita. Indeed, Tasso's more convincing characters are women. His own temperament was tainted with effeminacy. His poem, beautiful as it is, is nearer to the mood of grand opera than to great epic.

Still, taking him for what he is, Italians rate him as one of their four supreme poets, Dante, Petrarch and Ariosto being the other three. Curiously, he holds this high place in spite of himself. For in submission to pseudo-classic theory and reactionary clerical prudery working upon his undoubtedly diseased sensitiveness, he would have suppressed the *Gerusalemme Liberata*, creation of his own free genius, and did sanction publication only of the *Gerusalemme Conquistata*, a pitifully emasculated and stupid revision. Even with allowance for mental disorder, Tasso's story dramatically illustrates the prevailing loss of personal independence in

Italy consequent upon her loss of national independence. The *Gerusalemme Liberata* was, like Sannazaro's *Arcadia*, saved only by a literary piracy.

Perhaps, again, the extraordinary freedom and frankness of Benvenuto Cellini's autobiography are due to the fact that he seems to have had no intention of publishing it, at any rate during his life. Although circulated in manuscript, it was not printed until 1728. Also, neither scholar nor man of letters, he was totally free from the cramping influences of current academic rules and standards. He wrote as he would, and with a power of evoking the very substance of things seen or enacted such as no literary realist ever or anywhere has surpassed.

Consequently, his story is not merely *his* story. It is a series of revelations—through an individual temperament, to be sure—of Renaissance society in Italy—and to some extent in France—in its heights and depths. For if Benvenuto was at home in Bohemian quarters, as artist he had the entrée to courts and drawing-rooms. His picture, accordingly, is a valuable corrective of Castiglione's idealized one as giving the nakeder truth of Renaissance society.

To resume. After 1530 Italian literature, as well as Italy, lost its independence. To repressive political censorship were added ecclesiastic and academic. The Catholic reaction which culminated in the Council of Trent of 1570 became inquisitorial in inverse proportion to its real appeal to Italian educated classes. Piety became the fashion, but it was only a fashionable piety. Under the hard glitter of court life were frivolity and cynicism. Orthodoxy was a pride of caste. Cultured Italy disdained the northern Protestants as cultured Rome had disdained the early Christians—less for heresy than for social crudity, as barbarians. For the rest, it was easy to conform—and talk about other things. The cost of not doing so was found out by Bruno and Galileo, and others who might venture to discuss live issues of belief or knowledge.

Hardly less rigorous than the Holy Inquisition was the academic criticism,—virtually, that is, the criticism of Academies. From these edicts were issued with the solemnity of official decrees. They professed the authority of the ancients, especially of Aristotle and Horace; but the literary precepts of these and other classical critics and the practice of the poets were digested into a code of rules. This code every modern writer on peril of his reputation must follow, and might follow without necessarily reading a line of any ancient author whatever. The ludicrous consequences of such a literary method show themselves in a work like Trissino's *Italia Liberata dai Goti,* as will be illustrated hereafter.

The ceaseless critical theorizing of the Italians and their untiring clash of literary debate were not without profit. The classicist canon emerging, stultifying as it might be if followed in the manner just described, also proved a valuable discipline to really creative minds like a Ben Jonson's or a Racine's. With modifications, this classicist canon dominated European literature for two centuries to come.

In some measure, the mid-sixteenth century repeated the tendencies of the mid-fifteenth. At both times formalism strangled naturalness and spontaneity. But the activity of the printing-press had widened the general reading public, and given it a new independence. The ban on religious and political discussion could be enforced, but less easily on taste. Court and town alike demanded entertainment after their own hearts, regardless whether what they liked was properly "regular" or not. For the most part it was not. The experience of the elder Tasso is typical. Having begun his *Ama-*

digi according to the rules, he read a canto to the assembled courtiers. Before he had done, the hall was empty. So he started again, and threw all rules to the winds. Howevermuch classic forms might be praised and enjoined, the native sonnet remained the preferred lyric form, and was made the medium for every mood from sublimated platonic sentiment to ribald satire. The Boccaccian *novella* ran the gamut of thrills from romantic pathos to crude horror and cynical indecency. The *commedia dell'arte* with its caricatured local types, spontaneous dialogue and "gags," free business, bustle and horseplay made universal appeal, even to those who theoretically held the *commedia erudita*—comedy according to the rules—the only *right* comedy.

Italy's influence through these and other popular and non-classic kinds was no less than through her establishment and illustration of the classicist canon. The vogue of the sonnet spread throughout Europe. By his sonnets Ronsard, head as he was of the classicist school in France, really survives. Shakespeare would still be acclaimed had he written only his sonnets. The *novella* propagated itself by translation and imitation in French, English, Spanish, incidentally supplying plots, situations, characters to the drama of all three countries. Apart from more general influences, the *commedia dell'arte* shaped the comic genius of Molière.

II

DANTE

TO start with Dante in a discussion of the Renaissance calls for explanation. Is he not said to sum up the Middle Ages? Is not the *Divine Comedy* to be compared to a Gothic cathedral in contrast to a Greek temple or a Renaissance basilica? Dante was early recognized as *il gran teologo:* a "great theologian"—especially a Scholastic one—is hardly a Renaissance type. Dante's thinking was largely, if not chiefly, on political issues, and his point of view in these was reactionary, advocating restoration of a Roman Empire actually moribund, and loyalty to a Caesar not really Roman at all. "An upstart German prince" Dante's fellow-Florentines called the Henry of Luxembourg that Dante was hailing as "Caesar august and divine." Actually, they, not he, voiced the spirit of the incoming age of the separate sovereign nations of Europe.

All this is true. In his two major interests, in theology and politics—the science of God and the science of government —Dante held to medieval theory. Carducci, poet of the new Italian nation, scorns Dante's ideals of church and state while he exalts his "poetry." "I hate," he declares in a noted sonnet, "I hate thy holy empire . . .

> Empire and church are melancholy ruins
> Over which soars thy song and unto heaven
> Resounds."

[25]

No doubt Carducci's own nationalistic and sceptical views have led him to overstatement. Dante's Roman Empire may have gone to ruin, but hardly so his Roman Catholic Church. At the same time, I think it safe to say that the temper of church doctrine has changed materially since the Middle Ages. And I venture to think the most fundamental change is towards a more *humane* interpretation of dogma. For instance, churchmen would still agree, I suppose, that the damned are God's enemies, but I am confident that they would no longer hold to the opinion of their medieval predecessors that one of the joys of the blessed is to behold the sufferings of the damned.

Now the poet in Dante modified in very much the same way his theological doctrine. Dante is, and always has been, best known as the author of the *Inferno*. In consequence, he is commonly thought of as a stern, hard, vindictive man, given to putting his enemies into Hell. The picture is a libel. Dante put no private enemies into his Hell, only public ones, enemies of God and mankind. He is obedient to the injunction in the poem:

> "This thy cry shall do as doth the wind,
> Which beateth hardest on the highest peaks;
> And that is no slight proof of a just mind."
> [*Par.* xvii, 133-5]

Against wrong-doers in high places, recreant leaders and false guides, he is indeed scornful,—but only as against such. Carlyle, after all, read the truth out of the Giotto portrait of Dante when he saw "as foundation of it, the softness, tenderness, gentle affection as of a child," and, deeper still, recognized "a soft ethereal soul looking-out so stern, implacable, grim-trenchant, as from imprisonment of thick-ribbed ice." No doubt no one—not even with Scotch second-sight—could have seen all this from that one dimmed portrait alone, but the characterization, allowance being made for the Carlylean rhetoric, is, I think, a true one. Intellectually, Dante was "tough-minded" enough, of tremendous mental grasp and logical precision. The architecture of the *Divine Comedy*, at once colossal and delicate, is sufficient evidence of his virility of mind. But in temperament he was of extreme, of feminine sensibility.

This native sensibility continually moves the poet to modify the rigours of dogma accepted by the *"gran teologo,"* the "great theologian." As Pascal said, *"le coeur a ses raisons."* As an orthodox believer, Dante surely accepted the doctrine of original sin and its consequence, the vitiation of natural human impulses; yet nevertheless he can say that naturally men are of good will, well-meaning:

> "Ben fiorisce negli uomini il volere."
> [*Par.* xxvii, 124]

But though good in the bud, their will is blighted in the fruit by the false guidance of greed-ridden leaders. So are they more sinned against than sinning.

> "False guidance is the cause, as thou canst see,
> Which makes the world to be so full of guilt,
> And not your nature's own depravity."
> [*Purg.* xvi, 103-5]

"E non natura che in voi sia corrotta"—such a dictum would have been, I think, anathema to St. Augustine or St. Thomas, not to say Calvin or the author of the *Imitation of Christ.* On the other hand, trust in natural human impulses was the very basis of the philosophy of such typical Renaissance thinkers as Lorenzo Valla and François Rabelais.

Still more patently unorthodox was Dante's attitude towards certain of the damned. He should have been, as I have said, at the least indifferent to the sufferings of God's enemies. He is well aware of this. His own Virgil rebukes him for weeping at the tragically deformed soothsayers:

> " 'And art thou yet
> Among the other fools?' my Leader cried.
> 'Here lives true piety when pity dies.
> Who is more reprobate than he that scans
> The doom of heaven with protesting eyes?' "
> [*Inf*. xx, 26-30]

Dante does not hesitate to break a solemn promise to a damned spirit, merely remarking

> "That to be rude to him was courtesy."
> [*Inf*. xxxiii, 150]

On another occasion he kicks—accidentally, to be sure—a helpless culprit in the face. He is not in the least sorry; and when the same individual refuses to give his name, Dante pulls out a handful of hair. Now this is not very sporting, but it is quite orthodox.

But the poet is delightfully inconsistent. Towards certain sinners his Virgil urgently enjoins "courtesy" (*Inf*. xvi, 13-18). Dante himself swoons in pity for Paolo and Francesca, is affectionately reverent towards his old teacher Brunetto Latini, is admiringly eager to hear Ulysses, is passionately indignant at the horrible fate of Count Ugolino and his sons. In all these cases, and some others, human pity defies orthodox piety. The Renaissance speaks.

Again, in his picture of Purgatory Dante humanizes a repellently inhuman medieval conception. His master in theology, Thomas Aquinas, imagines Purgatory as a dark underground cavern alongside of Hell. About its only difference from Hell is that its torments are not everlasting. It is in effect a debtors' prison, where "toll of tears" is taken for sins unpaid for in life. An exacting God—one is tempted to say a supreme Shylock—demands it.

Dante would not have denied the validity of this legalistic conception of divine justice, but he transforms it imaginatively into a gracious and humane symbolism. The dark underground cavern becomes a tall mountain, sunlit by day and starlit by night; and on its top is a pleasant shaded garden tended by a lovely maiden. The pilgrim penitents pass through pain and torment, but they suffer joyfully; for they take their penance, not as the enforced payment of a debt, but as a desired cleansing of their souls, a beautifying of these for the heavenly bridals to come. God is for them no Shylock, but the Good Physician.

This humanity, or humaneness, of the *poet* Dante might be, if you will, only an emotional response, an impulse of the heart, and not a reasoned philosophy of life—like humanism, the gospel of *humanitas* of the Renaissance. There are humane hearts in all times. That the poet Dante, having such an one, sometimes oversteps the narrow bounds of his medieval creed would not by itself justify taking him out of the Middle Ages.

There is another Dante, however, a *prose* Dante, who does formulate a philosophy of life soberly justifying in principle the humanity of his poetry, and uplifting it from a passing mood to a permanent ideal. He presents this ideal as the premiss of his essay *On Monarchy*. He says: "The proper business of the human race as a whole is to actualize constantly the total potentiality of the possible intellect." By "possible intellect" Dante means the human mind, the conscious intelligence which distinguishes men from beasts. Consequently, the ideal presented is that of the fullest possible development of what is essentially human in us, of *humanity* itself.

Dante has not only presented this ideal of fully developed humanity abstractly; he offers a symbol—one might as well say a personal illustration—of its realization in the Virgil of his *Comedy*. Virgil is the "gentle sage who knoweth all" (*Inf.* vii, 3), "sea of all sense" (*Inf.* viii, 7), upon whose model Dante in the poem perfects his own humanity, is given the freedom of all his human powers (*Purg.* xxvii, 130-42). His Virgil anticipates in principle the complete or universal man, *l'uomo universale*, of the Renaissance. And Dante himself—again in principle—anticipates Renaissance humanism as a gospel of life.

It is not indeed surprising that he should have done so. For he exposed his mind thoroughly to the very influences that were to shape Renaissance humanism. I mean of course the classics. If he read less widely in these than some of the scholars of the following age, he read deeply—he claims to have had the *Aeneid* virtually by heart—and fully enough to have grasped the notion of *humanitas* as the ancients understood it. Besides, Dante Alighieri was no ordinary reader.

For him, not only is Virgil the model of perfected humanity, but Virgil's *Aeneid* has for its end—as nearly three centuries later Edmund Spenser was still to say—"to fashion a gentleman or noble person in vertuous and gentle discipline," —type, that is, of perfected humanity. Carrier of this lesson is Aeneas, who is therefore a parallel symbol to the Virgil—or better, to Virgil's alumnus, the Dante of the *Commedia*. So, in the fourth book of the *Convivio* Dante presents various actions of Aeneas as allegorizing virtues apposite to the four ages of man's life. Such reading of allegory into

the classical poem is no doubt a medieval misconception, but
—as Spenser shows—it is a misconception that persisted
throughout the Renaissance, and indeed after.

Dante was also intimately read in classical authors who
would more explicitly inculcate the gospel of *humanitas*.
Aristotle is of course for him *the* Philosopher. But Thomas
Aquinas had, if I may so say, thoroughly *scholasticized* Aristotle for Dante. The humanity of and in Aristotle's teaching
would be less apparent to him.

It is quite otherwise with Cicero. By Dante's own testimony in the *Convivio* Cicero *On Friendship* first after
Boethius taught him the consolations of philosophy. And by
citation and quotation Dante shows familiarity with other
works of Cicero.

Now Cicero is the very "fountain-head" of the ideal of
humanitas; and "so far as the records of literature allow us
to see, first discussed and consciously portrayed the ideal that
he called *humanitas* and was the very type of that ideal for
Lactantius and St. Jerome in the fourth century, for Bernard
of Chartres and John of Salisbury in the twelfth, and for
Petrarch and Poggio, for Bembo and Erasmus in the new
humanism of the Renaissance." [1] Assuredly, I think, the name
of Dante Alighieri must be added to that list.

"To Cicero," continues Professor Rand, "clearly, the adjective *humanus* connotes not so much 'humane'—though this
idea is included too—as 'humanized,' 'civilized.' *Humanitas*
is the quality that one acquires in the process of developing
the best that there is in human nature. (*Does not this come to
the same as Dante's ideal of actualizing every potency of
man's highest faculty?*) A man thus humanized will be the
opposite of 'wild,' 'brutal,' 'bestial.' (*Dante accuses his*

[1] E. K. Rand, *The Humanism of Cicero*, Proceedings Amer. Philos. Soc.,
LXXI, 4, 1932.

fellow-exiles, who had behaved in ways unbecoming gentle-men, of 'bestiality.') He will be mild, gentle, merciful, compassionate, benevolent. He will be loyal to duty, upright, virtuous. He will have the social graces, possessing tact, courtesy, forbearance of others, *savoir faire*. In a group of cultivated people he will contribute his share to the conversation, master of the ready word, of wit, of banter, of urbanity. These diverse accomplishments, and others related to them, are exhibited by the contexts in which Cicero has set the word *humanus* or by the adjective with which it is paired. In contrast with the *homo ferus*, 'the wild man,' they present a mirror of the gentle-man." And finally, Cicero's humanism "not only may be reconciled with religion, but needs religion for its existence. The humanist will not dwell in his own perfection or in the pleasant society of his friends, but will make his soul immortal by reverencing the power supreme and by devoting his life to the state."

Full restatement for the Renaissance of this doctrine awaits the *Courtier* of Castiglione; but nevertheless in his *Convivio* Dante sketches a like portrait of the gentle-man, the man of *gentilezza*, emphasizing similar traits. Indeed, he often cites Cicero as his authority—even for the assigning of apposite "habits and behavior" to each age. The emergent figure—like Cicero's own ideal type—is a cultivated and gracious man of the world, certainly no medieval saint or ascete. Dante stresses for *youth* discipline and the habit of obedience, but no Spartan harshness of regimen. On the contrary, the youth must have "suavity," or graciousness, to win him friends. And it is fitting he give heed to his body, that it may be sound and beautiful. Especially becoming to man's second age, his *prime of life,* is courtesy,—not only politeness, but helpfulness. *Gioventute* and *giovare,* to help, have a common root. Then in the third age—*middle-age* we should call it—is due ripeness of wisdom, the virtue of the counsellor—the statesman or at least the good citizen. Dante, demanding of this age that it be "affable," cites Cicero for warrant: "And this age carries with it a shade of authority, because of which people listen to it more willingly than to a younger age, and by longer experience of life it ought to have better and handsomer information to impart." Finally, the last age of all—*old age* from sixty on—should be of meditative repose and pious devotion. After *humanitas*, *divinitas*. Surely, Dante would have his gentle-man heedful of the observances of religion all his life long, yet it is nevertheless striking that no mention whatever is made of them in connection with any age but the last. It is Cicero's point of view. Cicero's gentle-man turns to religion only in his old age. And the same point of view is expressed by Cicero's Renaissance disciples, Petrarch and Castiglione.

In the *Convivio* the gentle-man is defined in the abstract. The *Commedia* is full of concrete touches and specific traits revealing him. There is no question as to what race the highest type of man would belong. He would be Roman, of "the *gentle* seed of Troy," (*Inf.* xxvi, 60) and noblest of all peoples (*Mon.* II, iii). He would have to be Roman; for only in the Roman peace, the *pax Romana*, of Augustus has man been able to attain to the full *humanitas* of a Virgil. By a few words Dantes makes us see the type—as he saw it in the gardens of the "noble Castle" in Limbo. The Castle symbolizes, I think,—at least on the historical plane,—Rome itself, with what went to the making of its history and culture.

> "People were there with serious eyes and slow,
>   Of great authority in their demeanor;
>   They spoke not often, and in voices low."
>
> [*Inf.* iv, 112-4]

This sober and reserved dignity is for Dante an essential mark of the gentleman. All his movements must be measured. It is "haste

> Which robs of dignity whatever act."
> [*Purg.* iii, 10-11]

True Roman is the leonine pose and poise of Sordello. "Aloof and lonely, . . .

> How haughty was thy mien,
> O Lombard soul, and scornful, and thine eye
> In turning how unhurried and serene!
> Never a single word it deigned to say;
> Suffered our coming, only watching us
> All like a lion couching at its prey."
> [*Purg.* vi, 58, 61-6]

The more humane side of Dante's ideal—its sensitive courtesy—appears in the "delicate scruple," as Professor Grandgent calls it, that disturbs Dante as he passes along a line of blinded penitents:

> "I felt that I did outrage as I went
> Seeing those others, and myself not seen."
> [*Purg.* xiii, 73-4]

The humanistic ideal of a personality developing itself to the utmost through increase of knowledge and experience explains Dante's apparent invention of, and sympathy with, Ulysses' last voyage and its motive:

> "The zeal to have experience of the world,
> And of the vices and the worth of men."

And the whole episode is also anticipative of what Jacob Burckhardt calls the "thirst of discovery" of the Renaissance.

Dante expresses also another characteristic craving of the age of humanism to come,—that for *fame*. It is sometimes said that he craved it even while—as a good Christian—condemning, or at least contemning it. I do not think this is true, —not as it is true with Petrarch, for instance. Surely Virgil, the all-wise guide, would not thus erroneously spur on his pupil to the quest of fame:

> " 'Henceforward,' said the Master, 'of this guilt
> Of sloth beware; not lying upon down
> Is fame to be attained, nor under quilt;
> And he who goes without it to his grave
> Leaves of himself such vestige upon earth
> As smoke in air, or foam upon the wave.' "
>
> [*Inf.* xxiv, 46-51]

True, as against vainglorying, Virgil stresses the transciency of fame:

> "Nought but a breath of wind is human fame,
> Which bloweth now from here, and now from there,
> And but for changing quarter changes name."
>
> [*Purg.* xi, 100-1]

But then human life itself is transient,—which however does not mean that we should not make the most of it. Dante certainly thought and acted as if we should.

We have heard Dante stressing, after Cicero, the duty of his gentleman to the state. So Castiglione makes the whole culture of his courtier converge to that end. And so Dante himself lived up to his own ideal,—while he could as an active statesman in Florence, afterward in exile as an urgent advocate—to the public and with princes—of his policies.

The *De Monarchia* sums his political theory under three theses: first, that to develop the full humanity which is his

[35]

end on earth, man must have peace—to be had only under a world-wide monarchy; secondly, that this necessary world-monarchy is by divine ordination the Roman Empire; thirdly, that the Holy Roman Empire owes its authority to God directly, and not through the Pope.

Medieval and reactionary as this doctrine sounds,—as the patriot-poet Carducci in his sonnet declared it to be,—yet there are forward-looking aspects of Dante's argument. Its premiss—that self-development, culture, civilization are dependent upon peace—is hardly debatable. And the prescription for peace of an international tribunal with power, a super-state,—for in principle as such he justifies the imperial authority,—is at least not unfamiliar today. His third thesis implies, in effect, separation of church and state,—a policy partially realized during the Renaissance and the Reformation, but perhaps not even yet finally achieved.

Still, I recognize the dangers of such interpretation by the light of later, and perhaps deceptively similar, ideas. Be it conceded, then, that the essay *On Monarchy* is in method and outlook fundamentally medieval. Such is not the case, I think, with the political message of the *Commedia*. The theoretical tenets may remain unchanged, but they are urged to a practical end, a special interest. The essay prescribes for world-peace under the aegis of Rome,—a consummation devoutly to be wished, but obviously remote. But in the explanatory epistle to be prefixed to the poem Dante declares that the end of the work is "practical," and also "manifold, —to wit, near and remote." The practical end is to bring "those living in this life" from present misery into felicity, the felicity of peace,—and *"in this life."* Realization of such an end for the whole world would be indeed "remote" enough. But Dante's interest in the whole world—in the world outside of Italy—was, I think, decidedly theoretical.

Italy is for him "the garden of the Empire." A nearer and dearer end would be to bring that garden back into flower,— even if there might be little promise in sight for the outlying fields of the earth. After all, original Eden was but a small part of the habitable earth.

Now if that aspiration for the emancipation of Italy be— as I think it demonstrably is—the inspiring motive of the *Commedia,* then the poem is no epic, as Carducci would have it, of a lost cause. Roman imperialism is transformed into Italian nationalism. The enemy to be overcome, as throughout—overtly and by transparent allegory—the poet insists, is the usurped temporal sovereignty of the Pope. And Dante has been finally victorious,—not in his own time, nor in the Renaissance when Italy was altogether enslaved, the Pope abetting,—not even in 1870, for the Pope then submitted only to force,—but when in the *Concordat* of February 11, 1929 Pope Pius XI voluntarily renounced all but a merely nominal temporal dominion on the ground that— as he said almost in Dante's own words—it tended to excite cupidity in those whose power and possessions should be spiritual. Considering that the Church had banned the *Monarchy* for such allegation, I know of no more signal triumph than this.

There is another difference between the *Monarchia* and the *Commedia.* The essay is only an argument; the poem is an argument and an appeal—*ad hominem.* The poem is dedicated to Can Grande della Scala, to whose "magnificence" Dante, in the poem, is counselled to turn for aid in his need. (*Par.* xvii, 70 *et seq.*) Dante's need is for *power* to carry his aspiration into effect, to actualize by arms the deliverance which he could but plead for by words.

Earlier—in the years from 1310 to 1313—Dante had looked to Can Grande's principal, Henry VII, who had come

"Ere she was ripe, to straighten Italy."

He had died, defeated by papal treachery. But while he lived, Dante's open letters to him, to the potentates and peoples of Italy, to the recalcitrant Florentines, all make it clear that Dante's passionate concern was for Italy,—at least for nothing outside Italy. No doubt, within Italy he was concerned most intimately for his beloved but perverse Florence and for his own fortunes. Still, he writes as an *Italian* patriot.

Henry VII had died, but his cause in and for Italy had not died. During the rest of Dante's life the imperial throne was vacant. Two rival claimants only succeeded in rending Europe between them. Hence in Italy, his title indisputable, Henry's Captain and Vicar General, Can Grande, continued in the name of the Empire to conquer and control the city-states of Lombardy. Lombardy pacified, he might then turn to adjacent Tuscany. Lombardy and Tuscany together formed a dominion that had enabled the "good" Countess Matilda to defy an Emperor exceeding his right. Why should not Can Grande, holding this same dominion, defy a usurping Pope?

Under Matilda, Florence,

"Sober and chaste, abode at peace with all."
[*Par.* xv, 99]

In his vision, Dante is led back to an Eden presided over by a "Matilda." Is the *personal* allegory—there are other aspects —difficult to interpret on these premises? We have only to imagine Can Grande, once victorious, to be possessed by the spirit of the "good Countess."

If the young Deliverer could go so far, he might well go farther. And Dante, as he says in the superscription to his epistle-dedicatory, will pray for the "perpetual increment of his glorious name." The poet believes him capable of things "incredible." (*Par.* xvii, 91-3.) He might yet redeem not only north Italy, but all Italy. And it may be said that such faith in Can Grande was by no means peculiar to Dante, or to Dante's generation. Two centuries later, Paolo Giovio attributes to the young Lord of Verona—he died at twenty-nine—a genius administrative as well as military that, had he lived, might have fully justified Dante's expectations. Fortunately, the poet died first.

A gospel of *humanism,* substantially after Cicero, and a proclamation of *nationalism,*—in these two fundamentals Dante certainly preludes the Renaissance. He does so, however, by himself, making no school. There is this important difference between him and Petrarch. He was a harbinger, a precursor; Petrarch a pioneer and leader.

The most obvious and intimate connection between Dante and the Renaissance, however, is in the matter of language and style. Unfortunately, his elaborately designed work on vernacular eloquence, *De Vulgari Eloquentia,* was not completed. It was to have had at least four books. Only the first book and a portion of the second are extant. But the general outline of his theory is clear.

The work evidences again the warmth of Dante's nationalism. He admits that literary, or classic, Latin is supreme, in that in it the flux of the spoken idiom has been shaped into a permanent art-language, or "grammar," by supreme artists in prose and verse. Similar, if less perfect, shaping has been given to the three idioms derivative from Latin,—the idiom of *oïl* or French, of *oc* or Provençal, of *si* or Italian. And Dante insinuates an at least potential superiority to the last named.

A stable and national language is built up eclectically out of the *best* of local usages, or dialects. That is the gist of Dante's theory. It is the dominant theory of the Renaissance everywhere. But of course the question immediately arises, Who is to determine what *is* best? *Gentle*-folk, replies Dante, and learned folk—courtly and curial folk—yes, to a certain extent. So we speak of "the King's English," meaning the sovereign speech of *all* the land, not of this or that part of it. But there is a higher jurisdiction, a superlative usage,— that of the poet, artist of the word. His standard is his own, —the cultivated taste of genius. And his cultivation must be in the school of his superiors in kind,—the master-poets of antiquity, makers of the art-languages, the "grammars," of Rome and Greece. So Dante proudly imagines himself made a sixth in the "fair school" of

> "the lords of that exalted song
> That soars above the rest on eagle's wing"—
> [*Inf.* iv, 95-6]

Homer, Horace, Ovid, Lucan and the "all-highest," *altissimo*, Virgil, to whom he acknowledges everything:

> "My master and my author verily,
> Thou only art the one from whom I took
> The seemly style for which men honor me."
> [*Inf.* i, 85-6]

Dante's *"italiano illustro,"* like Du Bellay's *"françoys illustré,"* is an eclectic work of art modelled upon the classics. The clay to be moulded is the mother-tongue. Doubtless, Dante enriched his native Tuscan less from other dialects, or by Latinisms and neologisms, than his eclectic theory might suggest (the *Cinquecento* was to divide on the issue of eclecticism *versus toscanità*); but then Du Bellay and Ronsard were inconsistent to the same degree. It remained for Du Bartas to denature French by imitating Greek compounds, and for Spenser (*crede* Jonson), "affecting the Ancients, *to write* no language."

Dante's imitation of the classics is not mechanical and by rule, but vital and spontaneous. Sidney, echoing Du Bellay, urged imitators of the ancient authors, "most worthy indeed to be imitated," not just to copy "their figures and phrases," but to "devour them whole, and make them wholly theirs." Dante so *digested* Virgil,—wrote like him by becoming like him. "*Le style c'est l'homme.*" Dante felt Virgil—as reflected in his writings—to have been the perfection of Cicero's gentle-man, and delights in drawing *his* Virgil after that model, emphasizing his sweetness, dignity, courtesy, his scrupulous honour (*Purg.* iii, 8-9), his fastidious scorn of vulgarity (*Inf.* xxx, 130 ff.), his modesty (*Purg.* xxi, 103 ff.). It was—at least principally—from the absorption of these and kindred qualities that the disciple formed within himself the touchstone of taste in the making of a language and of a poetic style both "illustrious" without peer. Dante's language is today less archaic than Shakespeare's English, though the English poet is nearer by three hundred years. And to appreciate the magnificence of Dante's achievement in poetic style, we must remember that the only vernacular poem previously produced in Europe even comparable to the *Commedia* was the *Roman de la Rose,* which in point of style is to the *Commedia* as a spinet to a full orchestra. Dante's poem, like his Mount of Purgatory, rises alone from the level sea.

Now it is possible that I may seem to have proved too much,—to have lifted Dante out of the Middle Ages altogether. That would of course be quite wrong. It is true, I think, that Dante's eager discipleship of Virgil, and of other poets and philosophers of ancient Rome, did modernize him to a degree not commonly recognized. We have been too exclusively preoccupied with the Christian mystic and moralist, and with the love-poet, and have relatively ignored the humanist and patriot. Still, although Dante was indeed the understanding disciple of Cicero and Virgil, he followed with equal ardency authors in every sense medieval,—theologians and mystics, scholastic metaphysicians, encyclopaedists. Consider the intellectual and spiritual luminaries—*illuminationes Ecclesiae*—to whom he pays homage in the heaven of the Sun. His method of argumentation—in the doctrinal parts of the *Commedia* itself, especially of the *Paradiso*—is altogether scholastic. He is a symbolist, an allegorist. The Beatrice of the *Vita Nuova* is, though dimly drawn, human—even playful in her puzzled mockery of her incomprehensible lover. In the *Paradiso* she is hardened into a hieratic symbol,— at best into a Mother Superior, as frosty as holy, and distressingly didactic. Only once—in the discreet cough at her neophyte's vainglorying in his Roman ancestry (*Par.* xvi, 1-15)—does she show a really human touch. Dante was nourished also on medieval poetry, romance, drama. His comic relief of the Demons (*Inf.* xxi-xxii) is characteristic medieval clownage,—the clownage of the mystery play in the marketplace. Doubtless also, even while study of the classics was leading him towards humanism, his more insistent and persistent absorption was in divinity. His contemporaries did not call him *il gran teologo* for nothing. Nor is it inconsistent to say that the central message, the focus of the argument, of the *Commedia* is not religious but political,—namely, insistence upon the necessity of stripping the Papacy of temporal power. For Dante believed in such action not only as rationally expedient for human welfare, but even more as obedience to Christ, who had said: "Render·unto Caesar the things that are Caesar's." Otherwise, the divinely "magnificent plan" of redemption would be thwarted,—indeed was now being thwarted. Dante's political policy was for him also Christian piety.

In sum, the great Florentine, colossus-like, bestrides two epochs, but his face is more than half turned towards the future.

Dante's love-poetry defines and celebrates the special influence perfecting his endowment of full humanity, and directing his desires towards divine things. This influence is love kindled by beauty, for him personally incarnate in Beatrice. She herself is made to say of him that, both by inheritance and by divine grace,

> "This man in his new life, potentially,
> Was such that admirable proof in him
> Would have been made by each right tendency;"

and that

> "My countenance some season was his stay;
> To him that while unveiling my young eyes,
> I led him with me looking the right way;"

and that the desires kindled in him by her were leading him

> "to love that Good
> Beyond which aspiration there is nought."
> [*Purg.* xxx, 109-23, xxxi, 22-4]

In principle, the platonic love-poetry of the Renaissance glorifies likewise the regenerative influence of womanly beauty and goodness. In both cases Goethe's text is anticipated:

> "Das Ewigweibliche zieht uns hinan."

This love-poetry of the Renaissance derives—however il-legitimately—from Plato, though no doubt the love-philos-ophy which Dante represents, also enters in. Dante's own love-poetry is a development from the courtly love-lyric of the troubadours of Provence. He was directly influenced by the work of some of these, especially, as he himself testifies, by the deliberately obscure and artificial Arnaut Daniel. Arnaut appealed to one taste of Dante's,—not the finest. I mean a predilection for the ingenious in craftsmanship, the subtle and esoteric in expression. Under the predominant influence of Virgil, poet above all of clarity, this irritating predilection is largely subdued in the *Commedia,* but Dante's earlier lyric poetry is much affected by it.

Dante's praise of Arnaut is put into the mouth of Guido Guinizelli of Bologna, a mid-thirteenth century philosopher and poet, "father"—according to Dante himself—of the school of the "sweet new style." He was for Dante's love-lyric what Virgil was for Dante's allegorical epic, and his philosophy of Love underlies all Dante's poetic expression. Dante is frank and modest in his gratitude, hailing Guini-zelli as

"Father of me and of my betters, who
Used ever sweet and gracious rhymes of love."
[*Purg.* xxvi, 97-9]

In brief, Guinizelli's achievement was to give truth and sincerity to a love-lyric which had been a literary pose. So in effect his disciple Dante declares to a representative of the older school, Bonagiunta da Lucca, whose spirit questions him in Purgatory. Dante says:

"I am one who, when
Love doth inspire me, note, and as within
He dictates I go heralding to men."
[*Purg.* xxiv, 52-4]

Bonagiunta sees the point, and humbly admits its truth. Dante sings a sincere love; he, Bonagiunta, and his fellows did not. This is the crucial difference.

> " 'O brother, now the knot,' he said, 'I see
>   Which from the sweet new style I hear held back
>   Guittone and the Notary and me.
> Clearly I see how your pens ever go
>   Following him who dictates, faithfully;
>   And verily with ours this was not so.
> Who seeks distinction elsewhere, could divide
>   Not by a hair the one and other style.'
> And he was silent, as if satisfied."
>
> [*Ib*. 55-63]

This distinction between professions of love sincere and insincere is not, however, what the modern reader might perhaps suppose. Dante does not mean—at least does not simply and necessarily mean—that he really is in love with a girl, or in love with a real girl. The point is that, even if he were, the *style* of his homage, as expressed in his verse, would be insincere, unless it be understood his homage is paid in its fulness not to the lady for her own private sake, however desirable she be, but for something she represents, or reflects, or is a symbol of. So Catholics kneel to the Pope as Vicar of God,—as God vicariously present. The Pope may himself be a holy man, but it is not for that they kneel. The worshipful something somehow present in the lady might be a pure ideal, a Platonic Idea. Later, in the Renaissance Maurice Scève and (after him?) Samuel Daniel implied this intention by addressing their love-lyrics to Délie and Delia, anagrams of *l'Idée* and *Ideal*, and Michael Drayton his openly to *Idea*. Or, the worshipful something might be concrete and personal,—the Virgin Mary for instance, whose handmaid

Beatrice is said to be, and whose virtues Beatrice is said to reflect. Obviously, either way there may be an actual lady in the case or not. Either way the poet's homage is not to her, but through her—to the ideal or divinity behind her. Even if she be actual, he would not praise her for herself in just the way he does. It would be extravagant, perhaps—ridiculous.

Ridiculous evidently the young Florentine matron of the *Vita Nuova* thought the ecstatic worship of her poet. As he ruefully admits, she and her friends laughed at him. She did not understand—how would she?—that his adoration was not of her, but of the divine in her. She might have felt him—*almost*—as Olivia did Malvolio, to be slightly mad. Later, in Paradise, she understood.

Dante's poetic homage could be sincere because it was religious. The daughter of a burgher of Florence might incarnate divine goodness and beauty. Religious homage was the quality of the *dolce stil nuovo*. But "the apes of Provence" —Bonagiunta and his kind—could not be other than affectedly insincere. Their verbal genuflections and servile protestations—feudal homage and courtly gallantry—were altogether out of the picture in democratic and commercial Florence.

Indeed, even in twelfth century feudal Provence poetic homage to ladies had become affectedly extravagant. Women of rank had achieved a high degree of culture. As *grandes dames, chatelaines,* they were accustomed to the subservient homage of their retainers; as *femmes de coeur, de sensibilité,* they complacently accepted an homage of gallantry without reserves. It was a highly feminized society. Husbands were much away on their wars; lady-wives were left to their own devices, and with a superabundance of leisure on their hands. Clever and witty, they amused themselves with games in

which these qualities were given play,—jousting with words
as their lords with lances. A natural arena between the sexes
was Love—its tenets and predicaments, its casuistry. Set de-
bates on amorous issues were the order of the day. The same
thing was to recur in the elegant and feminized society of
the Renaissance,—in Boccaccio's Naples, Castiglione's Urbino, Lyly's London.

To a large degree the minstrelsy of the troubadours was
also a polite and witty diversion, a game of love played by
set rules. As the game developed, the rules—like those of
contract or golf—became numerous and complicated, called
for codification. One Andreas, *capellanus*, or chaplain, of a
noble *chatelaine*, set himself to the task, and at the beginning of the thirteenth century published a treatise, the full
title of which is *Liber de Arte honeste Amandi et de Repro-
batione inhoneste Amoris*. An art of love reminds of Ovid,
but as the second part of Andreas's title implies, the tone is
far from Ovid's cynical levity. Andreas's book reads like a
legal code, and is largely responsible for the notion that
there were actual Courts of Love in the Middle Ages.

Fundamental in the code of courtly love is the inaccessibility of the lady of desire. She is by definition "merciless
Beauty." She is also secret—to be addressed by a name of
fancy, or through another lady acting as a screen. Her lover
prostrates himself before her—*verbally*—as a vassal before
his lord. Indeed, this artificial love-making is a translation
into terms of gallantry of feudal obeisance and homage. Occasionally it exalts the lady still higher, doing her reverence
in terms appropriate to "Our Lady." But this too, I think,
was only a more daring flattery, an audacious *façon de parler*
without mystical or symbolic intent.

This obsequious and worshipful attitude was assumed by
the troubadour no matter what his own rank. The first and

not least poetic of them, William of Poictiers, was Duke of Aquitaine. But in the court of Love all are servitors. In point of fact, the far greater number of troubadours were actual servitors of the high-born ladies to whom they addressed their humbly fervent verses of love. Usually—as in Renaissance courts later—these protestations were meant, and taken, as no more than gallant compliments. Naturally, such was not always the case. The heights of inaccessibility might now and then be scaled. The ban upon the quality of mercy was sometimes strained. Then proved indeed was the value of the rule of *secrecy*. We shall see how in Boccaccio's poem Pandaro honestly believes that observance of secrecy makes it quite permissible for cousin Cressida to give herself to Troilus. But I do not know if that view would have held in Provençal society.

The bequest of the troubadours as poets of courtly love—they wrote on other themes too, especially political—was a marvellously refined and subtle phrase-book for polite love-making, set in a rich variety of intricate metres, and with music.

All this elegant culture was abruptly threatened in 1208, when Pope Innocent III sent Arnold of Citeaux and Simon de Montfort to extirpate from Provence the Albigensian heresy. And they did—with pretty much all else worth while. Certain of the alarmed and empoverished troubadours took refuge at the Sicilian court of the anti-papal emperor, Frederick II. Fascinated by their minstrelsy, Frederick himself, his son Enzo, and his prime minister Pier delle Vigne composed vernacular imitations. From Sicily—chiefly at least—the fashion spread into northern Italy; so Dante calls all Italian love-poets prior to those of the "sweet new style" the "Sicilian school." Although he is proud that there should have been—even briefly—an imperial court poetry in Italy, he admits that the Emperor's Italian, the Sicilian dialect, was a sorry medium. Apparently, however, Pier delle Vigne fascinated him —as had Arnaut Daniel—by ingenious conceits and word-turns. Thus the shade of Pier, self-slain, is made to declare:

> "Against disdain my spirit put her trust
> In dying, and by her disdainful choice
> Unto my just self made myself unjust."
> [*Inf.* xiii, 70-2]

Dryden commended these "beautiful turns on words." They were rampant in the conscious rhetoric of the whole Renaissance.

There was a rather special insincerity in any imitation of the languishing troubadour lady-cult by Frederick or his courtiers. The social attitude of the Sicilian court was in one respect antithetical to that of Provence. It was indeed half Moorish,—certainly orientally contemptuous of women. Frederick is said to have maintained a harem. In any case, women did not, as in Provence, socially and culturally rule.

If in Sicily troubadour love-making was thus mere literary make-believe, in romantic Germany there was one startling example of literal sincerity by the code. In 1255 appeared Ulrich von Lichtenstein's *Service of Ladies*,—his own amazing love-story and *vita nuova*. Ulrich took the troubadour code, as the French say, "at the foot of the letter." He actually did —or said he did—what the Provençal poet without expectation of belief professed. For instance, to prove his loyalty, he sent his lady the pledge of one of his fingers cut off by himself.

Counter to this peculiar sincerity, but also different from the insincerity of Frederick's court, contemptuous of women, was the insincerity of the poets affecting the troubadour style in the north Italian communes,—Bonagiunta da Lucca and his kind, the "Sicilian school." In their *bourgeois milieux* there were neither ruling *grandes dames* nor slaves of the harem, but worthy God-fearing maids and matrons. *Ultra*-courtly, *ultra*-chivalrous wooing might not be a mockery, but was certainly an affectation. No young business or professional man would really make love that way. It was not done.

Yet the troubadour lyric was too beautiful—as poetry—to be discarded. How to give it life, make it true to living conditions,—that was the problem. And by a single poem—at least to the satisfaction of his disciples—Guido Guinizelli solved it. In his *canzone* beginning

"To the gentle heart repaireth ever Love,"

while sacrificing nothing of troubadour elegance, he yet sang in sincerity and truth. Curiously, although Guinizelli wrote much, he wrote nothing else like this *canzone*. For Dante— and I believe for the consensus of modern opinion—the *canzone* by itself inaugurates and defines the "sweet new style" of Dante and his circle,—Guido Cavalcanti, Lapo Gianno, Cino da Pistoia and others.

Fundamental in the Provençal courtly code is it that only a *gentleman* can in the proper sense of the word *love*. Common folk merely mate and breed. Gentlefolk must needs marry too,—for family and dynastic reasons; but that has really nothing necessarily to do with love. Guinizelli changes the whole colour of the conception by making two words of *gentleman*. Rossetti translates:

> "Let no man predicate
> That ought the name of gentleness should have
> Even in a king's estate
> Except the heart there be a gentle man's."

In the original two words are added: *da virtute*, "by virtue." A man is "gentle" not by caste or wealth, but by virtue, character. Only such a "gentle heart," *cor gentil,* is moved to true love. Indeed, Guinizelli affirms that love is the essential quality of the gentle heart. So in principle Dante sums Guinizelli's doctrine in the one line:

"Love and the gentle heart are one same thing."

And the gentle heart, which is love, is awakened into activity of desire by beauty. Once awakened, it rests not until desire is satisfied.

Desire of what? it may be asked. Upon the answer to that question hinges indeed the whole matter. The Provençal troubadour's answer—supposing him willing to make it— would have been simple. Courtly love had nothing to do with marriage,—except negatively. Indeed, according to Andreas, for such love only women already married were eligible. And besides, a regal *chatelaine* did not in those days marry a retainer. She would not have been allowed. In most cases her sued-for *favour* was just that,—the favour of a lady-patroness in return for a gallant compliment neatly and musically turned. It might take the form of a smile, a gift, the poet's maintenance. Only on rarest occasion was there the personal wooing of a Ruy Blas.

The desire of Guinizelli's "gentle heart" is for neither kind of favour, but solely for permission to contemplate and worship that in the beloved which had evoked it,—the beautiful. So in the *Vita Nuova* Dante declares his bliss to be solely in his words of praise of his lady. And the gentle heart being gentle *da virtute,* "from virtue," the beauty which is its desire must also spring from virtue, be not of earth but of heaven. Guinizelli excuses his seemingly idolatrous praise of his lady on the ground that hers indeed was "an angel's face." So Dante declares—in the words of Homer—of the young Beatrice: "She appeared to me daughter not of mortal man, but of God." Staled by frequence, repeated in a thousand vain and amatorious compliments, the comparison has become trivial. It is hard to realize how fresh—and startling—it was in the fourteenth century. And Guinizelli and his disciple meant more than a compliment,—meant definitely that what the truly gentleman loves in his lady *is* the "angel" in her, the angelic qualities that shall make those possessing them to be—in the words of St. Mark—"as angels in heaven." Fulfilment of the desire of such love can be only in heaven, where the angel that is to be, is. And the lover must win his way there too. Beatrice promises her lover, the penitent, that in the hereafter, when his sins have been remitted, his earthly task done,—"thou

> of that Rome where is a Roman Christ
> Shalt be forever citizen with me."
> [*Purg.* xxxii, 101-2]

That is the "favour"—the grace or *mercede*—of the lady of the *dolce stil*. He and she will be blessed together—"as the angels in heaven," as Augustine and Monica, but assuredly not as the humanly passionate lovers in Rossetti's *Blessed Damosel*. There is small comfort for the romantically minded in the gospel of love of Guinizelli and Dante.

That gospel is, obviously, a Catholic Christian conception, and quite distinct from the Platonic Love of the Renaissance. Rigorously, in the latter philosophy of love, there is no union of lover and lady ever. Her beauty merely starts him on the quest for Beauty in itself, is the first rung of a ladder towards the ideal. That reached, the ladder is kicked away. But of course Renaissance Platonism was not always rigorously logical. The philosophy of love of the *dolce stil* gave it a new shading, less mystical than Dante, less inhuman than the metaphysical Platonists. Beautiful women came to be hailed as refining personal and social influences.

Dante's desire of union, or better communion, with his lady angelical is to be realized in heaven. The tone of his love-poetry, therefore, is one of hope and cheer. Only before he had come to understand this true end of the highest love had his tone been querulous or plaintive. With his "first friend" and closest rival, the second Guido, this was not so. The whole key of Guido Cavalcanti's love-lyric is minor. He affirms the supersensuous desire of the *dolce stil*, but—as it would seem—denies the heaven, the life after death, in which such desire is alone attainable. And so Cavalcanti's desire, frustrated, turns to "gentle Death," the deliverer,—to the boon of oblivion.

It is curious that the Italian poet who follows Dante, and who for the Renaissance eclipses Dante's fame as a poet of love, not only found his lady in Provence but also in some considerable degree reverted to the mood of the Provençal troubadour. I mean Francesco Petrarca,—Francis Petrarch to the English,—whose Laura was a lady of Avignon.

III

PETRARCH

WE often, in a kindly mood, say of a lovable but rather weak person that he is very human. Turning from Dante Alighieri, one feels, I think, Francis Petrarch to be very human—in that sense. A great genius indubitably, not only in lyric poetry, but in the apostolic gift also of perfect self-surrender to a cause, and so in the power to impart his enthusiasm to others. His cause was ancient Rome. He lived himself back into the spirit of her culture sensitively, passionately. Perhaps because his learning was not too philosophically profound, it was the more widely communicable and influential. And his faith in the divine rightness of the ancients gave him strength to combat every medieval shibboleth and superstition. It was a vicarious strength. He himself was not strong, but vacillating, self-distrustful, introspective to an almost morbid degree. He had the itch for self-expression of the romantic temperament, a formidable *furor scribendi*. His correspondence was enormous, yet always carefully studied for publication. If he ran out of living correspondents, he wrote to dead ones,—dead except by fame,—to Cicero, Seneca, Quintilian, Titus Livy, Horace, Virgil, Homer. He had the vanity of the professional artist, the petted celebrity. Even loyal Boccaccio is bound to admit that "he was most fond of honours and display, more so perhaps than quite would be expected of his illustrious merit." He was jealous of his renown. When he was old and famous, four young Venetian philosophers, once his guests, referred to him—perhaps mischievously—as "a worthy, indeed most worthy, but illiterate and ignorant man." He at once wrote a little book about it. As a good Christian he would rather, he protests, be held worthy than learned, but world-wide testimonies force him to admit that he *is* learned. As for his young friends, they should be jailed for libel, and perhaps, being Averroists, burned as atheists.

The poet's father, Ser Petracco—the son made it Petrarca for euphony—was banished from Florence along with Dante. After various wanderings, Petracco in 1311 settled at Avignon. Young Francesco, who had been born at Arezzo, was now seven. In 1316, set on making a lawyer of the boy, Petracco sent him to the University of Montpellier, and four years later to that of Bologna. He had sternly repressed his son's literary inclinations, once even throwing his books into the fire,—and salvaging only a Virgil and a Cicero to placate the frantic lad. In 1326, however, Petracco married again; and apparently left to their own resources, Francesco and his younger brother Gherardo entered the service of the Church. Gherardo became a monk, but Francesco never proceeded beyond minor orders.

Independent at last, young Petrarch plunged at once into letters, and into the gay life as well of the rich commercial centre and brilliant Papal capital that in the previous two decades Avignon had become. Looking back from old age, he admits that he was good-looking, also that the price of fashion was sometimes high. In a letter to his brother he recalls the agony of tight shoes squeezing one's feet "*quam gravi et quam continui bello,*" and the "piratical torture of curling irons." "How often," he says, "sleep, which application of these delayed, their effects made impossible! . . . And what

[55]

blisters we used mornings to find in our mirrors on our inflamed foreheads, so that we who were fain to display our hair, were forced to veil our faces! Sweet are such things in the doing, but in memory dreadful." (*Epist. fam.* X, iii.)

By his own account it was a year later, in 1327, and on Good Friday, that the young dandy saw in church her whom he calls Laura, and was at once enamoured of her. But although thereafter he dilates upon every shade of his devotion,—by no means always a purely spiritual devotion,—he observes punctiliously the code of secrecy. We do not really know who "Laura" was. A certain Laura de Sade, wife of an Avignonese gentleman, made a will on April 3, 1348, and in it directed that she be buried in the Franciscan church of the city. Petrarch's "Laura" died of the plague on April 6, 1348, and was buried in that church. The coincidence is striking, but hardly proof positive. According to the code the poet-lover should not indeed have addressed his lady openly by her real name, even her real Christian name. But after all, seeing that nothing came of the affair but the poems themselves, does it really much matter?

In 1337, after ten years of shifting residence and some foreign travel facilitated by the bounty of the Colonna family, Petrarch established himself not far from Avignon, but in the lovely and secluded valley of the Sorgue at Vaucluse. To him in retirement there came simultaneously from Paris and Rome invitations to appear and receive the laurel of supreme Poet. After a decent show of hesitation he, son of ancient Rome, accepted the call of the Roman Senate, and was crowned on the Capitoline on April 8, 1341. It was the triumph of his life.

He was only thirty-seven. His life was barely half over. During the rest of it he was famed and fêted as few men of letters have ever been. Princes, popes, peoples contended for the honour of his presence and the profit of his *eloquentia*, his Latinity,—the political and diplomatic value of which he was the first to make evident and to exploit. To him not "salty tasted another's bread"; for he accepted it not as charity, but as a right. Successive popes conferred upon him profitable benefices. Florence restored his father's confiscated property. The Emperor Charles IV created him a Count Palatine. At Milan, where he lived from 1353 to 1361, the Visconti made him not only their ambassador to Venice, Prague, Paris, but also their intimate friend. At Venice, from 1362 to 1368, he occupied a palace conceded by the Senate. (In return, he pledged the bequest of his library,—a pledge for some reason never redeemed.) Finally, from 1370 came retirement on the little farm at Arquà among the Euganean hills, cared for by his natural daughter Francesca, until on July 19, 1374 he was found in his study, his head dropped upon his book.

It is a stirring life-drama, yet one interrupted just so often by *entr'actes* of self-withdrawal. In Petrarch the ambitious and somewhat vain man-of-the-world was ever at odds with the scholar and poet, almost the contemplative recluse. He wrote a *Praise of the Solitary Life*. The theme was a conventional one of the late Middle Ages. But not Vaucluse alone proves his praise not all literary. Solitude and the peace of nature were for him recurring necessities. He seemed, Antaeus-like, to draw new strength from the soil. He was rarely sensitive for his time to natural beauty. He climbed Mt. Ventoux for no other reason, apparently, than to enjoy the view. The idea was fantastic—then. Yet, as Boccaccio says, the other Petrarch loved "honors and display," and fed on applause. No one ever liked better being a celebrity, or inveighed more against invasion of his privacy. Fame was to him the forbidden fruit, desired the more eagerly for being forbidden. He professes envy for the peace of his cloistered brother, yet defends "human glory" even against St. Augustine. In the dialogue which, being an intimate self-confession, he called his *Secretum* (and for once declined to publish), he is reminded by Augustine that even if he should succeed in producing a "rare and distinguished work," it could not reach far in all space or in all time. But Petrarch rather bluntly asks to be spared the old trite reflections of the philosophers. "If you have anything better to urge, pray produce it; all this sounds very fine, but I have never found that it helped me. I do not ask to be God and to possess eternity and to fill heaven and earth. I am a mortal and I desire only the mortal." To Augustine's horrified protest he sturdily retorts: "There is a certain justification for my plan of life. It may be only glory that we seek here, but I persuade myself that, so long as we remain here, that is right. Another glory awaits us in heaven, and he who reaches there will not wish even to think of earthly fame. So this the natural order, that among mortals the care of things mortal should come first: to the transitory will then succeed the eternal; from the first to the second is the natural progression." [1] In a sense, Dante already had implied this progression of human concern in his setting the earthly paradise *on the way* to the heavenly, felicity here before felicity hereafter. But Dante's allegory is abstract and remote. One hardly realizes the full force of the implication. Perhaps, in this connection Dante himself did not. For Petrarch the issue between thisworldliness and otherworldliness was an ever present and pressing one. It is in principle the Renaissance against the Middle Ages. And in this rebellious retort to St. Augustine the Renaissance triumphs. Earthly glory may be transitory enough, but the best among men long for it. Messer Francesco longed for it

[1] To Professor James Harvey Robinson is due the credit of calling attention to this highly significant passage. I use also his translation.

above all things,—against whatever residual scruples,—and assiduously worked for it,—even, to be vulgarly frank, *worked* his friends for it. His surprise at the double invitation to receive the laurel-crown was somewhat the surprise of the political nominee. He writes (and publishes the letter) to his patron and friend, Cardinal Giovanni Colonna. The thing is "almost incredible!" he says. In point of fact, both invitations were the result of careful intriguing, especially on the Cardinal's part, but with the full cognizance of the poet.[1]

Petrarch himself always attributed his laureateship to his Latin poetry, beside which his Italian rhymes were mere pastime. The work that was to bring him enduring fame was, as he believed, the epic *Africa*. Unfortunately, however, this was a masterpiece more appreciated in the promise than in the performance. The poet says of it in his *Epistle to Posterity:* "It did not fail to arouse the interest of many before they had seen it." *But not after*—he might alas! have added. The poem—so far as it was completed—disappointed great expectations. Its inspiring motive is nobly patriotic. Through the man of Africa, Scipio *Africanus,* "high Providence," as already Dante had said,

"Defended for Rome the glory of the world."

It is the same motive that inspired Petrarch's own noble ode, *Italia mia.* But this last was a lyric cry. Petrarch's genius was not epic. Only one or two lyric moments break the flat monotony of the *Africa*.

More important is Petrarch's prose Latinity. Here he hails Cicero as master and model; and in general may be said to inaugurate the Ciceronianism which in its later extravagance was to incur the wrath of Erasmus. Petrarch's imitation, however, was not slavish or stilted. In his *Letters,* especially, his

[1] See G. Koerting, *Petrarca's Leben und Werke,* Leipzig, 1878, p. 161.

Latin style, while still classic, is individual and sparkling. Amazing is its advance upon the cumbrous Latin prose of the preceding generation, of Dante. Indeed, for ease and naturalness Petrarch's epistolary style is nearer to Erasmus's than almost any between.

Leader in the movement of humanism as Petrarch was, —far more deliberately and critically, and in many more directions, than Dante, as well as vastly more influentially,— there are still singular survivals of medieval prejudice in his thought and feeling. Perhaps most medieval of all is his *prose* attitude towards women. While giving deathless fame to one woman, he defamed all women. Listen to his characteristic summing-up of the sex: *"Foemina . . . verus est diabolus, hostis pacis, fons impatientiae, materia jurgorum, quâ caruisse tranquillitas certa est."* ("Woman is a real devil, an enemy of peace, a source of impatience, a matter of strife,—and to be without her is to be assured of tranquillity.") The gracious sentiment is from his edifying *Remedies against either fortune.* One is rather glad he had not better fortune with Laura.

The serious context would seem to forbid taking the passage as humorous; and indeed such indictment of the daughters of Eve the temptress is a monkish convention rooted far back in the morbid asceticism of the Dark Ages. Vowed celibates, tempted by their own natural appetites, put the blame on women. Throughout the Middle Ages—and after—womankind continued to be a stock subject of masculine satire. Jean de Meung's second part of the *Roman de la Rose* is—in secular literature—the most formidable indictment. But I am not sure that he is quite in literal earnest, and that Christine of Pisa's spirited rejoinder is not largely *literary.*

A concise dictionary, so to speak, of female malice is the fifteenth century *Alphabet de l'imperfection et malice des*

femmes of one Olivier. The cumulative effect of the whole
"alphabet" is startling. Here are a few letters: Woman is

Avidissimum animal	(Avaricious animal)
Bestiale baratrum	(Bundle of beastliness)
Duellum damnosum	(Damnable discord)
Falsa fides	(Faithless faith)
Garrulum guttur	(Garrulous gabbler)
Kaos calumniarum	(Chaos of calumnies)
Mendacum monstrosum	(Mendacious monster)
Regnorum ruina	(Ruin of realms)
Vanitas vanitatum	(Vanity of vanities)

I have no doubt M. Olivier is being funny. At the same time
he might, if pressed, have cited grave and reverend authority
for every one of his counts. Petrarch I am afraid is serious.
In certain prose moods he shows himself quite the medieval
moralist. In certain moods his love of Madonna Laura herself appears to him a temptation and a sin.

Still, most of the time he is assured that his love of her
leads to higher things, to heaven. She is his Beatrice.

But this way of putting it would have greatly angered
him,—as implying imitation of Dante. In a letter to Boccaccio,
who had humbly tried to win him to Dante, he denies having
read Dante. He was fearful, he says, of imitating unawares,—
he who had made a boast of imitating Virgil and Cicero! It
is typical humanist snobbery; and the whole letter is a masterpiece of damning—and damnable—faint praise, of evasion and
jealous vanity. A pity,—especially when we remember Dante's
own generous acknowledgment to Guinizelli, the greater poet
to the lesser.

Moreover, it is hard to believe Petrarch. His *Canzoniere*,
or sonnet-sequence—as we say, though other forms than the
sonnet are represented,—repeats the dramatic crises of the

[61]

Vita Nuova: The sudden and almost mystical meeting and enamourment; the repulse by his lady; her death; her forgiveness and intercession in heaven; his imagined meeting with her there. Even the temporary turning for consolation to another is there. As Dante pays Beatrice the greater tribute of the *Commedia,* so Petrarch pays Laura that of the *Trionfi.* Both are "visions" and in *terza rima.* Both emphasize the redeeming of the poet by the grace of his lady. And there are, moreover, innumerable coincidences in diction, phrase, metrics. It is all natural and proper. Literary progress is made that way. The original artist is not the one who refuses every apprenticeship, but the one with a strong enough personality to attain final independence.

There was no occasion for Petrarch to deny his master. No one would question his originality. Even in following the *dolce stil,* he conforms it to his own temperament, *is* original. In mood, manner, music he further *sweetens* the "sweet style." For no poet ever is Spenser's phrase more descriptively apt,—"linkèd sweetness long drawn out." And it is not a cloying sweetness.

Looking more deeply to the informing spirit of his love-lyric, I would say that Petrarch *humanizes* Dante. Though he also symbolizes his lady,—especially as inspiring him to the laurel her name signifies,—she yet stands out as a living, breathing woman. There is given the unescapable impression of a real love-affair. Proving it a fiction would not alter the effect.

Petrarch introduces his love-story in a tone of penitent regret for a youthful folly:

> "You who now hear in vagrant rhymes the sound
> Of sighs wherewith I entertained my heart
> When I was other than I am in part,—
> Still in the meshes of young folly bound:

For moods inconstant when I would compound,
Weeping, between vain hope and vainer smart,
Where there is one who knows by proof love's art
There may be pity, if not pardon, found.
Yet hearing well how on men's lips my name
A byword has been long, oft and again
At mine own self I am myself dismayed;
And of my vanity the fruit is shame,
Yea, and repentance, and discernment plain
That things men joy in are as dreams that fade."

That may be the way the poet, grown old, felt he ought to feel. But he almost certainly did not,—not for long, or long at a time. "Vanity" in the sight of God his love may have been; but the fruit of it, as he complacently realized, was not "shame" but glory. Writing after Laura's death, he protests:

"Had I imagined that so dearly prized
Would be the voices of my sighs in rhyme,
Out of my sighing in that olden time
More and in style more rare had I devised."

But now Madonna is dead; he has lost his "sweet file." Indeed, in those days

"I sought to weep, but not from weeping honor.
Now were I glad to please; but she on high
Unto her presence calls me, mute, forspent."

Another time he is satisfied—not without justification—that

"these thy praises in my rhymes composed
Mayhap shall set on fire a thousand souls."

Dante had found in the name of Beatrice—*beatitude;* the name of Laura signifies the *laurel*—reward of fame. She and her poet's song of her immortalize each the other. Incidentally, to the very end of his life he continued to polish the verses in which his youthful folly was recorded.

I said that in Petrarch's love-poetry, as in comparison with Dante's, the *woman* stands out. Laura—the living Laura—is no mystic dim-seen maiden, whom to look upon is a benediction, but to touch would be a profanation. Dante tells of Beatrice's appearance only that she was of the "color of pearl," and that he first saw her clothed in red, and next in white. And these particulars are probably also symbolic. Petrarch paints and repaints Madonna Laura. Hers is a most palpable and luxuriant beauty. Her poet glories in the pink-and-whiteness of her face, framed in blond tresses,—"like white roses with red in a golden vase." He dilates upon the lustrous "topazes," her eyes,—upon the whiteness of her bosom, "beside which milk would be a losing foil." He descants upon "her manners meekly proud, her gentle disdainfulness proudly meek." We feel ourselves in a gilded *salon* among opulently fair ladies such as Titian or Rubens were to paint. And the lover of Laura living is not always like the timid and worshipful one of the *Vita Nuova*. He is at times rather the bold gallant, even a wooer more passionate than the Dante of the *Pietra* ode. (Curiously, he voices this more sensual mood only in the artificial sestina.) He can be playfully impudent in his compliments,—as when he professes jealousy of his "rivals," those "homicidal mirrors, which," he tells her, "you have worn out gazing in." Unlike Dante, he sees much of his lady; she sings to him; scolds him for not visiting her; pouts when he goes off on a journey; in fine, breathes hot and cold like what Sir Thomas Overbury calls "a very woman." Now and then he rebels, spinning variations on the ancient theme—

"Woman by nature is a fickle thing."

[64]

Or he may, with frantic indignation, deny an alleged indiscretion:

> "If ever I it said, be mine her hate
> Whose love I live by, and whose loss must kill:
> If I it said, few be my days and ill,
> My soul in bondage to a loathly mate:
> If I it said, curse every star my fate;
> And by my side let be
> Anguish and jealousy;
> Let my sweet enemy
> Grow fairer ever, ever less compassionate!"

In general, even though unrewarded, he is resigned:

> "It still consoles me that to pine for her
> Far worthier is than to have won another."

And when all is said,

> "His death is sweet who dieth for sweet love."

One feels fairly certain, however, that the lover who so talks of dying for love is in no great danger of doing it.

Overbury again, in his "character" of "a very woman," concludes that "her chief commendation is, that she brings a man to repentance." So Laura brought Petrarch to repentance. But he acknowledges it without Overbury's irony. Altogether unlike Beatrice on earth, Laura in heaven is nearer to Beatrice *beata*. Still, there is a difference. She is less the saint, more the woman,—a woman now as lovingly tender as on earth she had been coquettishly cold. From being the "merciless beauty" she is become the "Blessed Damosel." Indeed, the sonnet describing Laura's entry into Paradise has a markedly Rossettian intonation. (My translation can but hint at it.)

> "The chosen angels and the spirits, blest
> Citizenry of heaven, that first day

My lady passed among their bright array,
About her, worshipful and wondering, pressed.
'What splendor is this? What bliss new manifest?'
Each whispered each. 'From where men go astray
Never in all this age hath winged its way
Spirit so fair unto this place of rest.'
She, in her soul's new dwelling gladsomer,
Peer is of those whom God hath highest placed;
And nathless now and then she turneth her,
Looking if I still follow, and goes slow-paced:
So every will and thought I skyward spur,
Because I hear her pray that I make haste."

Also, his imagined first reunion with her in heaven is in the
key of the *Blessed Damosel*,—the key of personal romantic
love:

"My thought upbore me unto where she was
Whom upon earth I seek, nor find again:
There, in that sphere which moveth to love's laws,
I saw her, lovelier and of less disdain.
My hand she took, and said: 'Here shall we twain
Yet joinèd be, unless desire deceive:
She am I who thee brought to so long pain,
And mine own day fulfilled ere it was eve.
My weal is more than mortals understand:
I wait but thee, and that by thee loved so—
My veil of beauty, harbored there below.'
Ah, wherefore hushed she, and let go my hand?
For at her words, so tender and urbane,
Almost it seemed I might in heaven remain."

As I say, this is a Rossetti-like picture of idealized romantic
love. Laura *beata* is never the cool, aloof Mother Superior,
the teaching and preaching symbol, that at once in Paradise
had discoursed to Dante upon the nature of the spots on the

Moon. At the very last perhaps Beatrice is touched to a tender humanity. After his final words to her of gratitude and appeal, Dante says:

> "And thus I prayed; and she from that far place
> Smiled, as it seemed, and looked once more at me;
> Then to the Fount Eternal turned her face."
>
> [*Par.* xxxi, 91-3]

Laura in heaven is always the tender woman eagerly awaiting her lover. The poet's appeal to her is still a human appeal; and this no doubt is the deepest reason why the coming humanized age preferred Petrarch to Dante. The unknown sixteenth-century enthusiast in *Tottel's Miscellany* was only expressing the judgment of Europe, contemporary and for generations to come, when he exclaimed—and in a Petrarchan sonnet:

> "O Petrarke hed and prince of Poets all!"

Petrarch humanizes the *dolce stil nuovo,* the love-song of the "gentle heart," of the *Vita Nuova.* For the theology of love he substitutes its psychology. The *Vita Nuova* records the grand crises of a conversion. Connecting these crises are only such incidents as are in the retrospect revealed to have been symbolically and prophetically significant. Petrarch builds from similar crises, but fills in with love's accidents from day to day, from mood to mood, for their own emotional interest. No happening is too slight if touching his love or his lady, no conceit that occurs to him too trivial. It strikes him that he is like a snared bird—*a sonnet;* that Madonna is the Sun of his life, and that away from her all is black night —*a sonnet;* that her very name proves her "the air" (*l'aura*) he must breathe to live,—proves her no less the coveted "laurel" (*lauro*) and precious "gold" (*l'oro*)—for each pun *a sonnet.* But she is the candle, he the moth—*a sonnet.* Her disdain is the winter of his discontent—*a sonnet.* She smiles, and spring returns—*a companion sonnet.* He steals a glove of hers; is made to give it back; is sorry he did give it back—*three sonnets.* And so on, and so on. He bewails her absence, her frown, her sickness, her death; he paints and repaints every feature of hers, every trait—until we hardly see the forest for the trees. Its author says that in the *Roman de la Rose "L'Art d'Amors est tote enclose."* So, even more truly, Petrarch might say of his *Canzoniere.* The sequence is a veritable handbook for lovers, a storehouse of amatory stage-properties,—and all exquisitely fashioned.

It is all beautiful,—or at the least, pretty,—but too often less love than gallantry. There is too often an intonation of smartness, even of smugness. Hence Shelley's cruel comment, that many of Petrarch's sonnets "begin with a sob, but end with a simper." The sonnet telling of his enamourment on the holy day of Christ's own Passion, should it not speak with seriousness, with reverence? And what have we but a carefully turned, smartish conceit?

> "It was the day when dimmed was in the sun
> For pity of his Maker every ray
> That I was taken, dreaming not *that* day
> To be by your eyes, Lady mine, undone.
> That day occasion seemed there not to shun
> The shafts of Love; and so I went my way
> Serene and unsuspecting: my dismay
> Thus in the common dolour was begun.
> Love found me with mine armor laid aside,
> The way wide open to my heart through eyes
> That now for tears are gates of overflow.
> To pierce me with his arrow in such wise
> I deem it not for Love a cause for pride,—
> Nor yet for you that hid from me his bow."

Pretty, graceful, playful, yes—at least in the original; but we are no longer in the cathedral with Dante; we are in the drawing-room, the *salon*. It might be an eighteenth-century abbé speaking. The *dolce stil* has been transmuted into *vers-de-société*. Gabriel Harvey, Edmund Spenser's friend, passed a notable Renaissance judgment upon the poet of Madonna Laura. "Petrarch," wrote Harvey, "was a delicate man, and with an elegant judgment graciously confined Love within the terms of Civility." His poetry, continues the Cambridge don, is "the grace of Art, a precious tablet of rare conceits, and a curious frame of exquisite workmanship; nothing but neat Wit and refined Elegance." This is perfect, absolutely perfect,—from the Renaissance point of view. One thinks more highly of the ponderous British humanist for it. But in the degree that his judgment is right, Petrarch may be said to have receded from the sincerity of the "sweet new style" back into the mood and manner of the Provençal troubadours, "courtly makers" meaning not precisely what they said of loving, but saying it with "neat Wit and refined Elegance," and "graciously confining *their* love within the terms of Civility."

Although indeed the poet of Laura has moving depths unplumbed by Harvey, an authentic "sob," it is nevertheless Harvey's Petrarch that was to become

> "Hed and prince of Poets all"

for the Renaissance in the matter of love. Presently, a new code of courtly love was to be formulated,—so-called Platonic love. It was to have the colour of a religion of beauty; and of this religion the Petrarchan lyrics—especially sonnets —were to make up the hymnal, the prescribed ritual of song. By worship of feminine beauty and charm cruder men were to be "refined to higher things," as one of them—Dr. John Donne—put it.

Petrarch's sonnets, in matter and manner both, became thus the preferred lyric model of the whole European Renaissance. Du Bellay, spokesman of the *Pléiade*, sets them alongside the "noble genres" of antiquity, worthy to be imitated. In England and Spain especially, translation and imitation of them inaugurated the literary Renaissance for those countries. So English Puttenham testifies as to Wyatt and Surrey and their fellow "courtly makers." The Spanish Petrarchist Boscán himself tells how in 1526 he was persuaded by the Venetian ambassador, Andrea Navagiero, to give the sonnets a Castilian dress. And as Wyatt was seconded—and polished—by Surrey, so was Boscán by Garcilasso de la Vega.

Dante's lyrics preluded his greater tribute to Beatrice—the *Commedia*. Petrarch's lyrics preluded what seems to have been intended as his greater tribute to Laura—the *Trionfi*, or "Triumphs."

These are visionary and symbolic pageants, moralizing the poet's love-story. He sees in dream the God of Love upon his war-chariot, followed by his train of captives—the great lovers of history, duly named, and among them himself, Petrarch, with a fair maiden, not named. Love is leading them all in triumph to Cyprus; when Laura, marshalling in battle array the chaste ones of all time against the Tyrant, rescues his prisoners, and hangs up as a votive offering his bow and arrows in the temple of Chastity at Rome. But then alas! comes Death in his Triumph, to whom even Laura must bow. The bereaved poet then turns for consolation to imagining the Triumph of Fame, only to confront the fame-destroying Triumph of Time. But at last is revealed to him the truly consoling Triumph of Eternity, in which he may share his lady's blessedness.

This allegorical narrative is undramatic and unreal. One after the other the personifications—Love, Chastity, Death,

Fame, Time, Eternity—appear upon triumphal chariots
drawn by emblematic beasts—elephants, unicorns, oxen—and
followed by representative types. It is all frigid enough, if
pictorially interesting. Indeed, the *Trionfi* have survived
chiefly in pictorial art.

They do bear witness to the poet's classical enthusiasm.
Their very title—"Triumphs"—suggests the processionals executed in relief on Roman arches, tombs, coffers, fragments of
which, not a little through Petrarch's own inspiration, were
being uncovered and gathered. One might say that the
Trionfi were more of a monument to Antiquity than to
Madonna Laura.

Like Dante, Petrarch believed in the divine right of the
Roman People to rule. But he was far from having Dante's
trained logical mind or political experience. Petrarch was the
complete man of letters, widely rather than deeply read. Indubitably a sincere and intense lover of his country, the
patria, he is a little confused as to what that *patria* might intend. It is indeed always the *Imperium* of the *Populus
Romanus;* but his understanding both of *Imperium* and of
Romanus seems to blur together the ancient Republic of
Scipio and Cato and Cicero with the Empire of the Caesars,
and as well with the purely theoretic sovereignty of contemporary Rome. His most famous patriotic poem, on the other
hand, has nothing to do with the ancient Romans, but is a
passionate appeal to his quarrelling fellow-Italians to unite
and take up arms against the foreign aggressor. It might have
been written in the time of the *Risorgimento,*—in fact became
a battle-hymn of that national uprising. Machiavelli, in the
ardent peroration of the *Prince,* had already quoted as a war-
cry the lines:

"Virtù contra furore
Prenderà l'arme; e fia'l combatter corto;

Chè l'antico valore
Nell'italici cor non è ancor morto."

(Prowess against savagery
Shall take up arms; and the battle be quick-sped;
For the ancient bravery
In true Italian hearts is not yet dead.)

But at other times—I daresay most of the time—Petrarch's imagination was obsessed by that characteristic illusion of the Middle Ages—and after perhaps: the conviction that the *Imperium Romanum* remained—and was ordained to remain —living and unalterable. Actual Rome in Petrarch's day was a slovenly village built over ruins, and dominated by the fortress-towers of a few locally powerful families in constant strife. Already by 1305 the Pope had removed his seat to Avignon. So far from governing the world, or even Italy, the people of Rome had no real government even for themselves—beyond the caprice of clans organized only against one another.

Under these circumstances one cannot but sympathize with Petrarch's generous enthusiasm for Cola di Rienzi's amazing effort to bring order out of chaos. Considering the human materials he had to use and the selfishness and treachery with which he had to deal, that Rienzi, virtually alone, should have achieved what he did, and for as long as he did, is one of the marvels of history. Making allowance for perfervidness of language then, one can, I say, understand and sympathize with Petrarch's tributes—in prose and in verse—to the ephemeral "Tribune of the Roman People." And one may pass the title of *Tribune*—as a name to conjure by. But one is dumbfounded to find a man of Petrarch's knowledge and experience taking it—and with all it implied—with serious literalness. Listen to a few sentences addressed to the people of Rome after Rienzi's downfall and imprisonment, calling upon them to rise and rescue him. "Invincible People," he begins, "to whom I belong, Conquerors of the Nations, . . . the supreme crime with which he [*your Tribune*] is charged . . . is his daring to affirm that the empire of the Romans is still at Rome, and in possession of the Roman People . . . If the Roman empire is not at Rome, pray where is it? If it is anywhere else than at Rome, pray where is it? If it is anywhere else than at Rome, it is no longer the empire of the Romans, but belongs to those with whom an erratic fate has left it . . . But believe me, if a drop of the old blood still flows in your veins, you may yet enjoy no little majesty and no trifling authority . . . You have but to speak as one. Let the world realize that the Roman People has but a single voice, and no one will reject or scorn their words. Every one will respect or fear them." [1]

Now all this is utterly unreal, utter bombast. One cannot but believe that Petrarch knew it, but—as emotional orators will—let himself go. The echo of the stirring words of his *canzone* "*Italia mia*," stirring as addressed to the potentially powerful whole people of Italy, must have sounded to the miserable inhabitants of fourteenth century Rome as a cruel irony. "Invincible People" indeed! How much the opposite Petrarch must have known: he had been in Rome.

Still, it is difficult to say how far self-deception may go,—especially with an imagination constantly feeding, as did Petrarch's, upon the past grandeur of what he regarded as his own people. It is not altogether strange if he sometimes confused past and present.

I make what may seem a trite reflection. It has, however, its point here, since out of this imaginative confusion of past and present came the most potent motive to the Renaissance

---

[1] Transl. by Robinson and Rolfe, *Petrarch*, Putnam, 1898.

itself in Italy. I mean the illusory conviction of its pioneers—among them, I think, Petrarch himself—that the past might literally become again the present, that the hand of time might be turned back a thousand years, that ancient Rome might come again to be as she was. The pioneer Roman archaeologist, Ciriac of Ancona, meant it literally when he said: "I go to awake the dead." The classical revival was to be not a matter of learning, but of living,—of *re*living the ancient life, for Italians the ancestral life.

It must be admitted that Petrarch himself achieved the antique Roman type far less than Dante, and that his passion for its virile dignity was, one might say, feminine. Like Shelley's "sensitive plant," he desired what he had not. And his contagious enthusiasm set his generation to desiring the same thing. For a hundred years after his death Italians in the degree of their cultivation and enlightenment set themselves to becoming ancient Romans. In many respects,—most of all in the practical and political qualities so preeminently Roman,—they ignominiously failed. But they Romanized their speech and taste, their arts and letters,—in a word their culture. And so under their tutelage did Europe. To a certain real degree it is owing to Petrarch that even in the twentieth century we are closer in thought and feeling to the time of Augustus Caesar than to the ten Christian centuries that came after him. For has not Christianity itself been humanized?

IV

BOCCACCIO

IN 1362, Petrarch wrote a sensible letter of advice to a certain younger literary friend. This friend had written about a visit from a monk, who came, he said, in the name of one Peter of Siena, a reputed saint. Peter on his deathbed, declared the messenger, had seen visions in which certain prominent men, including Petrarch and his correspondent, were shown to be damned—unless they promptly renounced, among other frailties, profane poetry. And Petrarch's friend, frankly worried, had seriously asked the elder poet if he did not think it would be wise to heed the monk's warning.

Petrarch's letter in reply is one of his wisest and most delightful. Assured that the monk is on the way to warn him too, he promises "to interrogate closely everything about him,—his age, face, eyes, dress, bearing, gait, even his tone of voice, movements, style of address, and above all, his apparent object and the upshot of his discourse." As for the warning that death is at hand,—that, remarks Petrarch drily, is no matter. Did he not know it already? But he is amazed that any man in his senses, saint or not, should propose to ban poetry as against piety. Was not the author of the *Psalms* a poet? In fine, Petrarch urges his young friend not to be frightened by such nonsense, but to go valiantly on in his service of the Muses. Still, he concludes cannily, if you do decide to renounce your secular studies, and to sell off your books, pray let me have first choice among them.

Fortunately, Petrarch's humour and good sense prevailed. The younger friend was Giovanni Boccaccio.

The tradition is that Boccaccio was born, out of wedlock, in 1313 in Paris of a Frenchwoman of rank and a travelling merchant from Certaldo, a town near Florence. One would like to believe this. It would account so well for the Gallic strain, the *esprit Gaulois*, in the *Decameron*.

Probably in 1325, the twelve-year-old lad, unwelcome in the household of his stepmother at Florence, was sent to Naples, apprenticed to a merchant. After six years, his father permitted his turning to the Law,—for which, however, he showed no greater aptitude than for business. Like Petrarch, like Pope, he "lisped in numbers," was a man of letters born.

Apparently, young Boccaccio was well recommended in the gay capital of Robert of Anjou. Like Petrarch at Avignon, he gave himself to more than letters. His romances show familiarity with Neapolitan high society, even of the Court. And it was with the young wife of a noble courtier, and she by repute a natural daughter of King Robert himself, that the romance began—about 1333—which was to colour nearly all of Boccaccio's writings, and—to take his own word for it —his life itself. The lady's name was Maria d'Aquino, but for her poet-lover she was always *Fiammetta*, "Flamelet." And she proved to be for him a devouring flame indeed. If Dante's attitude towards Beatrice is one of reverence, and Petrarch's towards Laura one of devotion, Boccaccio's towards Fiammetta is frankly one of passion. Now and again, indeed, ardent admirer of Dante, he presents Fiammetta in the rôle of a spiritual guide. But neither he nor she belongs in the picture. Whatever reality their affair had, it was not that kind of reality.

And, as he gives us to understand, Fiammetta first returned his love, and then jilted him, playing Cressida to his Troilus.

This was in 1338. About two years later, on account of financial reverses in the family, he was called back—much against his will—to Florence and an unsympathetic step-mother. His consolation was work. In the course of the next decade his abundant literary output brought fame, though not wealth. Later, like Petrarch, if more modestly, he was honoured by ambassadorial functions. In 1354, and again in 1365, the Florentine government sent him to the papal court at Avignon; in 1367 to Rome. The reason—in his case as in Petrarch's—was the reputation of *eloquentia*. These decorative envoys made the speeches; professional secretaries— "career men"—did the real business. One mission of Boccaccio's was indeed more personal,—namely, to offer the now famous poet and humanist Petrarch a chair in the *Studio*, or University, of Florence. It was in 1351, and Petrarch was at Padua. Though he declined, a friendship between him and Boccaccio was begun, which grew stronger with the years. On Boccaccio's side it was reverently loyal, almost filial; on Petrarch's benevolently protective, at times a little Olympian, Goethean. Curiously, the gay author of the *Decameron* was the more timorous character. He looked up still more worshipfully to Dante, whose life he wrote, and whose *Commedia* he expounded in the Florentine *Studio* at the very close of his life. This was in 1373, and was a welcome, if brief, consolation for the disappointments, poverty, pietistic remorse of his later years. A twelvemonth later, his health failing, he retired to Certaldo, and there died December 21, 1375.

He wrote the motto for his own epitaph—and for his life: *Studium fuit alma poesis.*

Boccaccio's first published work was a prose romance called *Filocolo*. It was begun in the early thirties, and, he says, at the instance of Fiammetta; but was probably finished after his return to Florence. It retells in seven books the medieval tale of *Flore and Blanchefleur*—adapted to the fashionable world of Naples, and insinuating his own love-story. Also, the young author—barely in his twenties when he began—airs his "new learning." The Greek title *Filocolo*—he had better have said *Filocopo*—is explained by him to mean *fatica d'amore*, "love's labors"—not yet, however, *lost*. The style is floridly Ciceronian, prolix and precious, full of long cataloguing descriptions. In short, the *Filocolo* is apprentice-work. Its fifth book, however, presents an interesting full-length picture of Neapolitan fashionable society at play—in a diversion which has its start in Provençal *chateaux*, and its further continuation in Renaissance courts and drawingrooms. I mean the game of "Questions," *Dubbii*. A circle of ladies and gentlemen debate, one lady presiding, some question, or doubt, usually in the casuistry of Love. In the *Filocolo*, thirteen love-questions are debated by a gay circle in a flower-garden on a summer afternoon. (We think of the setting of the *Decameron* to come.) It is a school of wit. Most of the questions have a long literary history before and after. One familiar question is, Whether 'tis better to have loved and lost than never to have loved at all. Another and ingenious one is raised again three centuries later in one of the eclogues of William Basse. A lady sits between two suitors. She and one suitor wear garlands of flowers. She puts her garland on his head who has none, and on her own head his who had one: to which suitor shows she the greater favour? It is quite possible to become argumentative over such an issue,—as some decades ago Americans did over Frank Stockton's *The Lady or the Tiger?* We find the game still prevalent in the full Renaissance. It was proposed after dinner at the court of Urbino, as Castiglione relates; and indeed the *Courtier* itself is the debate upon the question chosen—*What is a right Courtier?* In Elizabethan England, John Lyly makes the game the principal diversion at the Lady Flavia's dinner-party in *Euphues and his England*. Several of the questions there debated are from among Boccaccio's thirteen. Indeed, the discussion from the *Filocolo* was published in 1567 in English as a separate work, entitled *Thirtene most plesant and delectable Questions*, and went through two other editions in the century.

The *Filocolo* was followed a few years later—perhaps in 1343—by a work also inspired by Maria d'Aquino, but alas! in a very different mood and vein. It is called *La Fiammetta*, and is a step away from the romance towards the psychological novel. Fiammetta tells her story—or what is made out to be her story. She is in love with a certain Panfilo, who has been compelled by a stern father to leave her, and to go back to Florence. He has promised to return in four months. Like Troilus, like Madame Butterfly, she waits and waits, hoping and despairing. At last she learns he has married. Alarmed at her melancholy pining, her own husband takes her away for a change. In vain. She talks of suicide. Finally, at news that Panfilo is returning, she—still like Madame Butterfly—adorns herself for him. Still he comes not, and—she reminds herself, consolingly, how many other women have been in the same boat.

So with a malicious grin, Boccaccio turns the tables on the girl who jilted *him*. It is an easy kind of revenge, if one cares for it.

There are critics who insist that in this novel Boccaccio puts himself in the woman's place in also another sense,—that he shows an intimate knowledge of the feminine heart. I cannot presume to judge. I do know that his heroine is very voluble and very bookish, given to classical allusion, overflowing every minute into apostrophe and declamation. She pours out her heart in ejaculatory soliloquies, so setting a fashion for heroines of Renaissance fiction, and not wholly given over by Clarissa Harlowe.

In her display of classical lore, Fiammetta may have truly represented Maria d'Aquino. The "new learning" was getting fashionable, even among ladies. Boccaccio's own writings—after Petrarch's—were among the influences making it so. And he was reaching out beyond society novels, aspiring to become not only a poet, but a classic and epic one,—another Virgil perhaps. It was the common dream of Renaissance poets after him, as of Dante and Petrarch before.

So in the early forties, with versatile ease, Boccaccio wrote a series of narrative poems which, if not Virgilian exactly, yet had great vogue and international influence. I may begin with the *Filostrato* and the *Teseide*. Both were dedicated to Fiammetta.

Il Filostrato, explains the author to his lady, is "the man conquered and subjected by love—as we may see Troilus was ... His miseries are my story ... And if I vaunt the beauties and the charms of Cressida, you may know that I dream of yours." Boccaccio says nothing—*aloud*—about Cressida being also false as fair.

Actually, neither in mood nor in treatment is the poem epic or classic. It is another society novel, set to the manners and morals of fashionable Naples, in highly decorated verse instead of highly decorated prose.

Boccaccio's only access to the Homeric story was by the mutilated summaries and paraphrases of the Middle Ages—Benoit de Saint-More's *Roman de Troie*, Guido delle Colonne's *Hystoria Troiana*, the brief epitomes by Dictys Cretensis and Dares Phrygius. These gave names and general outline of the plot. There are introduced also some reminders of the poet's two admirations, Dante and Petrarch. But the real web and tissue of the tale are Boccaccio's own.

It is the festival of Pallas. Young Troilus, Hector's brother, strolls about the temple, chatting with friends, glancing disdainfully at the girls. He is proud of his indifference to the sex. Then—as the reader expects—his pose is abruptly broken by sight of Cressida in her widow's mourning—

> "Under white veil in sober-colored gown."

From that moment she is his life. To win her attention, he makes himself a hero in the war. One day, an intimate of his,

> "a Trojan youth
> Of lineage high and eke of noble heart,"

finding him in tears upon his bed, naturally asks the matter. Troilus petulantly begs to be let alone. He is dying, he says, —and he *wants* to die. Pandaro, the friend,—young in years, but old in experience,—understands. Perhaps he can help. Who *is* she?

But you cannot. She is your own cousin, sighs the dejected lover.

Friendship is stronger than kinship. Pandaro has no scruple.

> "Were she you love a sister of my own,
> I'd help you still to have your will of her."

Only, the affair must not be found out. Discovery would bring dishonour upon the family.

So Pandaro sets to work upon Cressida. He casually remarks one day that she is looking prettier than ever. Another has noticed it, too. *Who?* "Why, girl, He who made the first man, made never another as good until He made this one."

When Pandaro has got Cressida bursting with curiosity, he whispers—"Prince Troilus." Cressida stares; then "becomes as the sky which pales at dawn." "Troilus is far too grand for me," she exclaims. "And besides, I must not think of any man but my dead husband."

The tempter makes a show of indignation. A young woman like you has a right to love.

> "Lose not a moment; think how cold and gray
> Old age, or death, will steal those charms away."

Cressida yields. "Ah well, bid him be prudent!" Left alone, she reflects that after all, "to do as others do is no great sin!"

At Pandaro's suggestion, Troilus now presses his suit in a long epistle in Petrarch's amatory vein, exaggerated to florid sentimentality.

Triumphant at last after the long siege, Troilus thanks Pandaro for his loyal devotion as a friend and a gentleman. Neither young man for a moment suspects that anything shady has been done. Troilus does not see himself as a seducer, nor Pandaro himself as a pander. Troilus's only thought is how to repay the debt. If ever Pandaro should happen to admire Troilus's sister Polyxena, or even his famous sister-in-law Helen . . . !

There is no need to go on with the story. I have indeed tried merely to hint at the tone of it. To its morals applies very well Charles Lamb's defence of the Restoration drama. We are in a world of gallant and witty make-believe, and one —unlike the Restoration drama—entirely without verbal coarseness. No doubt, Neapolitan court-life is somewhat reflected, with its survivals from the code of courtly love—especially the prime statute of *secrecy*. Reflected more closely still, I should say, is that other love-code—the *Art of Love* of Ovid. But I do not think Boccaccio is concerned with any

serious reflection of, or upon, real life. He is writing to entertain—lightheartedly, if with perhaps a touch of sardonic
amusement at the frail shadows of human nature he is evoking. He is a little sorry for Troilus, yes; for, as he says,—
"his miseries are my story." But his more earnest concern is
with his art—his witty conceits, his ornately chiselled diction,
his limpid mellifluous verse.

Nor, in spite of many statements to the contrary, do I feel
Chaucer's mood to be very different. Because by him Pandaro
is called "uncle" of Cressida, we are often given to understand that the debonnair young friend of Boccaccio's Troilus
has been transformed into an elderly, lecherous pimp. It is
not so. On the contrary, Pandaro remains "brother" and devoted friend to the last, and no more immoral or cynical than
his Italian namesake. He is a gentleman by the code. Cressida too is still what Boccaccio made her,—not so much a
light woman as a light weight morally, thoroughly conventional, if sensual, and easily swayed. And, except for his
constancy, Troilus remains pretty much her male counterpart.
The main difference between Boccaccio and Chaucer is in
their own personal temper. Chaucer is more detached and
ironic, less suave and sentimental,—nearer perhaps to the
mature Boccaccio, to the comic spirit of the *Decameron*. It is
fair to remember, however, that English itself is more robust
than Italian, and Chaucer's stanza less mellifluous than the
octave. In fine, high praise, it seems to me, is due the English
poet not for altering, but for reproducing with extraordinary
accuracy, the spirit of the Italian poem.

In *Il Teseide* Boccaccio essays a really Virgilian epic. It has
twelve books, like its model, the *Aeneid,* even the same number of lines. But heroic numbers were not for Messer Giovanni. The only live portion of his twelve books is again a

love-story, a novellesque situation,—the very special triangle of Palamon-Arcite-Emilia. Chaucer wisely took out virtually only that portion for his *Knight's Tale*. He condenses to one-fifth Boccaccio's length. There are indeed certain scars of amputation. In reducing to a few lines Boccaccio's account of the war waged by Theseus against the tyrant of Thebes, Chaucer fails to explain the singular animosity of Theseus towards the two young captive Thebans, Palamon and Arcite.

The tale of the rivalry of these for the lady Emilia, Theseus's sister, appeals to the strong Renaissance interest in the issue of Love as against Friendship,—though in the present case the issue is hardly a live one. From the first glimpse of the lady by the two friends, their friendship has no chance at all against their resistless love for her. They revile each other, fight each other, most unchivalrously seize every opportunity to win. To be sure, at the very end Palamon, dying, commends Emilia to Arcite. It is, however, rather an eleventh hour act of generosity, and moreover one really determined by the gods.

In the course of the action another love-question is dramatized, namely whether Palamon's case is worse, who may see his lady daily, but is kept from her in prison, or Arcite's, who is free to go wheresoever he will except to Athens where his lady is. The lady, it must be said, has but little concern about the whole matter, but is throughout passively acquiescent.

As in all his earlier romances, Boccaccio abundantly farces his narrative with description—especially of the temples of Venus and of Mars—and also with philosophical reflection. This last Chaucer extends, drawing upon the doctrine of Boethius concerning Fortune.

Perhaps the greatest difference between the Italian poet and his English disciple is in the matter of style. When Boccaccio is languidly melodious and palely elegant in diction, Chaucer's verse is crisply vigorous, and his diction specific and coloured; also, his mood is at times one of mockery.

In these two poems of classical setting the influence of Dante is present, but slight. In two other works—*Ninfale d'Ameto* and *Amorosa Visione*—it is dominant.

Ninfale, "Nymphal,"—Michael Drayton uses the word,—is the feminine, one might say, of *pastoral*. *Ninfale d'Ameto* is a prose pastoral with verse insets. At the end, it turns out to be an allegory.

The scene is on the wooded slope of Fiesole. The time is at first autumn. The young huntsman Ameto, "uncouth and unkist," meets in the greenwood the nymph Lia. She responds to his advances, but tames his wildness. Separated during the winter, they meet again in the springtime; and on Venus' day she leads him to a temple by a clear spring, where are gathered shepherds and their nymphs, together with fauns, dryads, satyrs, naiads. Ameto is introduced to six nymphs coming two by two. The superlative charms of each are minutely and monotonously catalogued. They all then form a circle on the greensward, and the nymphs in turn recount their amorous experiences. It is a step from the circle of love-debate of the *Filocolo*, a larger step towards the story-telling circle of the *Decameron*. Indeed, the nymphs' tales are singularly like the later *novella*, and quite as free.

Hitherto there has been no suggestion of allegory. But now portents happen. Seven swans battle in the air with seven storks, and are victorious. A column of fire descends from heaven, and from it a voice speaks:

> "Light out of heaven am I, the One and Three.
> Beginning of all things I am, and end . . .
> He shall not go astray who followeth me."

Clearly, no pagan Venus is speaking. But Ameto is not left
to inference. Like Dante by Matilda in Eunoe, he is dipped
by Lia in the spring,—and his eyes are opened. The day is
really Easter. The nymphs declare themselves in the words
of Dante's Virtues:

> "Here we are nymphs, but we are stars in heaven."
> [*Purg.* xxxi, 106]

The suitors—or husbands—of whom they had told tales turn
out, surprisingly enough, to have been their own opposites,
the Vices. And some of these they redeem. Thus Lia, as
Faith, redeems Ignorance. Hope, as Fiammetta, cures Despair, who is Caleone, who is Giovanni Boccaccio. It is rather
mixed. Mopsa tells how, unhappily married, she had seduced
nice young Afron. It is a gay and racy story—until we learn
with surprise that Mopsa is really Wisdom, Afron Folly.

Manifestly, moral allegory is no more native to Boccaccio
than heroic epic. Whatever rôle he essays, the novelist
remains.

And so it appears again in the slightly later *Amorosa
Visione*, edifying allegorical vision though this purports to be.

In his dream, a fair lady appears, inviting him to follow
her in the way of true happiness. This feminine *Virgil* leads
him to a stately Castle, which has two gates, one strait and
narrow, the other broad and easy. Over the former is the
inscription over Dante's Hell, reversed:

> "*Recover* hope all ye who enter here."

The other gate, we learn, leads to Wealth and Power, and
other vanities of this world.

Boccaccio insists on trying the broad way *first*,—overstress-
ing perhaps Petrarch's argument that we may permissibly
seek the goods of this life *before* turning to those of the next.

Surely, the "broad and easy way leadeth to destruction!" The Guide, however, offers no objection. And after all, the gate opens into nothing worse than a spacious hall hung with pictured tapestries. The visitor's worldly enjoyment is purely visual and vicarious. He sees portrayed a Triumph of Love. Description of it fills fifteen cantos. It is almost a *résumé* of Ovid's *Metamorphoses* and medieval romance, recounting the loves of the Heroes—Jason, Theseus, Orpheus, and the rest, the tragedies of Aeneas and Dido, Lancelot and Guinevere, Tristan and Iseult,—and so on.

Finally, in the thirteenth canto, leaving all these worldly experiences for the shadows they are, the Poet is led into a pleasant garden, where are bevies of fair ladies, former friends—presumably of Neapolitan society. From among them Fiammetta advances—to be embraced by the angelic Guide, who now reveals herself as Virtue, and promises to lead them both by the strait and narrow gate to salvation. Meanwhile, she considerately leaves the pair to themselves. Ardent Boccaccio promptly offers to kiss his ladylove; but she demurs:

> "Ah, do not!
> Suppose that lady came, what should I do?"

Perhaps the bathos is deliberate. Boccaccio has an impish humour. He sincerely reverenced Dante, but he could not be Dantesque—for long. The temptation to sly mockery is too much for him. Artistically, the *Amorosa Visione* anticipates again that taste for word-painting already shown in Petrarch's *Trionfi*, and to be so strong in the generation of Poliziano, and after. A detail of curious interest—brought to light only in 1821—is that the initial letters of the tercets spell out three *ballate* of laudatory dedication to Fiammetta.

Certainly, if Boccaccio's love was only make-believe, he played at it hard.

There is one more poem to consider of these prolific forties. This is the *Ninfale Fiesolano,* or "Fiesolan Pastoral."

Again the poet seems to have started with an epic intention, only to be carried away by his love of a love-story. The epic matter is squeezed into the last sixty stanzas, and reads like a popular verse-chronicle. We hear how Prunello, son of the shepherd Affrico and Diana's nymph Mensola, became seneschal of Atalante, founder of Fiesole, and how from his ten children came the principal families of Florence. Such complimentary genealogy of legend was to figure largely in the narrative poems of Boiardo, Ariosto, Tasso, Spenser, and even in them takes on the naïve manner of a folk-chronicle.

Boccaccio has no heart in it. Six-sevenths of the *Ninfale* detail lovingly the love-affair of Affrico and Mensola.

Loving Mensola at sight, Affrico went to his fate forewarned. His own grandfather, for ravishing a nymph of Diana's, had been changed into a river, the Mugno. Now Affrico and Mensola both are changed into streams which, still known by their names, flow down the slopes of Fiesole.

Ovid's is manifestly the main influence here. Also, there is something of the naïve wantonness, the prurient innocence of the decadent Greek idyl, *Daphnis and Chloe.* A redeeming trait of real simplicity and rustic poetry is due to frequent imitation of Tuscan folk-song.

During these prolific years, young Boccaccio was also assiduously studying. He never became indeed the finished classical scholar that Petrarch was. But he amassed considerable erudition and achieved a fair Latin style. Linking his vernacular poems to his soberer Latin writings are sixteen Latin eclogues, mostly also of the forties, though two as late as 1363. As proclaimed in the twelfth eclogue, Virgil and Petrarch are the models. Some of the eclogues, like Petrarch's are allegories *à clef*. The poet is more interested in his secret meanings than in the beauties of nature he talks about. The seventh eclogue seems to confess an intrigue of the poet with a nun, who is also possibly shadowed in Mensola, vowed to the Virgin Diana. As an elegy for a daughter, the same eclogue has been presented, though not altogether convincingly, as a source of the Middle-English poem, *The Pearl.*

Boccaccio's prose Latin works are mostly encyclopedic textbooks of ancient history, mythology, geography, useful for their time and furthering the movement of humanism, but without literary importance in themselves. Not so his *De casibus virorum illustrium,* which may be translated as Falls —or Tragedies—of the Great.

Boccaccio's inverts Dante's plan. Instead of going to the world of shades, he—more conveniently—has the shades come to him in his study. They are anxious to remind living men of their sad reversals of fortune—as a warning.

The book is not only edifying, but entertaining. Its vogue was great, its influence wide. It was translated by the French Premierfait and the English Lydgate. It gave Chaucer materials for his *Monk's Tale.* The *Mirror for Magistrates* continues its genre; and so do—in dramatic form—the Elizabethan "True Tragedies."

A little earlier, Boccaccio had moralized a minor tragedy of his own. He had paid attentions, it seems, to a certain widow, and been snubbed for his pains. The *Corbaccio,* "Whip," of 1354–5 avenges him—not upon the widow alone, but upon all her sex. Ovid gives place to Juvenal and the ecclesiastics.

There is a frame story of Dantesque allegory. A man is lost in "the labyrinth of love"—the sub-title. A spirit from Hell comes to his rescue. Boccaccio is the lost man; the spirit that of the dead husband. This curious *Virgil* sympathetically warns his would-be successor that "Hell hath no fury like a woman—*scorned*" or not. Boccaccio reminds us of the painter of the *Campo Santo* at Pisa who, it is said, to pay off an old score, shows a woman carried naked to Hell on the back of a demon.

The *Decameron* was written between 1348 and 1353. It was avowedly intended—like all its author's Italian works, except perhaps the *Corbaccio*—for a feminine audience. In a flowery preface he explains his purpose. Suffering from unrequited love, he had found consolation in the pleasant talk of friends. The sting of the ancient grief has been extracted by time, but gratitude for the consolation remains. He would repay by offering solace to others in like affliction,—especially ladies, who, as they are at once more susceptible and more delicate than men, so also because of their shut-in and limited lives have fewer distractions than men. For them particularly therefore, these tales are designed—to be serviceable also as moral guides and warnings.

The spirit is one of polite irony,—spirit, if one had to pick, most characteristic of the Italian Renaissance.

Boccaccio's art is now fully ripened. The dramatic setting to the tales is perfect. We get a complete sense of naturalness. The meeting of the seven young Florentine ladies in church, where they had gone to pray for escape from the horrible plague, is most natural. Pampinea's suggestion of getting out of the doomed city,—the eager approval of the terrified girls, but hesitation to go alone in such times,—the lucky appearance of three young men-friends,—the small talk, broaching of the plan, and its acceptance with nonchalance by the youths,—all these expository incidents happen naturally, casually. And how the peace and loveliness of the *villa* stand out against the horrors left behind in the city! How naturally the story-telling comes about as a pleasant way of passing the long, vacant afternoons! And the first day there are no set themes; but as one tale led to another like it, there occurs to Pampinea the idea of some sort of program. To prevent the plan becoming too set and formal, Dioneo the irrepressible and impudent insists on being always last, and on choosing his own theme.

The program itself has a certain balance and connection, but without forcing. Ninth day, as first, was left open. As the tales of the first day had happened to be of *peril averted by ready wit*, so those of the second day were to be of *evil fortune unexpectedly turned to good*. The third day would tell, specifically, *how patience and perseverance win out*. Fourth and fifth days present *issues of love—unhappy and happy*. Sixth day reverts—with a difference—to *the saving grace of wit*. Seventh day bares *treasons, stratagems and spoils of wives*. Eighth day illustrates *the witty war of sex*. Tenth day proclaims *love's magnanimities*.

And each day, after their tales are told, the young people sing a *ballata*—sometimes to music and with dancing.

Unlike Boccaccio's other Italian writings, the *Decameron* is objective and impersonal. The author nowhere intrudes. Nor has he, I think, other concern than entertainment. Because he paints with frankness dissolute priests and charlatan monks and frail nuns, he has been hailed as a precursor of the Reformation. But he is by no means shocked by these naughty people. He as often laughs with them as at them. Indeed, he laughs *at* the deceived husband, however worthy, and *with* the erring wife, if clever. These things are outside morals, outside reason. Who cares whether the perennially close Scotchman in *Punch* is just to the Scotch? He goes—as a traditional butt. Boccaccio extracted the last laugh out of the traditional butts of his day.

[91]

He invented few of his stories. Most he took out of medieval romances, legends, chronicles, *fabliaux*, earlier collections of tales and anecdotes,—a few from contemporary happenings. It does not matter. He transmutes them all into something new and—*familiar*. The whole variety of human society from lowest to highest is given form and feature, becomes—by adoption at least—Italian. At one moment, we rub elbows with scum of the earth—thieves, lechers, parasites, hypocrites, whores; the next moment, we breathe a rarified air of chivalry and courtesy and loyalty, at times extravagant —as when a lover surrenders his love to a friend, and without any particular consideration of the lady's own feelings; soon again, we are among hearty, healthy plain people, somewhat gross of appetite and loud of laughter, but on the whole honest and good-natured, if fond of practical jokes. Boccaccio does not analyze, moralize, or dissect his characters. We meet them as we meet people in life. Some we get to know pretty well; others barely. It depends upon how well we must know them to get the point of the story. The several tales centering around the simple-minded Calandrino (VIII, 3, 6; IX, 5) would have no point unless the various traits that go to make him gullible and absurd were fully brought out. When we hear, on the other hand, of the converted Florentine Jew who visits Rome,—to the alarm of his converter, who knows how corrupt Rome is,—and returns stronger of faith, because, he says, no church could continue to exist in such rottenness without divine support,—we need no specification of character to appreciate the sardonic humour. (1, 2) And the same is true for the solemn absurdity of little red-headed, lively, rascally Friar Onion offering with unction his blessed wares,—wing-feathers of the Angel Gabriel, coals from St. Lawrence's gridiron. (VI, 10)

The effect of these and similar tales is partly from the situation itself, but as much from the gravely ironic manner of the telling. It comes close to what is called "American humour," to the dry and caustic humour of Mark Twain. It states with sober matter-of-factness something quite preposterous. Most of the looser tales are written in this mood. Boccaccio is rarely salacious. Nor is he being, as our modern "sex" writers proclaim themselves, "strong" and "frank." He is trying to be —and often is—merely funny. A few of the tales no doubt— fewer than popularly supposed—are beyond the pale of humour, are nasty. It is not altogether the fault of the times. Petrarch recognizes the impropriety; but for special reasons condones it. He writes: "Your book [the *Decameron*], written in our mother tongue and published, I presume, during your early years, has fallen into my hands, I know not whence or how. If I told you I had read it, I should deceive you. It is a very big volume, written in prose and for the multitude. I have been, moreover, occupied with more serious business, and much pressed for time . . . My hasty perusal afforded me much pleasure. If the humour is a little too free at times, this may be excused at the age at which you wrote, the style and language which you employ, and the frivolity of the subjects, and of the persons who are likely to read such tales." [1] Petrarch then, however, in his most Olympian manner makes an exception of the last tale in the work, that of the patient Griselda, which he says moved him so much that he is enclosing a Latin translation of it,—so raising it into enduring literature. (At least, Chaucer drew from Petrarch's Latin his own version in the *Clerk's Tale.*) One would like to know how Boccaccio reacted to his elder friend's condescension. Petrarch was writing indeed in 1373, twenty years after the publication of the *Decameron*. Still, Boccaccio himself was forty in 1353, an age only relatively tender, at

[1] Robinson and Rolfe, *Petrarch*, Putnam, 1898, pp. 191-192.

least hardly young enough to excuse an over-free humour. Doubtless Petrarch charitably set the composition of the tales too far back. The point is, however, that they did seem over-free to him, though perhaps tolerable in the vulgar tongue and for a frivolous reader.

In the tragic or pathetic love-tales, again, it is primarily the situation that counts. Isabella watering her pot of basil enriched by her lover's severed head (IV, 5),—Federigo slaughtering for his heartless lady's repast his pet hawk, last of his possessions: to feel the pathos of such situations we need not know intimately Isabella or Federigo. Do, in point of fact, Keats and Longfellow make us know them? I do not know that Shakespeare in *All's Well* especially individualized—or tried to—another of Boccaccio's heroines,—the Gilletta of Narbonne who wins over a frosty husband by a not attractive trick. It was the cleverness of the trick, without special regard to the personality of the trickster—Helena is indeed made human,—that appealed to Shakespeare and his audience as it had to Boccaccio and his.[1]

These considerations should modify, I think, the judgment often passed, that the Boccaccian *novella* is inferior to the modern short story, or novel, in that it is not focussed study of character. It is not. It is a *story*—something too many of our novels—problem, clinical, propagandist—emphatically are not. Both kinds no doubt have their place.

Admittedly, when Boccaccio does elaborate a character, it is as a type—as what Ben Jonson would have called a *humour*—rather than as an individual. Like Jonson—or, measurably, Dickens—Boccaccio centres the whole character upon a single dominant trait,—patience, constancy, greed, jealousy. It is but one step off from personification and allegory. The

[1] Cf. W. W. Lawrence, *Shakespeare's Problem Plays*. Macmillan, 1931. His argument would apply, I think, to the *Decameron*.

Trait, as it were, gets up and walks. Thus in the famous last tale of the collection,—the one Petrarch stooped graciously to translate into perdurable Latin,—Griselda *is* patience personified. She lives in literary memory as the female Job. Only, instead of showing patience before God, she is patient before her husband. She is the model wife in a man-made world. At least, so thought her creator and his friend, Boccaccio and Petrarch, and in sympathy the Renaissance. Does not even large-minded Shakespeare make his tamed Shrew exhort wives to set their hands under their husbands' feet? (V, ii, 136 ff.) Briefly, here is Griselda's story.

She is a country-girl whom a noble Marquis has condescended to wed. He is not a hard or cruel man, nor a snob. Indeed, he seems disturbed less by the possible social consequences of the *mésalliance* than by doubts of his young wife's constancy. He goes about testing her as if it were a duty. Some of his tests are rather stringent: he pretends to put her two children to death; he sends her off into poverty and neglect; he appears to install a rival in her place in his house. What all this proves,—beyond his manifest need of a sound thrashing,—is not clear. However, when she has taken it all with sweet meekness, he graciously reinstates her,—and they are supposed to live happily ever after.

And now listen to the enthusiastic verdict of the gallant Poet of Laura: "Anyone, it seems to me, amply deserves to be reckoned among the heroes of mankind who suffers without a murmur for God, what this poor peasant woman bore for her mortal husband."

Obviously, no lesser part of Boccaccio's art is his style. He narrates with an ornate and smoothly rhythmic suavity of manner, now and then relieved by spicy and colloquial dialogue. He still indulges—especially in serious and romantic tales—in long and detailed passages of description, of word-painting; but he has acquired too the evocative single touch, the expressive specific epithet, which makes us really *see*. Also, the *rococo*, pseudo-classical ornamentation, the "precious" mannerisms of apostrophe, soliloquy, word-play have been cleared off. Boccaccio has forged a truly classic prose,—a prose that was to be *the* model of the Renaissance. Its suave rhythms are to be heard even in the Spanish of *Don Quixote*.

It is hard to appraise the *Decameron* justly. The *unco' guid* and the cynical *dilettante* alike make it harder. As a whole, the work is indubitably one of the half dozen great expressions of "The Comic Spirit"—in Meredith's sense of the term—which, remaining humane, yet views humanity with humorous detachment. But Boccaccio no more than Aristophanes or Rabelais restricts his ironic amusement to the decorous and decent. For elect readers their sense of humour may be a sufficient antiseptic to what may well poison the generality. There are those who may enjoy a smutty story for the fun, not for the foulness, in it. A more fastidious taste might decline the fun at the price. There seems no more to say.

In any case, the *Decameron* has been one of the four or five most influential books in literary history. Its imprint is found on the poetry and drama, as well as fiction, of all countries. By an odd, yet not wholly inept, caprice of fame, its author is the hero of a popular comic opera of today.

V

VALLA — FICINO —
BENIVIENI

"SO that these four causes concurring, the admiration of
ancient authors, the hate of the schoolmen, the exact
study of languages, and the efficacy of preaching, did bring
in an affectionate study of eloquence and copie (*copiousness*)
of speech, which then began to flourish. This grew speedily
to excess; for men began to hunt more after words than
matter; more after the choiceness of the phrase, and the round
and clean composition of the sentence, and the sweet falling
of the clauses, and the varying and illustration of their works
with tropes and figures, than after the weight of matter,
worth of subject, soundness of argument, life of invention,
and depth of judgment . . . Then grew the learning of the
schoolmen to be utterly despised as barbarous. In sum, the
whole inclination and bent of those times was rather towards
copie than weight."

This judgment was passed by Francis Bacon in his *Advancement of Learning* (L, lv, 2). He is thinking rather of
sixteenth century England, but his words apply equally well
to fifteenth century Italy,—only for the factor of "efficacy of
preaching" might better be substituted efficacy of public oratory in all kinds. The cultural influences of the Humanists
were indeed great. I have hinted at a few of these influences
in my introduction. But to discuss them with greater fulness

would take us far away from our real concern, which is literature. I do not forget that the Humanists themselves produced an abundant literature; but apart from the fact that, as Bacon says, the "bent" of it "was rather towards copie than weight," the fact also that it was written in the dead languages of classical Latin and Greek has killed it for all but classical scholars,—and they for the most part scorn it. The literary historian cannot indeed afford to ignore so significant and formative a link in the development of European literature, but the task of analysis of this Neo-Latin and Neo-Greek literature is outside the scope of this book and my own competence.

Of course, there are a few exceptions to the general deadness of humanist writings. One thinks at once of Erasmus's *Encomium Moriae,* or Praise of Folly, and of More's *Utopia,* which have taken their place as world-classics. But certainly the Italian Humanists produced nothing remotely comparable.

As Bacon implies, the humanistic movement was on one side destructive of the medieval edifice. Wrecking the old was a prerequisite to building the new. Naturally, the Humanists in general participated in the wrecking of medievalism, but there was one among them so preeminently equipped for the task, and dedicated to it, that one thinks of him as the wrecker *par excellence.* Moreover, his life covers the first half of the century (1505–57), the time more especially of revolt against the established. This is Lorenzo Valla.

It must be admitted that Browning's "Grammarian," that gentle and unworldly seeker after truth, that soul

"Hydroptic with a sacred thirst,"

hardly typifies the more outstanding Humanists of the *Quattrocento,* such as Valla and Poggio Bracciolini and Francesco

Filelfo. They were indeed great scholars and men of power and independence, but also spoiled favourites and hard-boiled egotists, place-hunters bitterly jealous of one another.

Perhaps these unlovely traits are essentials in anyone setting himself to attack idols, things precious to others, however unwisely so. The iconoclast certainly needs unusual self-confidence and a certain ruthless pugnacity. Lorenzo Valla had both. In the preface to his *Elegantiae*, a Latin phrase-book, he claims to have "better deserved of the Latin language than all who have written during the last six hundred years, whether of grammar, or of rhetoric, or of dialectic, or of civil and canon law, or of the meaning of words." This for his modesty; and for his pugnacity—a contemporary, on hearing of his death, exclaimed: "Oh, how is Valla silent, so used to spare nobody! If you ask me what he is doing, I say he is now biting the earth." (*Oh! come tace il Valla solito a non risparmiare alcuno. Se domandi cosa fa, morde adesso la terra.*)

So temperamentally equipped, Valla indeed attacked almost everything held venerable by the preceding age: Aristotelian logic—on which scholastic philosophy was based; monasticism, asceticism,—"Would that man had fifty senses," exclaims Valla, "since five can give such delight!"—exaltation of celibacy and virginity,—"I say what I feel," he declares, "courtesans and street-women deserve better of the human race than nuns and virgins"; Christian ethics themselves, for which he would substitute a frankly sensualistic hedonism. His subversive radicalism spares not even the marriage-bond, which, he says, aggravates the possessive instinct in men, and engenders the dangerous vice of jealousy. Did not Menelaus's stupid jealousy bring on a ten years war? Patriotism, again, when carried to the pitch of self-sacrifice, is altogether illogical. "I am not bound—am I?—to die for one of my countrymen. For two then? or three? How many must there be to make it my duty to die for them? And what is country but the sum of individual countrymen?" "Besides," he adds, "you die because you do not wish your country to die—as if for you dead your country were not already dead."

Now I have no doubt that thus playing the sophist, Valla is inviting a laugh. I have been quoting from his dialogue *De voluptate, ac de vero bono,* On Pleasure, or the Highest Good. This little work, appearing in 1433, purports to be a debate between three papal secretaries,—Leonardo Bruni, Antonio Beccadelli and Niccolò Niccoli. All three became famous humanists, Bruni also chancellor of the Florentine republic, Beccadelli the poet of the *Hermaphroditus* of famous Latinity, infamous substance, Niccoli connoisseur and passionate bibliophile. In the Dialogue, Bruni defends the doctrines of the Stoics, Beccadelli those of Epicurus, Niccoli those of Christians. Bruni is a mere straw man, easily knocked over,—a significant fact in view of the high lip-homage paid to Stoicism by most of the Humanists. Niccoli, as decorum demands, has the last word; but his argument for Christianity really makes it also a gospel of Pleasure—deferred to the next life. Beccadelli carries the real weight of the argument, and is manifestly spokesman for Valla. Valla makes him witty, perverse, iconoclastic, paradoxical, visibly bent on shocking Mrs. Grundy and the conservative mind,—a *Quattrocento* Bernard Shaw of sorts. He is in earnest, all the same. Before Rabelais and Rousseau he proclaims Nature right and the rights of Nature. "*Quod natura finxit atque formavit, id nisi sanctum laudabileque esse non potest.* (What Nature has determined and shaped cannot be other than holy and laudable). On this premiss—exactly as by Rabelais in his apologue of *Physie* and *Antiphysie*—the unnaturalness of so many medieval tenets is demonstrated. From this premiss and the observed fact that human nature craves more than anything pleasure. Beccadelli-Valla concludes with defiant emphasis: "You ask me if I say that pleasure is the Highest Good? I do so say, and bear witness, and affirm that nothing else is really good." And the highest pleasure we are presently told, is in the enjoyment of the senses; and the highest sense is sight; and the highest enjoyment of sight is in visible beauty. "Who prizes not beauty is blind in soul or body, and if he has eyes, he should be deprived of what he knows not the use of." And there is no greater beauty than the fair face of a woman. It is a very glimpse of heaven. *"Nam quid suavius, quid delectabilius, quid amabilius venusta facie? Adeo vix ipse in coelo intuitus jucundior esse videatur"* (For what sweeter, what more delightful, what more lovable than a fair face? Truly, scarce is the heavenly vision itself of more delectable seeming). Presently, this sentiment, indoctrinated by Platonism, will become the fashionable philosophy of the Renaissance everywhere, and will provide the one most dominant poetic motif.

Valla himself is, as I have said, the militant humanist *par excellence*. His hard aggressiveness is chiefly against the old order. An outstanding grievance is against the temporal usurpation of the Papacy. In this campaign, active from 1437, he was protected by his patron, the sagacious Alfonso of Naples. Valla was following in Dante's footsteps, but he did not, like Dante, confine himself to eloquent denunciation. His greatest triumph—and one of the greatest triumphs of the new philology—was his definitive exposure in 1440 of the so-called Donation of Constantine as a gross forgery. Applying linguistic tests, Valla showed that the Latin of the document was clearly, not of the fourth, but of the eighth, century. What a pity Dante was not alive! That supposed Donation had been for him the crime of the centuries, in effect a veritable repetition of the sin of the Fall of Man. And now at the touch of a grammarian's wand, its voucher and warrant vanishes away, and never is heard of again. For the answer of the Papacy was—silence.

By 1447 Valla had no further need for protection from the insulted Papacy. Then the scholarly Tommaso Parentucelli became Pope as Nicholas V. The humanist Pope called Valla to Rome as apostolic secretary, and loaded him with honours and emoluments.

Having overthrown all the old altars, Valla built up two new ones—or perhaps very ancient ones revamped—to Nature and to Beauty. But to the second of these the most outstanding intellectual leader of the second half of the century was to give a more spiritual colour and to establish an almost religious cult. Marsilio Ficino's life (1433–1499) overlaps Valla's, and extends to almost exactly the end of the century. In character, he might indeed have sat for Browning's "Grammarian." He was the eager truth-seeker, the modest master of learning, the lovable and inspiring teacher. His own master was Plato, and he inherited much of the serene tolerance and humanity of the Greek sage.

More lastingly significant than the doctrine he formulated and taught was indeed Ficino's temper of mind towards all sincere truth-seeking. Medieval thought in general had at least this in common with a free-thinking rationalist like Lorenzo Valla, that both were dogmatically sure, and intolerant of dissent. Ficino's attitude of mind was one less of hard rationalism than of "sweet reasonableness"—in Matthew Arnold's sense. He examined historic creeds, not to prove all but one wrong, but rather to see if all might not be at one fundamentally. It was in principle the position Emerson took. And to a large extent, Ficino gave immediate inspiration to the enlightened Englishman, John Colet, Dean of

St. Paul's, who in a time of bitterly warring creeds, offered for guidance the simple question,—"Why should we try to narrow what Christ has made so broad?"

Doctrinally, Ficino's master, and accepted "master of them that know," is Plato. He actualizes, so to speak, the poetic prescience of Petrarch, in whose *Triumph of Fame* Plato marches ahead of Aristotle. But Ficino read his Plato in the mystic light of Plato's Alexandrian disciple Plotinus. The *Enneads* of Plotinus are for Ficino climax and consummation of a development starting with almost the first dawn of truth-seeking. In one of Ficino's Epistles we read: "Once among the Persians under Zoroaster, and among the Egyptians under Mercury, a certain devout philosophy was born, the one consonant with the other. Then among the Thracians under Orpheus and Aglaophemus this philosophy was nursed. Under Pythagoras among the Greeks and Italians it attained its youth. Finally by the divine Plato at Athens it reached full maturity . . . Plotinus, however, first and alone stripped theology of these veils,"—i.e. of myth and fable and allegory.

I must not exaggerate. This passage is hardly a foreshadowing of the modern comparative study of religions,—unless indeed in the fashion that Bronson Alcott conceived it. The methods of Ficino and his followers were very far from what would today be regarded as critical. Profoundly influenced by the Cabbala and by degenerate contemporary Byzantine Neo-Platonism, they saw almost all prior "scriptures," to use Emerson's word, as carrying not only allegories but also cryptograms and other secret codes. Thus Ficino's most illustrious disciple, the amazingly precocious and gifted Pico della Mirandola decodes the opening verse of the Hebrew *Genesis,* and discovers in it a full and doctrinal proclamation of the Trinitarian creed.

I cannot say whether Petrarch spoke for more than himself when he set Plato before Aristotle, or indeed whether he intended only priority in time. But there was in the fifteenth century in Italy a certain reaction against Aristotle, due to his close association with abhorred Scholasticism. Thus Valla, though not a Platonist, was antagonistic to Aristotle, and defiantly attacked some of his most fundamental principles of Logic. The time was ripe for revolt against the long dominance of the Peripatetic philosophy which Dante had declared to be "virtually Catholic opinion." (*Conv.* IV, vi.) The later triumphant Aristotle of the *Poetics* was of course not yet. Still, Aristotle's philosophical supremacy was upheld throughout the fifteenth and sixteenth centuries by the Paduan school, of which Pomponazzo was to be the principal exponent,—though his most productive years were spent at Bologna. The Aristotle of the centre of free thought that Padua became, was quite another than the Schoolmen's. Departing from the interpretation both of these and of the Averroists, and basing themselves on the commentary of Alexander of Aphrodisias, recovered in the late fifteenth century, the Paduan Aristotelians interpreted the Master into a complete materialist. Possibly, Valla might have welcomed this Aristotle.

Alexander stressed precisely the opposite factor, *matter*, in the Aristotelian dualism—or seeming dualism—of matter and form, from that stressed by the Arabian commentator Averroes. But the practical result, from the human point of view, of Alexander's absolute materialism and of Averroes' absolute idealism is the same. According to both extremists, human individuality is a transient affair; immortality is categorically denied.

Naturally, open expression of such heresy was dangerous even in the relaxed state of the times. Pomponazzo the materialist was persecuted; Bruno the idealist was burned. Yet both used to the extreme the device of the "double truth," coolly rejecting under the compulsion of faith the conclusions just arrived at by rigorous reasoning.

The Paduan school had its revenge. From its naturalistic explanation of things was to spring in some part the scientific movement of the seventeenth century. And its fashionable rival, the Neo-Platonic school of Florence, though dominant throughout the Renaissance, is today dismissed as of little account.

Our present concern, however, is not with the merits or demerits of this Florentine school of thought as a philosophical system, but with its literary effects. And that these were indeed great and wide-spread will be apparent as we proceed.

In 1438–9 representatives of the Greek and Roman Catholic Churches met at Ferrara and Florence to seek a compounding of their differences. With the Greek mission came philosophers of the Neo-Platonic school still dominant at Byzantium and in the Peloponnesus. Especially distinguished were a certain Gemistho Pletho, a man of great if unmerited repute as a philosopher, and the Bessarion who remained to become a Roman Cardinal, and narrowly missed being made Pope. These men, especially these two, aroused a lively interest in Florentine intellectual circles. And whether in response to this new concern with Plato or his own personal interest or perhaps to both considerations, Cosmo de'Medici, patron and untitled prince of Florence, took under his protection the eighteen-year-old Marsilio Ficino, son of his physician, and had him trained in Greek language and philosophy that he might translate and interpret Plato. A quarter of a century later Ficino fulfilled the trust, and for good measure translated the works of Plotinus also. He also wrote an elaborate commentary, and other translations.

Ficino's life-aim was wider than merely interpreting and translating Plato. It was to harmonize Platonism with Christianity. Indeed, St. Augustine himself had declared Platonists to be near-Christians. And, reading Plato in the light of the mystical and trinitarian Plotinus, and freely interpreting the myths and mythology of the Dialogues as allegories, Ficino found no serious difficulty in his way. His disciple, the brilliant young Giovanni Pico della Mirandola, attempted a still more ambitious synthesis.

Even more than Plotinus, Ficino stressed the *Symposium* as containing the core of the Platonic system. In it is presented as the supreme mover and motive Love,—love of the Beauty, Goodness, Truth, which as one and in one is God. Indeed, Plato's *Symposium* may be taken as an expanded commentary on the Gospel text: "Thou shalt love the Lord thy God with all thy heart, and with all thy soul, and with all thy mind, and with all thy strength." For in the *Symposium,* the Wise Woman of Mantineia, Diotima, reveals the doctrinal significance of these specifications. She explains how God, seen by the mortal eye in all things beautiful, awakens vague but ardent longings in the *heart;* how these longings then move the *soul* instinctively to shape its life also in symmetry and harmony; and how at last the *mind* recognizes the heart's true object of longing as the Beauty, Goodness, Truth in one, which is God. To actualize such love is indeed to love "with all thy strength." So in the Christian Gospel precept is implied the Platonic "ladder of love" with here the three rungs of desire of sense (the *heart*), desire of will (the *soul*), desire of intellect (the *mind*). From this first and great commandment of Christ may thus be developed the whole system of Plato—according to the Florentines.

Now thus had taught Diotima, the Wise Woman; and Plato and Socrates, as it seemed, had sat at her feet. And thus these masters of wisdom, scornful as they might be of women in general, must nevertheless, it appeared, turn to a woman for revelation of the deepest mysteries of their faith—Beauty and Goodness and Love.

But one thing more was needed to fill out the Renaissance cult of Platonic Love as it came to be preached by Bembo and Castiglione and Michelangelo and Marguerite of Navarre and Maurice Scêve and Edmund Spenser and Philip Sidney and how many others. That one thing was to make a woman a teacher of love by *being* loved, to make the first object of desire, the love-awakening beauty, a woman's fair face. No such notion, of course, appears in the writings of Plato, or of Plotinus, or—so far as I know—of Ficino himself. They might admit that a woman's beauty might start the beauty-lover on his quest for Beauty in itself; but so might the beauty of a boy, a tree, a horse, a flower. Metaphysically, it would make no difference. The start is simply from any attractive object of sense. But men are not all, or altogether, metaphysically minded. When Lorenzo Valla set before all visible beauties a woman's fair face, he spoke not as a philosopher, but as a man. Moreover,—and the point is all-important,—for Italians the two supreme poets of their own—Dante and Petrarch—had celebrated the redeeming power of love as kindled by a woman's beauty. Their love-philosophy was not Platonism, but it was near enough to Platonism to merge easily with the new popular philosophy, and to offer models for the celebrating of that.

As time had gone on, disciples had gathered around Marsilio Ficino. Finally these had organized themselves into an academy with more or less formal rites and ceremonies. It is said that the bust of Plato was venerated by a perpetual light burning before it. One member, Cristoforo Landino, divided his homage between Plato and Dante, and interpreted the latter in the light of the former,—so reemphasizing the spiritual kinship of the two.

It is not surprising therefore that before long there issued from the cenacle a *canzone*—and in the vernacular too—in which Diotima's discipline of love takes its start from the love of a woman. At least, such may be inferred from certain lines of the poem, though as a whole it is metaphysical enough. It is by a Florentine poet of some repute—Girolamo Benivieni, and is entitled by him *Canzona dello Amore celeste et divino*. The sanction of the Platonic Academy is evidenced by its most eminent member after Ficino, Pico della Mirandola, writing an elaborate commentary. Indeed the *canzone*, as Benivieni declares in his preface, is a summary of Ficino's commentary on Plato's *Symposium*. "I have compressed," he says, "into a few verses that which Marsilio in many pages elegantly described." Pico treats it as a *summa* of Platonism, and at the same time as a complement to Guido Cavalcanti's famous *canzone* of Love, which he thinks dealt with profane, as Benivieni's with sacred love. Benivieni arrives at sacred love, but he begins at the bottom of the ladder—at love of sense.

One is tempted rather to pair Benivieni's *canzone* of Love with Guinizelli's. As the latter formulated the philosophy of the *dolce stil nuovo*, the former may be said to have inaugurated in doctrine the new Platonic style to come. As Dante followed Guinizelli, Benivieni's fellow-academician, Lorenzo de'Medici, followed him.

Still, in scope and structure Benivieni's poem is closer to Cavalcanti's. Also, both poems follow systematically a series of topics propounded at the outset. Quite possibly the Platonizing poet may have taken the older Florentine piece for his model. (Translations of both *canzoni* are given in the appendix.)

After a stanza of invocation Benivieni announces his theses:

"I tell how love from its celestial source
In Primal Good flows to the world of sense;
When it had birth; and whence;
How moves the heavens, refines the soul, gives laws
To all; in men's hearts taking residence,
With what arms keen and ready in resource,
It is the gracious force
Which mortal minds from earth to heaven draws;
How it may light, warm, burn; and what the cause
One love may earthward bend, one heavenward bear,
A third sustain midway 'twixt earth and heaven."

In his thought, then, the poet descends the cosmic ladder of love from the One to the Many, and then as one of the Many climbs back from desire of a particular sensible beauty to desire of Beauty universal and suprasensible. The course of love is a circle beginning and ending in God. So later, Pietro Bembo in Castiglione's *Courtier* will apostrophize sacred Love: "Thou, fairest, best, wisest, from the divine union of Beauty, Goodness and Wisdom derivest, and in that abidest, and to that through that as in a circle returnest."

Man, in this Platonic scheme, is—like Mahomet's coffin—suspended midway between earth and heaven. By his intelligence, shared by the angels, he is drawn upward. As a creature of sense, shared by the brutes, he is drawn downward. But it is within his power, as a free being, to break this equipoise, and to rise to angelic heights, or to sink to brutish depths. Benivieni's commentator and friend, Pico della Mirandola, expresses this idea in a famous *Oration on the Dignity of Man*. It has been often quoted, and deserves to be, for it voices eloquently and clearly the most concretely valuable intellectual deposit of a philosophy too often confused and fantastic. I mean the ideal of the perfectibility of mankind we have already seen adumbrated in Dante, and which has played an important part in modern philosophies. I quote Burckhardt's translation of Pico's words: " 'I have set thee,' says the creator to Adam, 'in the midst of the world, that thou mayst the more easily behold and see all that is therein. I created thee a being neither heavenly nor earthly, neither mortal nor immortal only, that thou mightest be free to shape and to overcome thyself. Thou mayst sink into a beast, and be born anew to the divine likeness. The brutes bring from their mother's body what they will carry with them as long as they live; the higher spirits are from the beginning, or soon after, what they will be for ever. To thee alone is given a growth and a development depending on thine own free will. Thou bearest in thee the germs of a universal life.' "

Benivieni divides the central portion of his *canzone* equally, stanzas three, four and five explaining the descent of Love down through the universe to man, stanzas six, seven and eight recounting its uplifting of man by a six-runged ladder to reunion with the One. This seventh stage of consummation he stops short of as being really beyond words.

The human soul builds its own house of clay, the body,

> "moulding such matter into form
> As thwarts now less now more its high designs."

This form, seen by another, passing through the eyes into the heart, may, if welcomed there, awaken love:

> "And sometimes will the sun that therein shines
> Stamp on another heart the imprinted form;
> Which, meetly matched, will warm
> That soul; and lodging there will erelong blaze

Far fairer in the rays
Of that soul's virtue; whence it is decreed
That loving hearts on a sweet error feed."

Already, in these lines the lover has climbed two rungs of
the ladder. He has fallen in love with a fair face, a fair
person. That is the first step. But then his loving fancy makes
his lady fairer than she really is,—or, if you like, than she
seems to others. We have all wondered, I suppose, what so-
and-so could see in so-and-so. Every Jack says of his Jill:

"She's all my fancy painted her;
She's lovely, she's divine."

But Jack's friends cannot see it.

Now when fond affection declares that *she* is the perfect
woman, it should perceive that what his love is really ador-
ing is the perfect woman, to which surely his Jill can only
approximate. The Chian painter who was commissioned to
paint the perfect woman assembled a large number of models,
each supplying a particular perfection that the others lacked.
So in the *third* stage of his progress, the intelligent lover
realizes that he really loves this composite lady, the perfect
type.

"From many fairs
That thought from matter tears
Is shaped a type, wherein what nature rends
For sense asunder, into one image blends."

It will be observed that this process of shaping the composite type from the traits of many individuals, is purely
imaginative, and not practical and experimental. Benivieni is
not recommending a Don Juan-like sampling or series of
loves.

But what the wise lover now realizes is that the beauty he

[111]

worships is not outside him, but within him. For after all how did the Chian painter know what model to select for what trait unless he had already in his imagination the whole perfect type? He was the artist of the beautiful; his various models merely supplied the predetermined forms and pigments. The inwardly known type he created at his own will.

Realization of the beautiful type as the lover's own creation is the fourth stage, the *fourth* rung of the ladder.

The *fifth* step is taken when there comes the further chastening realization that this imaginative creation is upon a pattern found in his *mind*. I mean an intellectual pattern, a complex of laws and principles of beauty, of proportions and symmetries. When the lover has analyzed beauty into its laws and principles, it becomes for him altogether abstract and immaterial. It is an idea, an ideal.

Now this intellectual pattern of beauty owes its validity to not being of the lover's own creation. As I said, he *finds* it in his mind. Moreover, unlike that personally preferred type of beauty created by his imagination, it is valid for all minds and forever,—assuming of course that he has really found it. Then indeed it is not only *his* idea, but God's Idea. It is poured into the human mind from the divine. In Benivieni's imagery, which reminds one of Dante's, it is a pattern of light cast upon the human mind by a ray of the divine Sun. And thus illumined, the lover seeking true beauty leaves earth altogether, and

> "soars to more refined
> And pure light circumfused about that Sun
> By whose eternal, one
> Glory illumined, loving, are made fair
> The mind, the soul, the world, and all things there."

This is attainment of the *sixth* rung.

There is a seventh stage—a landing stage, so to speak—when the soul enters into possession of the divine Beauty; but to take this step the soul must put off mortality, and take on immortality.

Pico in his commentary reminds us indeed that a mortal may by exception share momentarily in the bliss of the immortals. There are, he explains, two deaths. In the second death body and soul are separated finally. But in the first death the separation is temporary only. The body sleeps, while the soul goes on a heavenly excursion. As Milton puts it,

"the deep transported mind may soar
Above the wheeling poles, and at Heaven's door
Look in."

This first or false death is the Platonic—or more properly Neo-Platonic—ecstasy. In it, declares Pico, the lover may see the celestial Venus face to face, and hear her speak,—but no more. In the second or true death, however, when body and soul are wholly released from each other, then shall the lover's soul embrace and kiss the celestial Venus; and in that kiss his soul and hers shall intermingle and become as one in perfect union.

Underneath the amorous imagery, the close likeness to medieval Catholic rapture, *raptus*, the exceptional privilege of the living mystic, and beatitude, the common reward of the redeemed in heaven, is apparent. For the Florentine Platonists Diotima's dream came true in Christ's revelation. Indeed, these enthusiasts of a pagan philosophy retained more than ordinary Christian piety. Benivieni and Pico later enrolled themselves among Savonarola's Pietists, and renounced their secular studies. Ficino gave at least his sympathy to the great revivalist.

[113]

VI

LORENZO DE'MEDICI

IN 1469 Lorenzo de'Medici accepted the invitation of a deputation of Florentine citizens and politicians to "assume charge of the government of the city." The words are his own. And he accepts the proposal, he adds, "only for the sake of protecting my friends, and our own fortunes, for in Florence one can ill live without control of the government." The explanation is frank. It also seems to reveal the young magnate's conviction that a life without power would not be worth living.

The authority accepted by the banker's son was not official. It carried no title. The title by which Lorenzo is best known —*il Magnifico*, the Magnificent—was purely honorary—like our "the Honourable"; though it certainly fitted Lorenzo uniquely. One might say that he ruled as a virtual dictator by tacit consent. Florence was still subject to her regularly elected officials, but the selection of the ones to be voted on was in Lorenzo's hands. In that respect, he was something like an American Boss. But in the open use of his authority he was perhaps a nearer anticipation of a Mussolini or a Hitler.

At barely twenty-one Lorenzo would hardly have been chosen on his own record, but rather as the heir of the Medici wealth and power personally acquired by his grandfather, the great Cosmo. In that sense, his preeminence was hereditary. He was not a self-made man—a new prince in Machiavelli's sense—like certain other despots of the period. Also he had been given an education such as few royal princes have enjoyed.

At the same time, a dictatorial authority outside the law exercised by a private individual must be precarious, especially among a people like the Florentines, fickle and turbulent, democratic by tradition and constitution. To maintain control over them, and particularly in a period of extreme unrest within and of peril from without, called for rare political genius. Undoubtedly, Lorenzo started with a piece of good luck. The outrageous conspiracy of the Pazzi clan, bitterest rival of the Medici in Florence, connived at almost certainly by Pope Sixtus IV, proved a complete boomerang. The last touch of horror was given by the scene and signal for the attack—the high altar and the bell of the mass. The partial success of the conspirators in murdering Giuliano de' Medici only increased popular sympathy for his surviving brother, and incidentally removed a potential rival. Ten years later, in 1479, Lorenzo, by visiting in person Ferdinand of Naples, enemy of Florence, and notoriously treacherous and cruel, and by sheer persuasion detaching him from alliance with Rome,—Lorenzo amazed his countrymen by his personal courage, and delighted them by his astute diplomacy.

No doubt, however, Savonarola was right when in a pamphlet *On the Rule and Government of the City of Florence,* written immediately after Lorenzo's death in 1492, he declared that it is absolutely incumbent upon a tyrant to keep the people amused, "so that they think about themselves and not about him," and in every possible way to shine in their eyes—"even in trifling things, as in gaming, conversation, jousting, horse-racing, learning and all undertakings else, wherever competition offers, making it his business always to be first and foremost." The austere reformer does not name Lorenzo, but there can be no doubt whatever that

[115]

he means him. And it is certainly true that, whether or not from dark policy, Lorenzo the Magnificent did "make it his business always to be first and foremost," and not least in such "trifling things" (*cose minime*) as "learning" and letters. And in these, if indeed he enslaved Florence politically, he set himself to free her.

We have seen how during the century from the deaths of Petrarch and Boccaccio in 1374 and 1375 Italian literature had been neglected as a matter of principle. I may quote again Boccaccio's dictum that "things in the vernacular cannot make a man of letters," for it was the watchword of the age. To achieve enduring fame, one must write in the enduring Latin or Greek.

Rarely has a boycott been so effective. After the phenomenal creative outburst of Dante, Petrarch and Boccaccio, virtually nothing of significance had been produced in the vernacular. On the other hand, by the very nature of the case only a small proportion even of literate Italians could really savour a masterpiece in Latin or Greek. Yet outside the charmed academic circle, there were doubtless many who still cherished the Tuscan masters, not to speak of the common people with their oral literature of sermon and song and tale. The manifest need in the situation was of a middleman to bring the two classes together,—one far-seeing enough to recognize that the future of literature in any nation must lie in the national living language, and at the same time be deeply enough imbued with the new classical culture to lead in the refining of the vernacular and in the enriching of what might be said or sung in it by the beauty of classical art and the humanity of classical thought. Lorenzo was preeminently fitted for such a middleman. For he had both the endowment of genius and the requisite education. Also, as *Magnifico* of Florence, he had the power to make his words listened to, his example followed. If, as Savonarola somewhat ungraciously hinted, he "made it his business always to be first," in the rehabilitation of Italian literature he *was* first—in time and tendency and in some things perhaps in quality.

The young Lorenzo was tutored by humanists whose own fame rested chiefly upon their Latin writings. But one among them had made a highly significant breach in the humanist ban upon the vernacular as a medium of serious and learned writing. Cristoforo Landino, ardent disciple of Ficino in the new Platonism, was a no less ardent admirer of Dante. And he wrote *in Italian* an elaborate commentary on the *Commedia*. Incidentally speaking, he inread into Dante's thought much that was Neo-Platonic. But the more significant fact is that he wrote in Italian exalting an Italian poet, the same that at the beginning of the century a fellow-Florentine had relegated to the reading of "butchers and bakers and such-like folk." Now Lorenzo de'Medici was certainly independent enough to have discovered Dante and the other early Tuscan poets for himself, but as certainly Landino's example and influence fostered the young critic's predilection.

The tradition is indeed that this patriotic literary interest of Lorenzo's bore early fruit. As the story goes, in 1465 eighteen-year-old Lorenzo paid a visit to the thirteen-year-old prince of Naples, Federigo, who was breaking a journey at Pisa. In the course of the following year Lorenzo sent to Federigo a volume of early Tuscan poems, selected by himself, and introduced by a rather high-flown epistle, in which, principally, the Tuscan language is defended and the Tuscan poets appraised. The whole undertaking is declared to be in response to the young Neapolitan's "laudable desire" to become acquainted with these poets. There is also added—by request—some of Lorenzo's own poems.

It is a charming picture,—that of these two princely youths

so earnestly concerned with high things. And it is a fittingly dramatic overture to the revival of Tuscan poetry fathered and furthered by the mature Lorenzo. Incidentally, the edition itself is of no mean value.

But alas for the picturesque in the annals of the past, which is forever being sobered into commonplace! Recent Italian scholarship [1] would set the whole episode forward by ten years, when an extant letter from Luigi Pulci to Lorenzo at Pisa refers to the presence there of Federigo; whereas there is evidence against the supposed meeting there in 1465. Eighteen-year-old Lorenzo, with or without assistance, might have compiled the anthology and composed the epistle, but —at the "laudable desire" of a thirteen-year-older? That is a little strong—even if Federigo was the one flower of a rather villainous family. There are other objections. For instance, four of the poems of Lorenzo's own appended to the collection touch upon the death of the Simonetta who was the "lady" of Giuliano de'Medici, and who died in April, 1476. Furthermore, one codex of the collection attributes the epistle to Poliziano. But this last indignity is, if warranted, less regrettable in that Lorenzo at least himself re-elaborated the essential argument of the epistle in a commentary on a full and dramatized collection of his sonnets and *canzoni* of love made also in or about 1476.

In this commentary defending himself for writing in the vulgar tongue, Lorenzo presents four tests to be applied to a language. The first is intellectual. A right language expresses fully and finely the concepts of the mind. The second test is aesthetic. A right language has harmony and sweetness. The third and fourth tests are extrinsic. A language

[1] Michele Barbi, *Studi sul Canzoniere di Dante*, Firenze, 1915, pp. 220 ff. Professor Barbi's conclusions are accepted by Vittorio Rossi in a new edition of his *Quattrocento*, 1933.

gains credit when significant and useful things have been said in it, and when the range of its use is wide. Proudly, in evidence for the first three tests Lorenzo offers the Italian works of Dante and Cavalcanti, Petrarch and Boccaccio. Even so, he declares that Italian is only in its "adolescence," and that yet greater things may be expected from its maturity. And the range of its use and influence will widen with "the prosperous success and expansion of the power of Florence (*fiorentino imperio*)."

Also, Lorenzo feels it incumbent upon him to defend his writing of love. He rests his apology upon the joint authority of Dante and Plato. Love it is, he says, that "makes actual virtues which are in the soul potentially." In this phrasing speaks the *dolce stil nuovo*. That is true love, he says, that loves but one, and forever. This is a rare thing, and presupposes a rare degree of perfection in lover and beloved. But "whoso loves one thing alone and always, takes not care for other things; and therefore cuts himself off from the errors and sensual delights into which commonly men run." Loving worthily, he will strive ever to make himself worthy of the beloved. "As the image of the beloved is ever present to his heart, so is it present to all his deeds, praising or blaming them according to their merit, as a true witness and attendant judge not only of deeds but of thoughts as well." Here speaks, as it seems, the Phaedrus of the *Symposium*. Such love, declares Lorenzo, "is the subject of my verse." And this Platonic apology for love echoes and re-echoes through the Renaissance. Thus, for instance, Edmund Spenser:

"Such ones ill judge of love that cannot love,
Ne in their frosen hearts feele kindly flame.
Forthy they ought not thing unknowne reprove,
Ne naturall affection faultlesse blame
For fault of few that have abusd the same;

> For it of honor and all vertue is
> The roote, and brings forth glorious flowres of fame,
> That crowne true lovers with immortall blis,
> The meed of them that love, and do not live amisse."
>
> [*Faerie Queene* IV, Introd., 2]

Emulating the *Vita Nuova*, Lorenzo introduces his poems of love by narrating the occasion and circumstances of his enamourment. The "appropriate (*conveniente*) beginning of this new life" of his, he says, "was a death." It was the death of young Simonetta Cattaneo, Giuliano's "lady," which moved, he says, all the city to compassion. She was so fair that no lady was jealous of her, but praised her beauty as something divine. Death could not rob her of her beauty, but she made death beautiful. And Lorenzo is saddened by her loss even to longing himself for the remedy of death.

In this part of his commentary the influence of Cavalcanti accompanies that of Dante. Love's tragic note is sounded. And the conclusion is in the key of Cavalcanti's appeal to death for death:

> "Gentle death, refuge of th'unfortunate,
> Mercy, mercy with clasp'd hands I implore:
> Look down upon me, take me, since more sore
> Hath been love's dealing: in so evil state
> Are brought the spirits of my life that late
> Where I stood joyous, now I stand no more,
> But find me where, alas! I have much store
> Of pain and grief with weeping: and my fate
> Yet wills more woe if more of woe might be;
> Wherefore canst thou, death, now avail alone
> To loose the clutch of such an enemy.
> How many times I say, Ah woe is me!
> Love, wherefore only wrongest thou thine own,
> As He of Hell from his wrings misery?"

Lorenzo concludes his fourth sonnet touching Simonetta with the lines:

> "What should I do? what turn to in my need?
> Alas that guerdon may I hope alone
> From death, that is how tardy to give heed!"

The dead Simonetta has impressed the image of her beauty upon his heart. And in the light of this *remembered* ideal beauty "I cast about in my mind," he says, "if any other was in our city worthy of so great honor, love, and praise." "For some space of time" the quest was unavailing. But on a day, in a public festival, he saw her. "Incredible desire" is awakened in him. The dead lady has been to him as the star Lucifer which preceded his new Sun.

This is Platonic fiction. It is Platonic in that it explains the awakening of love by an outer visible beauty accordant with an inner ideal image of beauty which is itself a reminiscence of more than earthly beauty. Lorenzo feigns that the testing image came from the face of "la bella Simonetta" glorified in death, unearthly. The story in the commentary is fiction, because we know that the enamouring lady was Lucrezia Donati, and that Lorenzo's relations with her had extended back to before 1467, in which year he had defended her beauty in a tourney.

Still, the fiction is *ben trovato*. By it Lorenzo inaugurates that most typical and prolific literary species of the Renaissance, Platonic love-poetry. Also, in his sonnets and *canzoni* themselves he sets—with a certain qualification—the type which is to prevail, namely imitation of Petrarch with an infusion of Plato. The qualification is that Lorenzo adheres more than later Petrarchists to the austerer mood and manner of Dante and Cavalcanti. Indeed, there was a melancholic strain in Lorenzo's temperament to which the second Guido, poet of tragic love, was sympathetic.

Dante had followed the *Vita Nuova* with the greater tribute to Beatrice of the *Commedia*. So to the greater glory of Laura Petrarch followed his *Canzoniere* with the *Trionfi*. Lorenzo in his turn follows his *Canzoniere* with the *Selve d'Amore*. Through the serenely facile octave stanzas of this poem runs, almost hidden, a thread of Platonic love-story, holding together the many little panels of word-painting after the manner of Ovid and Boccaccio. Boccaccio-like was the long cataloguing description of Lucrezia's charms in the commentary on the *Canzoniere*. Indeed, although the younger Tuscan may affect the solemn tones of his elders, his mood is fundamentally different from theirs. His is a new generation, a new world. Intellectually adept as he may be in the new Platonic notions, he is not really a mystic, but a young man-of-the-world, and mundane. If in the *Selve*, loyal pupil of Ficino as he is, he climbs in profession the Platonic ladder of love from love passionate to love contemplative, from beauty carnal to beauty spiritual, his tone does not quite ring true. We feel the pose, the attitude of a young literary exquisite.

Dante's first meeting with Beatrice, indeed his every meeting, is a religious experience, a crisis of the soul. Petrarch, though he may somewhat cheapen the association by a tone of epigram and conceit, yet does associate the conversion of his heart to Laura with the solemnity of the Passion of Christ. He met her, as he tells us, on a Good Friday. Even Boccaccio stresses his first seeing Fiammetta in church, as if his passion gained thereby a kind of sanctification. But now Lorenzo meets his Lucrezia—*at a ball*. And in the *Selve*, the Dantesque solemnity with which his enamourment is announced is itself mocked by the frivolous setting and sug-

gestions of an art of love in action far nearer to Ovid than
to Plato or Dante. Listen:

> "Fair ladies to the music moved their feet,
> Dancing, a-tingle with sweet love each breast,
> Fair youths I saw fair maidens shyly meet,
> And hands by hands one instant softly pressed,
> Glances and signals, sighs—love's art complete—
> Words meaningful to one, blind to the rest,
> Posies let fall with innocent-seeming art
> To be caught up, kissed, hidden next some heart.
>
> Amidst the pleasures of that brilliant place
> My lady fair, my lady of delight,
> Outgracing all, yet lending all her grace,
> Stood in a garment of transparent white,
> Pleading in parlance mute and new the case,
> With her eyes to my heart, of love's high right:
> 'Come,' said she unto me, 'dear heart of mine;
> Here, here is peace for every will of thine.' "

Dante's angelical lady has stepped down from her pedestal
—into Society. His Beatrice has given place to another, to
Shakespeare's Beatrice, Benedick's "dear Lady Disdain," who
even when conquered will love "no more than reason," and
for whom love is a "merry war" with many a delectable
"skirmish of wit."

But Lorenzo ever surprises us. Among his sonnets there is
one of poignant realism, and from the woman's point of
view. In two codices the sonnet carries the startling superscription: *"Sonetto fatto al duca di Calavria in nome di una
donna"* (Sonnet done for the Duke of Calabria in the name
of a woman). One would give much to know what lay behind this statement. Was it a jest, or a remonstrance? The
Duke was certainly brutal enough with women, but then

[123]

Lorenzo was hardly one to throw stones. Maybe it was only an exercise on a set theme. At any rate, here is a rough idea of the sonnet:

"Enough to have robbed me of my liberty,
Turned me from path of virtue and misled,
Without desiring too to see me dead
At age so tender and so cruelly.
All without pity you abandoned me;
And in my pale and wan face might be read
True presage of a life to be quick sped;
And now I care not I am fair to see.
Nor can I think of aught else than that hour
Which was occasion of my tender sighs,
Of my sweet martyrdom and woeful gain;
And had not fond remembrance still the power
Unhappy lovers' hearts to tranquillize,
Death would have put an end to so great pain."

It is not a great sonnet. The original does not come near to the dramatic poignancy of a Dante or a Shakespeare. Still, it measurably approaches Drayton's famous

"Since there's no help, come, let us kiss and part,"

and it stands by itself among Lorenzo's poems, voicing a mood of humane pity too rare with the poet-potentate, but none the less a real mood.

Certainly humane in Lorenzo is his love of intimate nature, particularly flowers. He paints these in the settings of his poems with the same delicate care as some contemporary artists in their pictures. A favourite Renaissance motif is *Carpe diem*. It is over and over figured in

"Gather ye roses while ye may."

In the *Corinto* the motif is developed under this figure. But Lorenzo personalizes the setting, presents himself in his own beloved rose-garden:

> "Into a little close of mine I went
>   One morning, when the sun with his fresh light
>   Was rising all refulgent and unshent.
> Rose-trees are planted there in order bright,
>   Whereto I turned charmed eyes, and long did stay
>   Taking my fill of that new-found delight.
> Red and white roses bloomed upon the spray;
>   One opened, leaf by leaf, to greet the morn,
>   Shyly at first, then in sweet disarray;
> Another, yet a youngling, newly born,
>   Scarce struggled from the bud, and there were some
>   Whose petals closed them from the air forlorn;
> Another fell, and showered the grass with bloom;
>   Thus I beheld the roses dawn and die,
>   And one short hour their loveliness consume."

So the picture is presented. The moral is then drawn at some length. I have quoted Symonds's translation. He then sets beside it his translation of Poliziano's exquisite *ballata*, beginning with its refrain:

> "I went a-roaming, maidens, one bright day,
>   In a green garden in mid month of May."

It has the same motif, the same imagery. Only it is lyrically light and swift whereas Lorenzo's narrative is rather pedestrian. And Symonds will not refrain from the invidious comparison. "It might almost seem," he says, "as though Poliziano had rewritten Lorenzo's exercise with a view to showing the world the difference between true poetry and what is only very like it." One must agree—as to artistic expression. Still, Lorenzo saw and felt what he wrote; Poliziano apparently wrote from what Lorenzo wrote. We must at least concede to Lorenzo in that case the original poetic impression.

Lorenzo himself indeed very often painted not directly from nature, but from—especially—classical word-painting of nature. And here his artistic inferiority to his dependent and friend is most patent. But yet again, it is fair to remember that the patron in all probability both set the example and supplied the model. His *Selve d'Amore* is a chain of word-carved cameos strung together on a slender thread of Platonized love-story. Poliziano's *Stanze* represent precisely the same kind of thing—much more exquisitely done. To many, however, I suspect that the *Selve*, reflecting as they do the vital personality of Lorenzo, may be as good, or even better, reading.

Lorenzo experimented in various classical kinds. After pastoral Virgil, he sang the loves of the Arcadians, Corinto and Galatea. After Ovid—and perhaps with some reminiscence of Boccaccio's *Ninfale Fiesolano*—he told how the nymph Ambra, pursued by the amorous river-god Ombrone, is changed by Diana, the chaste goddess, into a rock, still washed, as one may see, by the penitent waters of the Tuscan river. And Ovid's lusciously erotic tone is echoed in the *Amori di Venere e di Marte*, anticipatory in type of so much in the full Renaissance, especially of the "bower of bliss" motif perfected by Tasso and Spenser.

Lorenzo had many other poetic moods, from austerely pious to lewdly profane. To please, it is said, his pious old mother, he composed *laudi*, hymns, full of unction and not seemingly insincere, and a *sacra rappresentazione*, or religious play. To justify membership in the Platonic cenacle presided over by Ficino, he discoursed in the *Altercatione*, or Debate, of truths abstract and abstruse. To amuse the wits of his circle, he parodied Dante—and the Petrarch of the *Trionfi*—

in the *Beoni,* the Topers, a procession of thirsty Florentines to an abandoned cask of wine in the suburbs, identified as they pass by an undignified *Virgil,* and an irreverent *Beatrice.* It is Rabelaisian to a degree. To appeal to the coarser taste of the populace he packed his carnival songs with an obscene undersense. But we cannot assume that in all these moods he did not also please himself. He was many-sided, and knew no inhibitions. Machiavelli, who admired him enormously, yet deprecates his hero's lapses from Roman dignity, as for instance in his addiction to wine and women, practical jokes, and horse-play with his children.

If Lorenzo the artist adapted himself spontaneously to many seemingly incongruous moods, there is one mood in which Lorenzo the man reveals himself most naturally and pleasantly. I mean his hearty liking for the countryside and for country-folk. The fifteenth century Tuscan peasant was far removed from the yokel of northern Europe. For one thing, he was in daily contact with the local gentry, who spent much of their time in their villas—as Lorenzo himself at Careggi. And Lorenzo took a leading part not only in his own tourneys, horse-races, processions, but also on May-day danced with the country-girls to roundelays, *villanelle,* of his own composing.

He knew his peasantry at first hand, intimately and sympathetically. He imitates their folksong as for the time being one of themselves. He does not treat it as raw material to be refined into something new and strange. Perhaps the chief difference between him and the peasant-singer was that he was alive to the humour of situations that the peasant took solemnly.

His best imitation of folksong—and it is generally regarded as his best work—is *La Nencia da Barberino,* in which the young peasant Vallera celebrates his lass in rivalry with the best Petrarchist of them all. For he had overheard these amourists of the villa. His poem follows the formula of a sonnet-sequence, only instead of sonnets there are the equivalents of the countryside—*rispetti,* so called because in them the rustic lover pays his "respects" to his sweetheart. The *rispetto* may assume various stanzaic forms. Here it is the octave stanza.

Now while Vallera has stored up in memory many Petrarchan phrases caught from the gentry, he sometimes gets them mixed. He opens in the grand style—almost:

> "I burn with love, and am constrained to sing
> Of a fair dame who devastates my heart."

A real Petrarchist would have said *lady,* not *dame.* However, while his cows are crossing, one by one, the ford, he will declare her beauty and his love:

> "I've been to market down to Empoli,
> To Prato, Monticelli, San Casciano,
> Colle, Poggibonsi, San Donato—see!
> And fine are Quinamonte, Dicomano,
> Figline, Castelfranco I'll agree,—
> San Pier, il Borgo, Montagna, Gagliano;
> But nowhere's any market half so fancy
> As down to Barberin', where lives my Nancy."

This high-sounding list is of little hamlets near by.

He bethinks him he ought to describe her, and gets as far as her lips:

> "Her rosy lips are like two bits of coral" . . .

Good. Next her lips—and a rhyme to "coral?"

> "And in between them are two rows of teeth
> Whiter . . ."

It is a hardish rhyme; but the farmer-boy is not stumped:

"Whiter by far than those of our young sorrel."

Again, a country lad finds no incongruity in these praises:

"Tender as frost is she, and to my taste
Luscious and sweet as any chestnut paste."

The English reader is reminded of Doron's rapture in Robert Greene's Pastoral:

"Carmela dear, . . .
When cherries' juice is jumbled there withal,
Thy breath is like the steam of apple-pies."

The sentiment is not altogether burlesque. To vigorous out-of-door young folks the delight of the palate is no vulgarism. Still, Vallera has thoughts above his stomach. He is even literary, in a way:

"I've likened you to Morgan the fair fay,
Who led away with her so many a peer;
I liken you unto the star of day
Shining above my little cot so clear."

Having praised his sweetheart, Vallera turns to his own tribulations:

"I am so crazy for the sight of you
I cannot sleep for brooding on your slights.
The family have discussed it through and through;
'Vallera,' they all say, 'she's yours by rights.'
Among the neighbors there's a great to-do
How I go prowling round your haystacks nights,
And while I keep on singing what I'm after,
They say you lie abed, and burst with laughter."

I said that Lorenzo was a middleman with power. He had the power of his own genius. He had in addition the power of personality and position to compel imitation and emulation. In his train—indeed in his household—were a score of artists in all kinds. Foremost in letters were Angelo Poliziano and Luigi Pulci, humanist and humourist. Each paid their friend and patron the flattery of imitation, and each coloured his imitation according to his own temperament. So in a companion-piece to the *Nencia* Pulci caricatures the peasant. Lorenzo's Vallera may now and then use homely idioms and imagery somewhat incongruous or even uncouth, but he is always decent and sometimes genuinely poetic. Pulci's Nuto is just coarse, though he may be amusing. He admits that his lass has her defects, but . . . well, one must not ask too much:

> "My Becky's just a little undersize,
> And limps—but not so as you'd really mind it;
> She's got a squint in one of her two eyes—
> But still, unless you tried you'd hardly find it."

La Nencia laughs at her moonstruck serenader; la Beca snores.

If Pulci—as I may venture to say—jazzes the folknotes, the elegant classicist Poliziano refines them into something else. His *La Brunettina Mia* turns Lorenzo's robustly natural folksong into a dainty idyl, exquisite song of an exquisite poet; the peasant is vanished away. The lyric is untranslatable; but I offer a rough sample:

> "My little nut-brown maiden,
> Where the clear spring plashes,
> Her face each morning washes,
> And tranquil breast.

Modestly she is dressed
All in a kirtle snowy;
Paints, powders, trinkets showy
    She despises.

She wears no strange disguises—
Ruffs, furbelows, pelisses,
Like your high-born misses,
    All airs and graces.

A garland of bright daisies
Set on her golden head,
She goes gay-spirited,
    Lissome and chaste.

Away she trips in haste
Sometimes—not that she flees me,
But only to tease me;
    Then back comes dancing.

Truly she is entrancing
My little gentle maiden,
Flower o'the thorn dew-laden
    On a May morning.

He joys, despite all scorning,
Who undespairing pursues her;
Blessèd the mortal that woos her
    Adorable dimples.

Mischief ripples and wimples
Along her lips so merry,
Each like a ripe strawberry
    Or ruby precious." . . .

This—at least in the original—is daintiest pastoral. It has
the characteristic of pastoral of being written outside and
above the life it describes. It is the poet acting the peasant,

not the peasant being the poet. Poliziano was the finer artist, but Lorenzo was the truer observer.

Of all Lorenzo's compositions probably the most popular and immediately influential were his carnival songs, *canti carnascialeschi*. They are of two types,—*trionfi* and *carri*. The former were sung in a mythological or allegorical processional—like the *Triumphs* of Petrarch; the latter in a carnival procession of the Guilds of Florence, each with its symbolic *carro*, or float. The songs for the *carri* were generally mock-encomiums and licentiously double-meaning. Those for the *trionfi*, on the other hand, were stately paeans. The most famous of these last is the *Triumph of Bacchus and Ariadne*, with its refrain so often said to be the *leitmotif* of the Renaissance:

> "Fair is youth and free of sorrow,
> Yet how soon its joys we bury!
> Let who would be, now be merry:
> Sure is no one of tomorrow."

Yet the age was one of half-truths, of violent contrasts and contradictions. What of Lorenzo's hymns to the Virgin? of Ficino's mysticism? of Savonarola and his *piagnoni?* of such puritanic scruple as Messer Dominici's, who laid down the rule of conduct that "a father must never show a glad countenance to his daughters, lest they grow fond of the masculine face?" Lorenzo himself was perhaps a poet of the joy of life; yet he was also haunted by melancholy; yet he was also the iron prince who could order the brutal sack of Volterra, could have a hermit's naked feet held in hot ashes "until," as an eye-witness puts it, "the grease dripped from them."

In Lorenzo, as in his age, sensitive refinement and callous brutality met.

VII

POLIZIANO

IN the fifteenth century, Montepulciano in southern Tuscany was a feud-ridden hamlet. There in 1454 was born Angelo Ambrogino, later called from his birthplace Politianus, or in Italian Poliziano. When Angelo was ten years old, his father, a lawyer, was murdered, and the boy was sent to Florence. There he studied under Ficino, Landino and Argyropulos, and astonished all by his precocious talents. His partial translation, begun at fifteen, of the *Iliad* into creditable Latin hexameters won him the title of "the Homeric youth," and—what was decisive for his future—a place by 1473 in the household of Lorenzo de'Medici. There he remained, more as a brother than a dependent while Lorenzo lived, and was at his bedside when he died. He outlived his patron by only two years. If Poliziano had reason to be grateful for Lorenzo's friendship and protection, so indeed has Italian literature. For without Lorenzo's stimulus and example, Poliziano might well never have stooped to composition in that vulgar tongue.

By vocation Poliziano was a humanist, probably the greatest that Italy produced. A profound and exact scholar, a revered and inspiring teacher,—filling the chair of Latin and Greek Eloquence in the *Studio* in Florence from 1480 to his death in 1494,—he was also a poet both in Latin and in Greek. He achieved a prose Latin style which stands out with Erasmus's for its spontaneity and individuality, from the prevailing servile Ciceronianism. He himself—and indubitably his contemporaries with him—held these to be his titles to lasting fame. His Italian poetry—with one partial exception—was by the way and "by request."

I say "partial exception," for the fragment known as *Stanzas Written for the Tournament of Giuliano de'Medici* was evidently planned as a monumental tribute to the house of Medici. Poliziano began it when he was in his early twenties. He broke off in 1478, when the hero of the poem, Giuliano, was murdered. He never took it up again.

Beside this fragment, Poliziano wrote a dramatic pastoral, the *Fable of Orpheus,* and a number of lyrics. The former was an occasional piece for a gala, and was virtually an improvisation; for its author himself declares that it was dashed off "in the course of two days, amid continual tumult." The lyrics were written from day to day, and set to music, to entertain the ladies of the Medici household.

Slight as is Poliziano's Italian poetry in bulk, its substance is even slighter. It would be hard to assemble from anywhere an equal number of verses so little satisfying Matthew Arnold's definition of poetry as a "criticism of life." And yet Poliziano's debonair Muse carried a message which became the dominating ideal of an epoch. I mean, of course, the ideal of neo-classic art.

Poliziano did not himself define or discuss this ideal; that was left for the theorists of the full and later Renaissance; but at the very outset of the epoch, he illustrated it with a perfection rarely surpassed—as art.

The common formula of Renaissance poetry was imitation of the classics. Later, this formula became codified into rules by which one might pretend to imitate without troubling to read. Such a procedure may well be called pseudo-classicism. The best critics of the period, naturally, deprecated such

[134]

mechanical methods, and urged what they called "digestive" imitation. Sir Philip Sidney may speak for these—and in fact he is echoing the French spokesman, Joachim du Bellay. "Truly," he says, "I could wish (if at least I might be so bold to wish in a thing beyond the reach of my capacity) the diligent imitators of Tully and Demosthenes, most worthy to be imitated, did not so much keep Nizolian paper-books of their figures and phrases, as by attentive translation, as it were, devour them whole, and make them wholly theirs."

Poliziano had not merely digested the Latin and Greek classics, he had constantly created in both languages poems almost equally good, and also expressive of his own temperament. He had made the classic manner his own manner. Imitation had passed into spontaneous likeness, and further—by the unconscious intrusion of his own thought and taste—into originality. He said of one of his Latin works: *"Multa et remota lectio, multa illum formavit opera."* The statement would hold of his most casual Italian poem. If it took him but two days to do the *Fabula d'Orfeo*, it had taken him years of "wide and deep reading" and "hard labor" to be able to do it.

When seventeen-year-old Poliziano was called upon by Cardinal Gonzaga of Mantua to provide entertainment for the visiting Duke Galeazzo Sforza, he conceived the idea of adapting the story of Orpheus and Eurydice to the form and ceremony of a Christian *sacra rappresentazione*, or mystery.[1] These religious plays were popular in Italy as in Europe generally, and were sometimes given elaborate settings. They dramatized the stories not only of Biblical characters, but also those of saints and martyrs. Lorenzo himself wrote one on St. John and St. Paul, two eunuchs martyred under Julian

---

[1] The *Orphei Tragoedia* published in 1766 is a "Senecan" revision, probably by Antonio Tebaldeo, a poet of the generation after Poliziano.

the Apostate. In appealing more to historical than to pious interest, he to a certain extent secularized the genre; still, in theme and treatment, his piece follows the accepted type.

Poliziano introduces us abruptly to a new world. His theme is still a martyrdom—but of love profane. The "saint" of this love appeals for mercy to the Queen, not of Heaven, but of Hell—and finds there no less courtesy. Disgusted by Eurydice's instability, the lover forswears love of womankind:

> "Mad is the man that yieldeth his own will
>   To woman's, or for her sake joys or grieves,
> Or turns a slave her pleasure to fulfil,
>   Or in her seemings or her sayings once believes.
> A thousand times a day she won't, she will;
>   Lighter she is than are wind-wafted leaves.
> Flee her, she follows; seek her, she will hide;
> Now comes, now goes, as on sea-beach the tide."

Enraged by this blasphemy against their sex, Mænads tear him limb from limb. And the piece ends with their frantic bacchanal with its suggestively tipsy lilt:

> "Let each follow, Bacchus, thee,
>   Bacchus, Bacchus, ohó! ohé!
> All ye thirsting, all ye thirsting,
>   Come be drinking, draw ye nigh.
> But thou wineskin, filled to bursting,
>   I'm for drinking also, I!
>   Thou'lt have plenty by-and-by;
>   Pass the flagon first to me.
>   Let each follow, Bacchus, thee!"

The mysteries ended with pious lauds. They began with devout invocations. In the nativities, the angel Gabriel was often the speaker of such. For the Angel of God, Poliziano substitutes the Messenger of the Gods, *angelus deorum*, Mercury. Again, in the Nativities there is a prologue in which appear the Shepherds, usually presented in a homely and humorous fashion. Poliziano too has a shepherd-prologue; but his shepherds are of Virgil's Arcady. Instead of kneeling in saintly prayer, as would the hero of a mystery, Orpheus appears, lyre in hand, singing in Latin sapphics the praises—of the guest of the occasion.

So at one step the religious drama is secularized. There is begun that characteristic and prolific dramatic genre of the Renaissance, the mythological pastoral, of which Tasso's *Aminta* is perhaps the culmination. Also, accompanied as it was throughout to music, the *Orfeo* is in effect the first Italian opera.

In the *Orfeo* Poliziano set classical matter to contemporary form. In the *Stanze* he partially reversed the process, treating contemporary matter in classical style. The octave stanza itself was already a popular Italian measure, but Poliziano may be said to have perfected it. Claudian before him had described with epic dignity Roman games and festivals, and of course there was the description of the games in the fifth book of the Aeneid. Also, just recently, Luigi Pulci had celebrated a tourney held by Lorenzo in 1469. Pulci, however, had followed to extreme the chronicle-like manner of the popular metrical romance which his *Morgante* was presently to make famous.

On January 28, 1475, Giuliano de'Medici held a tourney in honour of his lady, Simonetta Cattaneo; and himself won first honours. Simonetta died on April 26, 1476, and the poem was probably intended as a memorial to her. Probably, also, it was broken off by the assassination of Giuliano himself on April 26, 1478. Poliziano never finished the poem, but wrote instead a prose memorial in Latin against the Pazzi conspiracy, through which his hero was murdered. The extant fragment of the poem consists of the first book and forty-six stanzas of the second.

The first book tells how Cupid, in the form of a white stag, lures the heart-free huntsman Giulio to a glade, where the fair Simonetta is gathering flowers. In a few words she tells who she is, and departs; but the youth returns home, hopelessly smitten. Cupid, meanwhile, hastens in triumph to his mother's Cyprian domain, which is described. In the second book, Cupid praises Lorenzo as prince and compassionates him as lover, and urges that Giulio must emulate him by a notable triumph in arms for his own new love. Venus, consenting, sends a Dream to Giulio, heartening him to that resolve.

On this slender thread of narrative are strung one hundred and seventy-one stanzas of word-painting. It may be that the poem is fortunate for being a *torso*. If its main theme —the tourney itself—had been developed with proportionate decorative amplitude, the reader must surely have been more than surfeited with sweetness long drawn out. As it is, the modern reader can hardly do justice to the exquisiteness of Poliziano's lacquer-work. Its kind is staled by frequence in the age which follows. It suffers from its own potency as a model. It is a museum of classical miniatures, mythological, pastoral, allegorical. It is elegant, musical, frigid. There is not a fresh idea in it, not an imaginative suggestion, not a touch of real feeling; it is purest decorative art.

The pictorial felicity of the *Stanze* made them a quarry for painters as well as poets. Botticelli's so-called *Primavera* appears to have been really designed as a kind of frontispiece to the poem. In the central foreground is Simonetta, risen at Giulio's approach; and the painter scrupulously follows the poet's specifications:

"White is the maid, and white the robe around her,
   With buds and roses and thin grasses pied;
Enwreathèd folds of golden tresses crowned her,
   Shadowing her forehead fair with modest pride . . .
Reclined he found her on the swarded grass
   In jocund mood; and garlands she had made
Of every flower that in the meadow was,
   Or on her robe of many hues displayed;
But when she saw the youth before her pass,
   Raising her timid head awhile she stayed;
Then with her white hand gathered up her dress,
And stood, lap full of flowers, in loveliness." [1]

At the left of the picture stands Giulio (Giuliano de'Medici); at the right Spring escaping from the arms of Winter; in the middle the three Graces; in the background, Venus and Cupid presiding over all. Botticelli's Venus, again, presents in line and colour the word-picture of the *Stanze*, I, 99-102. And it has been surmised that Poliziano's treatment of the myth of Polyphemus and Galatea (I, 115-118) inspired Raphael's frescoes in the Villa Farnesina in Rome.

In the rest of Poliziano's vernacular poetry, the lyrics, there are three types. Some are decoratively ornate, like the *Stanze;* some are in the manner of Petrarch; some assume the measures and intonations of the Tuscan peasant's songs of Maying and of wooing. It is, I think, in these last, these sublimated folk-songs, that the art of Poliziano is at its happiest. True, under his handling, with the crudeness much of the humanity of folk-song is polished away. It is sometimes poignant; it is frequently precious. Of his wooing songs the most exquisite is *La Brunettina Mia,* which I have partially translated. It is an "idyl in porcelain." No peasant could have composed it; nor

[1] I, 43, 47. Translated by J. A. Symonds. The description reminds one of the decorated portrait of "Elisa" in the "April" of Spenser's *Shepheardes Calendar.*

could Poliziano—without a peasant's model in kind. On the other hand, a Tuscan peasant—of some native genius—could have composed Lorenzo's *Nencia da Barberino*. Lorenzo successfully imitates Tuscan folk-song; Poliziano transmutes it into dainties that remind of Tibullus or Catullus, or of Herrick.

To my thinking, his most perfect piece of all is the May-Song (*Canzon maggiajola*) beginning *"Ben venga maggio"* (Welcome May). The theme is all gaiety, calling for no deep feeling—which Poliziano seems unable, or disinclined, to express—and inviting no conceits—with which he too often masks his want of feeling. The subtlety of a musician's art is shown in the recurrence at the end of each lightly tripping stanza of the harshly sonorous word *maggio*, like a bass chord. Unfortunately, the English equivalent of *maggio*, May, has no sonority at all; hence the special musical effect of the song must be quite lost in translation. I can at best suggest the tone and movement.

> "Welcome May,
> And rustic scepter's sway!
> Hail, the merry springtime
> That to love disposes!
> Come, maids, in the ringtime,
> Each with him she chooses,
> Come, with wreaths and roses,
> Make ye fair the May!
> Come where green the grass is,
> Green the trees are turning.
> Have no fear, fair lasses,
> Every lad is yearning;
> Beasts and birds are burning
> All with love the May.
> Be not overweening:

Youth's a brittle jewel.
Grass again is greening,
Age knows no renewal.
Fair ones, be not cruel
To your loves the May.

. . . .

    Here comes Love with laughter,
Wreathed with rose and lily.
You it is he's after.
Fair ones, be not chilly.
First from which one will he
Pluck the flower of May?
    Welcome back the Rover:
Love, what is thy mission?
That each lass a lover
Crown at her discretion.
Gipsy and patrician
Love alike the May."

VIII

PULCI

IN the brilliant household of Lorenzo the Magnificent, Luigi Pulci was the jester and the jest. He was a man of many contradictions. Like so many other humorists, he had a deep strain of melancholy. He looked it. Filippino Lippo painted him in a fresco in the Church of the Carmine in Florence. Thin, pallid, beardless, snub-nosed, he looks—to use his own comparison—like a melancholy satyr. He is dressed in black from head to foot—he who spiritually wore the motley. His life was consistent only in bad luck. Born in 1432 of a once prominent family, he played many rôles during his comparatively short life of fifty-two years. Tradesman, farmer, miller, soldier, confidential agent, he proved again that rolling stones gather no moss. In 1458, at twenty-six, he wrote Lorenzo that he had nothing in the world except debts. And apart from Lorenzo's bounty, the condition was constant. Even in death he was unlucky. Unjustly accused of heresy— at the worst he jested rather frivolously on religious matters— he was buried in unconsecrated ground. His favourite son Jacopo was beheaded for a crime against nature. It is easy to see why this tragic humourist appealed to the author of *Don Juan*.

It was particularly at Lorenzo's table, between courses, that Pulci expended his gay talent. There he exchanged sonnets of ribald persiflage with Matteo Franco, chaplain of the household. There he recited his *Morgante*.

This last was begun at the instance of old Lucrezia Torna-buoni, Lorenzo's mother, who had asked him to rhyme for her some story of the Paladins. Pulci set to work upon a metrical romance of the people, and at first did little more than add burlesque embroideries to its narrative. He began about 1460, and by 1470 had done twenty-three cantos. Twelve years later he added five more cantos, based on another rhymed romance, narrating the rout at Roncesvalles. Because of these added cantos, the whole poem was now called *Il Morgante Maggiore*, "the Greater Morgante." It was published in 1483.

The street-minstrel, or *cantastorie*, was a familiar figure in fifteenth century Italian cities. He belonged to a professional class; and although his calling demanded a vagrant life, and an appearance of poverty, he often acquired a considerable competence. Often, too, like his ancestor, Homer, he was blind. Perugia and Florence at one time engaged official minstrels of the sort to relax city magistrates at banquets, or to kindle them with examples of antique heroism. Street-minstrels were also often brought in to entertain at private social functions, much as opera-singers are today.

The *cantastorie* usually took up his stand in a public square. There would gather about him a motley crowd of peasants, workmen, artisans, children, perhaps a *signore* or two. It would be a responsive audience. Poggio, in his *Facetiae* tells of a certain "*homo simplex*," who, hearing that Hector's death was to be related the following day, paid the *cantastorie* to put it off until the day after, it being a pity that such "an excellent good man" should die; and the tender-hearted listener kept on paying for postponement until his money gave out; and finally attended the death "*multo fleto ac dolore*." It would be a critical audience, too, vehemently objecting to any violation of traditional plot or character.

The *cantastorie* had certain rules of procedure. He began by a courteous salutation, first to the Good Lord, or the Virgin or some Saint; then to his audience. The former often took the form of a prayer for special guidance. For instance:

> "O Thou All-glorious Lord, supernal God,
>   Who guid'st and govern'st heaven and earth and sea . . .
> So do Thou, Father, govern now and guide
> This tongue of mine that I may tell of how
> The mighty name of Troy was once brought low."

Sometimes indeed, affecting the humanist, he invoked Apollo. This pious decency observed, he proceeded to compliment his audience:

> "Here in this street, here in this place I see
> An audience so great, so grand, that proud
> 'Twould make a millstone, not to mention me."

He accompanied his chant with a fiddle or guitar, adapting the music to the mood of his narrative. Always at a moment of suspense, he would break off abruptly, announcing continuation in his next, and specifying place and time:

> "For your return on Wednesday let me pray,
> Which is—to speak precisely—All Saints Day."

The *cantastorie* drew from ancient and medieval history and legend, between which neither he nor his hearers distinguished. They devoutly believed both, and made equally free with both. As to repertory, the Italian scholar Pio Rajna published a *Cantare dei Cantari*, or "Song of Songs," in which a *cantastorie* lists his wares for his audience to choose from. He can tell, he says, about "the joyous birth of our faith," about the Deluge and the Ark, of Abraham, of Joseph sold by his brethren, of King David, of Nebuchadnezzar, of the life of our Lord. He knows eighty-two *cantari* on the story of Troy, eighty on that of Thebes, twenty-seven on the gests of Theseus, eleven hundred and six on those of the Romans. He especially recommends these last—

> "For that each quality of good or ill
> Which Italy hath shown in wit and worth
> Rome gave it her."

And he runs down the list of the worthies—Kings, consuls and emperors, Greek as well as Latin—to Constantine. He can sing the loves and exploits of Messer Lancelot and Messer Tristan, the enchantments of Merlin, the adventures—"by the book"—of all the knights-errant, four hundred *cantari* of the Table Round, of King Arthur, the Grail. He knows by heart the ten cantos of Alexander, and so on, and so on. He concludes: "You have heard how I can sing of the Bible, and of Troy, of Alba, of Rome, and of all their chances, of Alexander, of the Greeks, of the Thebans, and every tale of the Paladins and Paynims; wherefore

> "Now choose among them which ye like the best."

It is safe to say that if it came to a choice, fifteenth-century Italians would have picked a tale of the "Paladins and Paynims."

This "matter of France" was early brought to Italy. Along the valley of the Po lay the route for pilgrims for Rome. For safety, these journeyed in numbers; and brought with them also minstrels to enliven the tedium of the journey by recitation of the national epics. Italians living by the way evidently shared in these entertainments, for by the beginning of the twelfth century records show Lombard children being named after the French heroes. Furthermore the Lombards began retelling the stories in their own way, though using still the French language and metre.

Even in France, the national epos of Charlemagne and his Peers was in reality a very complex product. It was based on chronicles in which survived elements of the heroic legends of the Franks who in the fifth century had conquered Romanized Gaul. It attributed to Charlemagne deeds and characteristics both of his ancestors and of his effete descendants. It assimilated love-stories from the "matter of Britain," the knight-errantry of Arthur's court, and fantastic "travellers' tales" of returned Crusaders. Rarely it maintained the simple and austere dignity of the *Song of Roland,* and degenerated at last into a curious medley of quixotic love-quests, Munchausen-like travels, and superhuman prowess.

Out of this varied material, there was developed in Lombardy a peculiarly Italian type. In the first place, the historical situation is simplified. All starts from a feud between two great French baronial Houses, that of Clermont and that of Mayence—the Italians called them Chiaramonte and Maganza. Heads of the House of Clermont are Roland, now Orlando, and his "cousin" Regnault de Montauban, now Rinaldo. Their inveterate foe is the traitor Ganelon of Mayence, usually called by the Italians Gano or Gan.

Gan is continually deceiving Charlemagne, *"il buon Vecchio"* grown—as in later Old French story—a little senile in his readiness to believe evil of his faithful paladins. So, in the typical Lombard plot, one of these—especially Orlando himself—is banished, or departs in a dudgeon. Undaunted, however, he wars single-handed against the paynim, performing prodigies of valour; until, betrayed by an agent of Gan usually, he is made captive. Often he is saved by a pagan maiden, who has fallen in love with him, and is later converted and baptized by him. Indeed he is continually converting the paynim—often *en masse*. Finally, he joins certain brother paladins who have set out to find him, and returns with them just in time to rescue Paris, besieged by overwhelming paynim hosts.

The formula was good for any number of stories, with incidental variations *ad libitum*. However incredible the exploit recounted, it was told with a matter-of-fact, chronicle-like particularity. Authorities are conscientiously given—especially the word of Bishop Turpin. Turpin was a Bishop of Rheims in the eighth century. An eleventh century Chronicle of Charlemagne's reign was fathered on him, and he in consequence was made father of all *romantic* lies.

The formula of the Italian "romantic epic" was shaped in Lombardy; but only when imported into Tuscany in the mid-fourteenth century, did it take on a truly Italian idiom and metre, *ottava rima*, or octave stanza.

The late fourteenth century metrical romance chosen by Pulci to adapt for the amusement of Lorenzo's household quite conformed to the type. The titular hero, Morgante, is a bad giant, who, conquered and converted by the self-exiled Orlando, becomes his faithful squire. To their prodigious exploits are added those of three other paladins—Rinaldo, Ulivieri, and Dudone—sent out to recall Orlando. But, as said, the main tissue of the story is not Pulci's. His contribution is partly by way of inwoven comments and asides, sometimes burlesque, sometimes ironical, sometimes quite serious. More significantly, he interpolated the brilliant episodes of Margutte, the dwarfed giant, and of Astarotte, the Platonizing fiend.

As Pulci completes him, Morgante is a cross between the loyal St. Christopher, charitable, genial, ready to do a good turn to anybody, and the ogre of the fairy-tale, gluttonous and gory. He acts as mast for a storm-beaten ship; having

[147]

slain single-handed a whale in the sea, he is bitten on the great toe by a crab, and so dies. His comrade, Margutte, was born to be a giant, but became stunted as a child. One of his literary ancestors was Sosia, the rascally clever valet in Plautus; and he is himself the literary grandfather of Rabelais' Panurge. His account of himself anticipates the picaresque novel. He is as proud of his vices as ordinary men of their virtues; but one merit he claims—that of never going back on a friend. His *credo* is culinary; his laughing candour almost disarming.[1] He is ingenious. Wearing enormous spurs, when a giant attacks him, he turns a handspring, and, striking his foe in the paunch, disembowels him. He suffers from his own sense of humour. Watching the awkward efforts of an ape to draw on his great-boots, he literally dies of laughing.

Astarotte is an obliging fiend. He not only provides Rinaldo with a winged horse for quick transit to besieged Paris, but rides himself in the beast's belly as guide and companion. Thence he instructs the paladin on many matters celestial and terrestrial, from the essence of the Trinity to the existence of the Antipodes. (In these episodes, Pulci may be dishing up things heard from the philosopher Ficino and the geographer, Toscanelli, both of Lorenzo's circle.) The learned devil is orthodox enough, and perhaps there is no more irreverence in the episode than in the habitually familiar handling of sacred things in the later Middle Ages and the early Renaissance. Astarotte also serves Rinaldo with delicious dinners, and shows that in hell too there is "gentility, amity, and courtesy."

In the added five cantos on Roncesvalles, Pulci more nearly approaches a genuinely epic tone. His model—the *Spagna*

---

[1] John Addington Symonds in his *Renaissance in Italy* (*Ital. Lit.*, Pt. I, Appen. V) brilliantly translates Margutte's merry account of himself; also, much of the conversation of Astarotte.

in rima, or verse-tale of the Spanish war ending in the rout at Roncesvalles—was more serious; perhaps also age had made him himself more serious. Yet, though his account of the disaster has both dignity and pathos, his sardonic wit is ever ready to break through. For instance, roused at last from his long lethargy by Orlando's tragic blast, Charlemagne prays that the sun may stand still until he can get to the pass dolorous. Joshua's miracle is repeated; but the King considerately still hurries.

> "Per non tenere in disagio più il sole"
> (To keep the sun no longer in a fix).

It is today easier to estimate the *Morgante* than it was in Byron's day. We know that the greater bulk of the poem is not Pulci's at all, but the work of nameless street-minstrels catering to the naïve taste of a casual and largely illiterate audience. When Byron started to translate the poem, he did not know that. He completed only the first canto, in which is relatively little of Pulci. Byron also acknowledges that he owed the manner of *Don Juan* to Pulci.

> "To the kind reader of our sober clime
> This way of writing may appear exotic;
> Pulci was sire of the half-serious rhyme,
> Who sang when Chivalry was more quixotic,
> And revelled in the fancies of the time,
> True Knights, chaste Dames, huge Giants, Kings despotic;
> But all these, save the last, being obsolete,
> I chose a modern subject as more meet."

The *Morgante* is a mirror of Florence in the first flush of the Renaissance—democratic, gay and frivolous, cynical and mystical, beauty-loving, jest-enjoying, childlike and learned. All its contradictions are reflected in the poem—including the spirit of contradiction itself.

[149]

IX

BOIARDO

DOUBTLESS much of the modesty in munificence of the Medici was due to consciousness of newness, of middle-class, and of dependence on the favour of a fickle, turbulent, democratic people. The family of Este in Ferrara offered a striking contrast. One of the oldest ruling families in Italy, indeed in Europe, it was accustomed to rule,—and its people to be ruled. Machiavelli in the *Prince* especially cites the House of Ferrara as an example of ancient hereditary rule, which need not dissemble its power. In point of fact, the Dukes of Ferrara delighted in displaying their power and wealth. We hear how Ercole I, on his accession in 1471, entered the city in truly royal state,—mantle of crimson brocade, collar of precious gems, bonnet studded with diamonds. When he travelled, his train was worthy of a Wolsey: one hundred and seventy-five mules, caparisoned in cloths embroidered with the ducal arms, for the heavy luggage; seventy-five mules, caparisoned in crimson velvet and tinkling with silver bells, for the wardrobe; five hundred horsemen in gold brocade, eighty huntsmen, each with four hounds in leash, squires in silver brocade—and so on and so on. So runs the contemporary account. Remember old Cosmo de'Medici, who, though master of Florence and *Pater Patriae* by acclamation, yet considered himself sufficiently princely in two or three yards of red cloth.

And the Court of Ferrara, more feudal than any in Italy,

was full of magnificence and chivalry. Tourneys were the order of the day. There was rigid observance of etiquette and precedence. As for the people—*canaille!* Espionage was perpetual; the crime of *lese majesté* swiftly and terribly punished; tolls and taxes were crushing. The luxury of the court had to be paid for.

The Este rule was progressive, too, in a way. It made Ferrara the first really modern city of Europe, with well-paved, broad streets. On the highway between Paris and Rome, it was visited by pilgrims and travellers from many countries, and so acquired a cosmopolitan air. It has been called the Paris of the Renaissance.

The Este princes, again, *condottieri* as they mostly were, uniformly patronized arts and letters, and—some of them—excelled in these. Alfonso, Ercole's successor and Ariosto's patron, was not exactly an artist, but he travelled in France, England and the Netherlands in order to study the industry and commerce of these countries; and, like Peter the Great, trained himself in various handicrafts, especially wood-turning and cannon-forging.

But under their humanity of culture and modernness of outlook the Este princes show barbarous traits. Indeed, their two-sided character strikes the eye in the series of medallion-portraits executed exquisitely by Pisanello. A certain analogy in physiognomy reveals itself between these medallions and the portrait-busts of the Roman emperors.

And the darker side of the Este character is again revealed in the chronicles of their house and rule. Under the sumptuous palace in Ferrara were imprisoned in noisome dungeons prisoners of state, perhaps guilty of no worse crime than of being in the way. Torture was still as cruelly used as in the darkest ages. In the palace itself crime was frequent. In 1425, a princess of the House was beheaded for adultery with a step-son; heirs, legitimate and illegitimate, had often to flee for their lives,—in 1471, assassins were sent after certain troublesome ones; Ercole I had to defend his throne against the bastard of a bastard; in 1493, this same Ercole was accused of poisoning his wife on discovering that she, at the instigation of her brother Ferrante of Naples, was about to poison him; in 1506, the two bastard brothers of Alfonso I and Cardinal Ippolito d'Este were imprisoned for life for an unnatural crime.

Also, under all the luxury and elegance there were indelicacy and, from a modern point of view, uncleanliness. A ducal bill for washing has been preserved. It is for an entire year, and is for ten *lire*—in present value about ten dollars. No doubt labour was then cheap, still . . . !

In Florence, the social life of Lorenzo's household was essentially masculine. Other reasons apart, his mother Lucrezia was too old as well as too simple-minded, his wife Clarice altogether too limited, to count—not to say lead—socially. Moreover, in bourgeois Florence woman's place was in the household, her function domestic. She had not yet emerged socially. In Ferrara, she had emerged. At the court of the Estensi, clever and highly educated women dominated fashions and tastes. Fed on poetry and romance, they exacted from their courtiers the ultra-refinements of chivalric, and—presently—of platonic, homage. And their courtiers, in turn, were refined by them, were being shaped into the type to be fixed in its fulness by Castiglione,—a type at once connoisseur and soldier and diplomat and gallant, adept at need with sword or pen or lute. Also, submissive to these feminine preferences was the courtier as poet, the "courtly maker." Behind court-literature is the court-lady.

At Ferrara, consequently, in the closing years of the fifteenth century, there was being developed a literary taste, asking for an art mundane and sensuous, spicy, gay, yet touched with sentiment and elegantly turned. Good form forbade bookishness,—the college-woman was not yet,—but deprecated illiteracy no less,—especially as to the classics. A decent respect for religion also was demanded,—however pagan the general tenor of living. One of Boiardo's characters remarks:

> "Methinks it fits not well the gentleman
> To be all day bent double over books."

And yet, on the other hand,

> "Like to an ox is he,—a stock, a stone,—
> Who not on his eternal Maker thinks,
> And without learning rightly think may none."
> [*Orl. Innam.* xviii, 34-4]

But at court, assuredly, the burden of learning, theological or other, was not a heavy one. A polite learning was asked, a polite literature. Compositions, grave and gay both, were addressed not to the private reader, but to an elegant audience assembled. Between courses at dinner, the blind minstrel Francesco—"*il Cieco da Ferrara*," as he was called—chanted his romance of *Mambriano*, a more fantastic and gayer sprout from the *Orlando Innamorato*. In villa-garden or palace-courtyard, translations or imitations of Latin tragedies and comedies—Seneca, and Plautus and Terence—were sumptuously presented, and often acted by courtiers and court-ladies themselves. The new invention of Poliziano—the dramatic pastoral—in the *Orfeo*, was imitated, with the plot out of Ovid, by the elegant and versatile Count Niccolò da Correggio in his daintily Arcadian operetta, *Cefalo*. Indoors, in the drawingroom, Antonio Tebaldeo improvised sonnets and madrigals of love, in Petrarch's manner, but with Petrarch's poignancy extracted, pretty air-bubbles of verse, or—for variety—epigrams, caustic but veiled, on some recent court scandal. Or, the story-teller Sabbadino outdid Boccaccio in the spiciness of his tales; or ribald Cammelli from Pistoia contributed facetious anecdotes, smuttily ambiguous. The Ferrarese ladies were not too nice as to what was amusing. On the other hand, they were as responsive to a delicately refined and high-toned appeal.

Matteo Maria Boiardo, Count of Scandiano and—from 1487—Governor of Reggio, was by birth and breeding of this court, responsive to all its humours. Besides being an Italian poet, he was a great gentleman and a finished classical scholar, a maker of charming Latin lyrics. Perhaps above all, in that rather heartless if brilliant society, he was a man of heart,—or, to use the eighteenth century word,—a man of "sensibility." It was the fashion to possess a motto. Boiardo chose for his motto—*Amor omnia vincit*. In 1490, for his fiftieth birthday, a medal was struck off in his honour. It bore on one side his portrait; on the other, his motto and a Vulcan forging arrows for Cupid while Venus holds his bow.[1]

By his own account, Boiardo discovered his "heart"—a real one this time, and no mere literary imitation—in 1469, on April fourth. On that day, at a festival gathering, he met Antonia Caprara. He was twenty-eight years of age,[2] and the love conceived for her was serious. He tells the story of it in a sonnet-sequence. It is like the avowed experience of Lorenzo de'Medici with his Lucrezia,—with this difference, that we can hardly take Lorenzo at his word; we can hardly help taking Boiardo at his. His love-poetry is perhaps not great poetry, but it is charming and touching. Reminiscent of Pe-

---

[1] The medal is reproduced in *Studi su M.—M. Boiardo,* Bologna, 1894.

[2] On the assumption that he was born in 1441. In giving this date instead of 1434, the usual one, I follow Vittorio Rossi, most eminent authority on the *Quattrocento.*

trarch, like most Renaissance love-lyrics, it is yet graciously
simple, untrivialized by conceits. One might describe the
sequence as a more sensitive, gentler *Astrophel and Stella.*
Also, if Sidney's sonnet of renunciation,

"Leave me, O love that reachest unto dust!"

be taken as concluding his love-story, then Boiardo's drama
has the same three acts,—jubilation at love won, despair at
love withheld, renouncement of human love for divine.

If Boiardo outlived his disappointment,—indeed, if truth
must be told, married happily in 1479, and became father of
a large family,—yet he never outlived the tenderness of his
early love. It is Antonia he invokes for the inspiration of his
Orlando Innamorato:

"Light of mine eyes and spirit of my heart,
For whom so sweetly I was wont to sing
Verses and rhymes of love with careful art,
Now to my story thy kind comfort bring."

He is said—I know not upon what evidence—to have modelled upon her his Angelica, whom Pio Rajna calls "the first
modern woman in fiction,"—charming and exasperating,
sometimes a coquette but always a lady. And unlike so many
sirens of romance, she needs no black magic to win men's
hearts.

Boiardo *could* have read Pulci's *Morgante.* But even if
read, Pulci's serio-comic masterpiece would have offered no
congenial model to the refined and sensitive Ferrarese aristo-
crat, the man of sensibility. The plebeian coarseness of
Pulci's style and humour would have repelled him; the pugna-
cious bluster and crude manners of Pulci's heroes would have
appealed little to his chivalrous sentiment—or to his audience

of fine ladies. I must not overstress the point, however. As compared with Ariosto a generation later, and much more with Tasso three generations later, Boiardo is virile and red-blooded; and the ladies he addressed—for all their classical culture—still relished the old fighting tales without softening or sugaring. We hear of Duchess Isabella herself sending to Venice for books, and demanding especially the ones that "contain battles, stories and fables, of moderns as well as of the ancients, and particularly about the paladins of France." [1] Also, we hear how she and Galeazzo Visconti beguiled the tedium of a journey by disputing upon the relative merits of Orlando and Rinaldo. This, however, was in 1491, and may have related to Boiardo's own heroes.

Still, I doubt if Pulci's vein would have pleased at Ferrara, —and perhaps not so much because he was rough, as because he was in temper and outlook *bourgeois*. His Orlando was a good, middle-class fighting-man, not a high-toned and knightly gentleman.

Moreover, though "the paladins of France" were still popular at the Ferrarese court, yet more sympathetic were Arthur's knights of the Table Round. This "matter of Britain" was early introduced into Italy,—perhaps by the Normans in Sicily. Arthur was reputed to be buried under Mt. Aetna. Several tales of the thirteenth century *Novellino* are from the Arthurian cycle. It was reading of the love of Lancelot and Guinevere that led to the undoing of Dante's Francesca and Paolo. And the very casualness of Dante's allusion to the Dame de Malehaut's cough

> "At the first error writ of Guinivere"
> [*Par.* xvi, 15]

[1] *Contengano batalie, historie e fabule, cossi di moderni come de antichi, e massime de li paladini di Franza.* Luzio e Renier, *Precettori d'Isabella d'Este*, Ancona, 1887.

would imply that the story was well known. There were also the subtilized and sophisticated "society novels" with Arthurian backgrounds of Chrestien de Troyes.

Now if the *motif* of the stories of Charlemagne's paladins was patriotic piety, that of those of Arthur's knights-errant was love. And the universal empire of Love—*Amor omnia vincit* —was Boiardo's motto—and poetic motive. Love, as he sings, has no rival but Death:

> "Unto its dance go young and old together,
> The lord so haughty and the lowly hind.
> No remedy has love, nor death has either:
> They both take everyone of every kind."
> [*Orl. Innam.* I, xxviii, 2]

After all, then, could even the doughty paladin Orlando have withstood Love? Assuredly not. Let us imagine, then, Orlando in love—*innamorato*.

Boiardo's happy thought was to combine into one the diverse appeals of the two medieval cycles of romance, Carolingian and Arthurian, by making a knight-errant of the paladin of paladins. Boiardo is quite explicit about it:

> "Now once upon a time Britain the Great
> So glorious was in deeds of love and war
> That still today its name goes gathering weight,
> And honored is King Arthur more and more;
> For that those banded knights of high estate
> In many a battle proved their worth of yore,
> And with their ladies went adventurous ways,
> So that their fame endureth to these days.

> "King Charles in France thereafter held high court,
> But his in all unlike that other shone,
> Although 'twas mighty and of good report,

And called Rinaldo and the Count its own;
Yet, since to Love it shut its gates, and fought
Battles for Country and for God alone,
'Twas not of such high valor and esteem
As that whereof I made at first my theme

"For Love it is that glory hath in fee,
And maketh men in worth and honor bright;
And Love it is that giveth victory,
And giveth valor to the armèd knight:
So I pursue the tale, begun by me,
Of great Orlando caught by Love's delight."
[*Orl. Innam.* II, xviii, 1-3]

Only, unhappily, Love brought Orlando neither glory nor
victory, but defeat and dishonour, inducing him at last to betray
at heart his country, *la Patrie,*—when he prayed God devoutly that

"The sacred banners of the lilies of gold
Might be o'erthrown, and Charles, and all his host."
[*Orl. Innam.* II, xxx, 61]

All for love—of a paynim girl who violently detests him! No
wonder worthy Bishop Turpin hushed up the matter.

Apparently, the Ferrarese poet of Love is not conscious of
the discrepancy. He is thinking rather of the testimony given
by Orlando to Love's omnipotence:

"Let it not cause, my Lords, astonishment
If of Orlando's love you hear the tale;
For whoso is the world's most insolent
Before almighty Love turns faint and pale;
Not powerful thews, not valorous intent,
Nor filèd blade, nor shield, nor coat-of-mail,
Nor other potent thing can so hold fast
But that by Love 'tis beaten not at last."
[*Orl. Innam.* I, i, 2]

To be sure, the paladin's surrender to Love is not generally known. In point of fact, it was kept dark by Bishop Turpin out of consideration for Orlando's reputation of invincibility:

> "Known but to few, indeed, is this romance:
> Turpin himself, they say, suppressed the story,
> Deeming that to the valiant Count, perchance,
> To write it down might prove derogatory;
> Since against Love he took a losing chance
> Who from all other rivals had wrung glory."
>
> [Ib. 3]

So by a wave of the poet's wand, the austere paladin is metamorphosed into a love-sick knight-errant,—*errant* in every sense. Boiardo goes still farther. He is not content thus to infuse a new and strange romantic motive into the spirit of an epic hero. He also combines with Carolingian, Arthurian machineries. Charlemagne has somehow got possession of Arthur's Round Table, for instance.

It is Easter at Paris, and high festival. Carlo Magno sits with his paladins at the "table round." The Saracen guests, as is their custom, recline upon mats. A tourney is in progress. Enter the paynim princess Angelica, amply guarded by four giants, and followed by her brother Argalia with the magic lance which later in little Astolfo's hands will do such wonders,—and later again greater wonders still in the hands of Spenser's lady Britomart. For still further security, Angelica wears a magic ring, which at need can render her invisible.

These precautions, indeed, are quite justified. Seducing all too well the Christian leaders, the perilous lady's charms emperil herself. The whole French court—to its Nestor, white-haired Namo—is immediately enamoured of her, passionate for her. Majestic Charles himself is perturbed. Orlando is lost to everything—dignity, duty, loyalty. *Amor omnia vincit.* He will desert Alda *la bella,* fight his cousin and brother-in-arms, Rinaldo, deny at heart his Country and his God. It is not love, but witchcraft,—though so far Angelica has used only her own natural charms.

But there is real magic in the forest, whither, pursued by Orlando and Rinaldo, Angelica flees. Exhausted, she rests beside two springs in the way, and drinks of one. Now it so happens that the water of this spring engenders love of the first person seen,—and she sees Rinaldo sleeping near by. Already he has drunk of the other spring—of hate,—and so spurns her amorous advances. And thereafter she still flees Orlando, but pursues Rinaldo, who flees her. Later indeed, the drinks are mixed again; and she, as at first, flees both; while they in mad jealousy come at last to fight for her— even before beleaguered Paris in sore need of their succour.

This confused love-chase forms the major action of the *Innamorato.* The *imbroglio* of A loving B, B C, and so on to perhaps X loving A, goes back at least to the pastoralist Moschus:

> "Pan loved his neighbor Echo; Echo loved
> A gamesome Satyr; he, by her unmoved,
> Loved only Lyde." [1]

It is enormously popular throughout the Renaissance, especially in the pastoral drama.

The situation has been designated "the cross-eyed Cupid"; and such a perverse and puckish divinity of Love is the one whose triumph is presented in the *Orlando Innamorato.* Indeed, the poem has much the air and effect of a fairy tale. Spenser's instinct was right in calling his derivative *mise-en-scene* "the land of faerie."

It is this quality of *faerie*—that is to say, a mixture of fan-

[1] Transl. by J. A. Symonds.

tasy and magic and capriciously romantic beauty—which most
of all distinguishes Boiardo's poem from Pulci's. The *Morgante* follows a verse-chronicle of ostensibly real persons and
events,—real, that is, for the credulously uncritical folk to
whom it was originally addressed. Pulci has preserved the
chronicle-like detail and tone, only travestying these by exaggeration and irony, and with humorous asides. Rabelais
later was to use similar methods. And even Ariosto, for all
his sympathetic imagination and the urbanity of his wit, was
nearer to Pulci's mood of travesty.

Boiardo does not travesty. He does not make chivalry a
laughing matter,—even while relating some of the extravagant exploits attributed to it by the popular imagination. He
indulges in few if any satirical or sardonic asides. Yet he is
by no means without humour,—and we catch a twinkle now
and then; but in the main he gives to his narrative, and asks
for it, the "willing suspension of disbelief which constitutes
poetic faith."

No doubt, the faith asked for is a rather childish one—
such as Barrie asks for in *Peter Pan*, only stretched hugely.
The love-chase between Angelica and Orlando and Rinaldo
reaches from West to East, and back again. It is mixed up
with two wars upon France,—by the African king Agramante,
who would "extend the law of Macon," and by Gradasso,
who from beyond farthest Ind comes coveting "Durindana"
and "Bayart," Orlando's sword and Rinaldo's charger. Battle
on battle rages also around the stronghold of Albracca,
wherein Angelica has taken refuge. Knight forever fights
knight—or lady-knight. They fight singly, or in groups, or
in pitched battles, or against wizards, or demons, or strange
hybrid monsters—orc, dragon, centaur, griffin, hippogriff. A
wandering damsel, fair and forlorn, may turn out to be a
baleful witch in disguise. There are enchantments every-

where. Angelica, at will, flies through the air; she has Rinaldo so transported for her pleasure to a sea-encircled bower reminiscent of Dante's earthly paradise; she speeds to his aid, riding a demon. Orlando, full-armed, jumps into a lake —to find himself on a greensward among dancing ladies, who conduct him to a crystal palace. The puny braggart Astolfo, possessed of the fated golden lance of Argalia, is— except when he forgets to take it—invincible. The sister fays, Morgana and Alcina, devise ever new magical traps for the Christian heroes,—only to fall into them themselves. In supreme appeal to the ladies of Ferrara, Bradamante appears, Rinaldo's sister and his peer in prowess. She cleaves an armoured knight in twain to the saddle. And yet

> "Her lips and nose and brow and every feature
> Were seeming painted by the hand of Love."
>
> [III, v, 41]

Sans peur et sans reproche, this very perfect lady-knight is to wed converted Ruggiero, flower of Saracen chivalry, and to bear the seed of the Estensi,—and to become, in letters, ancestress of British Britomart.

Boiardo's invention—or his memory—never flags. It must not. No more than Scheherezade can he afford a moment without its novelty, its new thrill. And dexterously he uses the street-minstrel's trick of suspending each adventure at the crucial moment, so whetting—but not for overlong—the curiosity, and drawing the reader on from suspense to suspense, from canto to canto. And unlike English Spenser, he is concerned to draw no moral from his tale, is cramped by no allegory.

For setting and landscape the medieval romancer collaborates with the humanist. Over his "land of faerie" are glimpses of antiquity,—pastoral glades and bowers, the cave

of Cyclops, the spring of Narcissus; but his word-pictures are
swiftly sketched. Action, ever action is the thing.

The first two books of the poem, running to sixty cantos,
were published in 1484. Of the third book, only nine cantos
and twenty-five stanzas were composed by 1494, ten years
later,—when Charles VIII of France invaded Italy, passing
by Reggio itself. Boiardo, patriotic and proud, was profoundly shocked and humiliated. Milton-like, he felt he
could write no more "in these noises." In a final twenty-
sixth stanza, and in an altered tone, he takes leave of his
light-hearted song as now unmeet while these Gauls in their
fury are setting all Italy aflame, but he promises that

> "Another time, if I be given strength,
> I shall relate the rest of it at length."

He himself did not live out the fatal year. But Ariosto fulfilled the promise for him.

Much as the *Orlando Innamorato* appealed to its own
immediate audience at Ferrara, in the eyes of the next following generations it had one fatal blot. Its style, nervous
and robust,—with many phrases from Dante,—seems today
admirably attempered to its matter, even if it is also sometimes rough and provincial—Lombardese. But presently, the
academic purism of the humanists in respect to Latinity was,
after the Italian revival, to be carried over to the vernacular.
Under the influence especially of Bembo, Dante's ideal of a
vulgaris eloquentia corresponding in its degree to the *eloquentia* proper of Latin was interpreted, one might say,
rather in accordance with his practice than with his precept.
Dante had prescribed a "noble vernacular" for high poetry
which should eclectically combine the best from all the dialects of the Italian peninsula, but in practice he had written
a nearly pure, if stylistically refined, Tuscan. And so also

Petrarch and Boccaccio. Consequently, early in the sixteenth century Tuscanism—*toscanità*—was made the critical order of the day. The *Orlando Innamorato* failed to meet the test.

It was indeed kept alive,—probably rather as supplying the prologue, so to speak, to the enormously popular *Orlando Furioso* than for its own sake. Also, it was kept alive only after being radically reconstructed. The most approved operation was performed by the witty and satirical, but unimaginative and shallow Francesco Berni. Berni gave the poem—as one might give a mutilated war-victim—a new face, Tuscan, smooth, smart, but expressionless, masklike. Not until the nineteenth century was the *Innamorato* looked at again in its true and native semblance, and given due honour.

X

SANNAZARO

ALMOST simultaneously in three political and cultural centres in Italy—Florence, Ferrara, Naples—came about a revival of vernacular literature. In Florence with Lorenzo the Magnificent it was a revolt against the humanistic ban. Lorenzo defended Italian, and wrote in it, with the proud conviction that it was capable of becoming as worthy a medium as Greek or Latin. And its "prosperous success" would be one, he prophesied, with the "prosperous success" of the people using it.

As both statesman and poet Lorenzo was able to effect both terms of the equation. He certainly, while he lived, made Florence prosperous, and made her language and medium of high poetry both by his own art and by that of those his example and patronage encouraged and assisted. In himself there were two distinct personalities,—one of a sensitive and delicate artist, and one of a sardonic and somewhat sensual cynic. His own poetry reflects both phases of his character; they are reflected separately and distinctively in the poetry of his two friends and emulators—Poliziano and Pulci. I daresay indeed, that they—especially Poliziano —influenced him as much as he them. At any rate, the body of literature they produced between them was characteristic of a democratic city-state in which upon *bourgeois* manners and customs had been superimposed a highly refined academic culture.

[165]

The city-state of Ferrara, on the contrary, was altogether feudal and aristocratic. Its learning and culture were less academic and more courtly. Its literary activities were virtually altogether of the court, and for the court,—and therefore very largely conformed to the taste and capacity of court-ladies. And fully representative of this courtly literature—at least of its poetry—were the Italian works of Boiardo, his sonnets and his romantic epic.

But true patriot as Boiardo was, as he speaks in that last silencing stanza of his *Orlando Innamorato*, he gives no sign of having chosen Italian, like Lorenzo, from patriotic conviction. His humanist education led him to compose—and well—Latin verse; but a courtier, he wrote for the court,—and more especially for the ladies of the court, and most of all for the Duchess Isabella. And for poetry as a courtly diversion the vernacular would be the natural medium. Trained in classic Latin as these high-born *Quattrocento* ladies and gentlemen may have been, for relaxation and recreation they would surely demand the everyday living tongue. And Boiardo gave them—to his own literary undoing, as it turned out—*their* living and everyday tongue, the Lombard idiom,—chastened and refined by the scholarly poet, no doubt, but still—for the purists presently to prevail —unforgivably *Lombard* and not proper Tuscan.

At least, the ruling house of Ferrara, and its court, were native. In Naples, king and court were alien. From 1438 had ruled, despotically, princes of the house of Aragon: Alfonso; his bastard, Ferrante; Ferrante's son, Alfonso II; Alfonso II's son, Ferrandino; Ferrandino's uncle Federigo.

These Spanish princes were indeed men of the *Quattrocento*. Themselves trained in the new humanistic culture, they were as interested in arts and letters as their contemporaries in North Italy. Ruling as foreigners, as "new princes" in Machiavelli's sense, they needed—far more than did the ancient and secure house of Este—to gild by every possible ornament their alien domination. Consequently, like another *new* prince, Napoleon Buonaparte, they were eager to find "a place for every talent." In display of their wealth and power they surpassed even the dukes of Ferrara. Duke Ercole journeyed with sumptuously caparisoned mules and horses; in Naples, to celebrate the conquest of Granada, a triumphal chariot was drawn by four elephants. And opulence of style is characteristic of Neapolitan literature itself.

The truly representative poet of *Quattrocento* Naples was an Italian, Giovanni da Ponte, Umbrian born in 1426, but from 1447 to his death in 1503 resident in Naples. A highly trained humanist, he wrote many works, both learned and imaginative, both in prose and in verse.

Pontano—as he was called from his birthplace—was a poet of originality and versatility. His preferred themes were characteristic of the Renaissance,—pagan joy-of-life and delight in all beautiful things. He sings the manicoloured magnificence of the bay of Naples, the high-coloured opulent charms of Neapolitan girls. He is singularly impartial in his loves, celebrating with equal ardour his mistresses, his wife, his babies. Some of his cradle-songs are exquisite.

Devoted to the furtherance of literature, he founded a literary society, which was called after him *Accademia Pontaniana*, and which outlived him for generations.

But Pontano wrote only in Latin.

A member of his academy, and a friend,—though younger by thirty-two years,—Jacopo Sannazaro was destined, and without really intending it, to make the one important contribution of Naples to the Italian revival. Sannazaro was of Spanish extraction; and although his family had been in Italy for several generations, his sympathies were still Spanish. Indeed, devotion to his prince and patron, Federigo, dominated his life. When finally, betrayed by Ferdinand the Catholic, Federigo went into exile in France, Sannazaro gave up everything to accompany and to serve him.

This devotion was not to country—not to Naples, still less to Italy, but to a foreign dynasty and a personal patron. Sannazaro hardly felt himself an Italian,—certainly not in the way Lorenzo or Boiardo did. As a young man he composed in the vernacular—besides the *Arcadia*—much verse, some humorous and some Petrarchistic; but his mature writing,—the writing by which he hoped to win enduring fame, —was all in Latin. He himself regarded as his masterpiece an epic in Virgilian style but on a religious subject—*De Partu Virginis,*—to modern taste a rather frigid *antiquing* of the Gospel narrative, but at least more sincere and in better taste than most humanist epics. In it Sannazaro expresses the common aspiration of nearly all Renaissance poets,—to be to his princely patron what Virgil had been to Augustus, or putting it more broadly, to be the Virgil of the new age. And the aspiration is remembered in the epitaph which Pietro Bembo wrote for him:

> "De sacro cineri flores. Hic ille Maroni
> Syncerus, musa proximus ut tumulo."
> (Give to the sacred ashes flowers. Here Maro
> In Muse Sincerus neighbors as in tomb.) [1]

Like Edmund Spenser in his *Shepheardes Calendar,* accordingly, Sannazaro followed Virgil's example by first trying his wings in "the low-flying pastoral." Only, as befitted his bay-side home, he wrote eclogues of fisher-folk instead of shepherds. His *Eclogae Piscatoriae* had international vogue

[1] This epitaph was copied on the tomb in Westminster Abbey of Edmund Spenser —another emulator of Virgil.

and influence. They are cited as models by Du Bellay in his *Deffence et Illustration de la Langue Françoyse*, referred to with respect by the "E.K." of the *Shepheardes Calendar*, and closely imitated by Phineas Fletcher in his *Piscatory Eclogues* of 1633.

In 1504, however, when Sannazaro, now nearly fifty years of age, returned from France after Federigo's death, he published the pastoral romance in Italian, composed some twenty years earlier, entitled *Arcadia*. This action did not mean that the humanist poet had been converted to the vulgar tongue as a literary medium, nor that he might not willingly have let his youthful performance die. But whether so or not, his hand was forced. The manuscript he had left behind him had been purloined and printed piratically, and with a text full of errors. Naturally the author could not see his work so misrepresented. Since it had to live, it might as well live right. So Sannazaro not only corrected and revised the text, but also added a new chapter to round out the story, before unfinished. He was particularly solicitous to purify his diction from all provincialism,—thus avoiding the rock on which Boiardo split, and also becoming one of the prime movers of Tuscanism, *toscanità*, as the true *vulgaris eloquentia*. A little later Pietro Bembo was to make this idea prevail in theory, and Ariosto—by his own account—was to give it definitive sanction in his *Orlando Furioso*.

It is a singular coincidence that two of the most important literary works, nationally and internationally, of the Italian Renaissance were preserved only by a literary piracy. The other case is Tasso's *Gerusalemme Liberata*.

Perhaps the mature Sannazaro still deprecated his *Arcadia* for being in the vulgar tongue. But certainly the term *vulgar* applies to the language of the work neither in its meaning of *inelegant* nor yet of common local usage. Lorenzo de'Medici and even fastidious Poliziano could use for literary purposes the dialect of even the Tuscan peasant with relatively little change. Boiardo's Lombardism was an offence to the purists that came after him, but I doubt if it detracts seriously from the modern Italian's enjoyment of his poem. But the Neapolitan dialect—or *patois*—was, and is, uncouth and mongrel. Almost by necessity, then, the Italian of the *Arcadia* is not merely bookish, it was book-made. The severer humanists of the previous generation had scrupulously purged their Latinity, their *eloquentia,* of every word or phrase not sanctioned by Virgil or Cicero. And now Sannazaro, before Bembo, gives assurance that he has never "used anything not to be found in good authors" (*fatto cosa che non l'abbia osservata in buoni autori*). And so far as Italian was concerned, "good authors" for him meant Boccaccio for prose, Petrarch for verse.

To Boccaccio the *Arcadia* owes also more than language and style. At least, Boccaccio's own pastoral *Ninfale d'Ameto* had similarly—although not indeed with equal balance—mixed prose and verse. And the love-story of Sincero, hero of the book, has been shown to combine into one the two stories of Florio and of Fileno in Boccaccio's *Filocolo*.[1]

Sincero's unhappy tale of love gives dramatic unity to the work. Rebuffed by the lady of his heart, Sincero has come to Arcadia seeking distraction. He has interested himself in the affairs of its pastoral folk,—their love-makings and merry-makings, their contests of song and dance, their rites and ceremonies. Like Childe Harold, he travels to escape from himself, from unhappy memories. But, again like the disguised Byron, he must tell us about himself, and devotes his seventh chapter to a recountal of his amorous misadventure. And in the twelfth and last chapter—that newly added one—he returns to and concludes his personal tale. Oppressed by a

[1] Cf. Michele Scherillo, ed. of *Arcadia,* introd., Turin, 1888.

premonition of evil, he is anxious to return home to his native land. Rather surprisingly,—for it is the first intimation of anything supernatural or allegorical,—his return-trip is facilitated by the kindly offices of a nymph, who conducts him adventurously by the subterranean channel of her dedicated river. Sincero arrives home—to find his ladylove dead. And the book ends mournfully with an elegy of farewell to his shepherd's pipe.

Admitting its Boccaccian literary provenience, Sincero's love-story without doubt reflects Sannazaro's own unreciprocated love for a certain Carmosina Bonifacio; but his biographers differ as to the seriousness of this passion. It does not, after all, so much matter. The thread of personal romance in the *Arcadia* serves principally to hang the pictured panels of pastoral life. Also, no doubt, Sincero's woes set the contrast of a note

"Most musical, most melancholy,"

against the merry pipings of the care-free shepherds.

Sannazaro is really the first returned traveller to tell of Arcady the Blest. I say *Arcady*, for Sannazaro's land (*very literally*) of milk and honey has little in common but name with the real Arcadia, tract of rugged mountains and ruggeder mountain-folk. Virgil indeed first associated the name with literary pastoral in the remark that two of his pseudo-shepherds were "*Arcades ambo.*" Polybius in his history of Greece stressed the simple-living and the fondness for song and song-contests of the Arcadians. And in his *Fasti*, Ovid, always given to magnifying the first Golden Age of simplicity and peace, and of springtime perpetual, found its reflection in an imaginary "Arcadia."

But to the making of Sannazaro's Arcady went—besides these hints—the whole paraphernalia of previous pastoral—

[171]

and yet more that was literary. With punctilious industry Scherillo has picked out in Sannazaro's text bits inserted from the Greek idyllists Theocritus, Moschus, Bion,—from the late Greek romances, especially Longus,—from Roman Virgil, Nemesianus, Calpurnius. Erotic touches are identifiable as from Ovid and Catullus, Claudian, Anacreon, Ausonius, Apuleius, Petrarch. *Prosa* X is an epitome of the *Georgics*. The whole work would appear to be an intricately built-up mosaic of borrowed bits. So far from offending as unoriginal, even plagiaristic, such literary Cosmati-work, so to speak, was especially to the taste of an age delightedly responsive to every reminder of classical antiquity. The same taste liked, analogously, to inset fragments of antique marbles into the walls of its palaces and public monuments.

To veneration of remote Roman ancestors, Renaissance Italians joined that of the near literary masters of the *Trecento*,—of Petrarch and Boccaccio even more than of Dante. There are some echoes of Petrarch in the *Arcadia;* of Boccaccio, as I have said, many. But what particularly pleased Sannazaro's more immediate Renaissance audience—and not in Italy alone—was the intensified echo of Boccaccio's Ciceronian style, his stately and balanced periods and sugared diction. It is Boccaccio indeed at his most urbanely serious. Even when he describes a pastoral merrymaking, Sannazaro himself is never merry.

In his introductory chapter he professes a love of simplicity,—not only of simple living but of simple writing as well. To write simply of simple folk sounds almost Wordsworthian. But listen:

"Wont most often are tall and spreading trees produced by nature upon rugged mountains, more than cultivated plants by trained hands trimmed in ornamental gardens, to please the observer; and much more among solitary groves do the wild birds singing upon the green boughs please him who listens than in crowded cities in their fine and ornate cages the tamed songsters. For which reason moreover, as I conceive, it happens that the sylvan songs cut in the rough bark of beech trees delight not less him who reads than the studied verses printed in the smooth pages of engilded books; and the waxen reeds of shepherds diffuse through flowery vales perchance a more pleasing sound than polished and precious flutes in pompous drawingrooms. And who can doubt that more agreeable to human minds is a fountain naturally issuing forth from living rocks bordered by verdant grasses than all others carven by art of whitest marble and resplendent with much gold? Assuredly, I think, no one. Wherefore, of this confident, shall I indeed amid these desert strands, to the listening trees, and to those few shepherds that may be here, recount rustic eclogues issuing forth from a natural vein, and present them as naked of ornament as under pleasant shades, to the murmur of clear-flowing springs, by the shepherds of Arcady I heard them sung; to whom, not once but a thousand times the mountain gods by the sweetness won did lend attentive ears, and the tender nymphs, forgetting to pursue the wandering beasts, left their quivers and their arrows beneath the lofty pines of Maenalus and Lycaeus."

It will be agreed, I think, that in calling Sannazaro's manner of describing country life *"urbanely* serious" I did not use an incongruous term. The literary pastoral is for the most part at least an *urban*, a citified, conception of country life. Even Theocritus painted his native Sicily to suit an exceedingly citified audience in Alexandria. Virgil bucolicized for the sophisticated court of Augustus. When Samuel Johnson, the irrefragible Doctor, defined a pastoral as "a poem in which any action or passion is represented by its effects upon a country life," his succinct definition must—in the light of the history of pastoral literature—be radically amended. A pastoral may of course be a prose piece, not a "poem." "Any

effects" must cover—indeed more significantly must cover—
"actions or passions" of city folk, court folk, literary folk
"represented by *their* effects upon a country life,"—effects
tending completely to *denature* it. Uncountrified, sophisticated people do not by giving their "actions or passions" a
rustic setting make them really rustic. A Phyllis *à la paysanne*
would not make butter or shell peas, or dare milk a cow.
Such things are not in *her* definition of a country—that is to
say, a pastoral—life. She would be rustic in a play-land where
the necessities of life do not exist, where all "action and passion" are of the heart, where only sentiment rules. That land
is Arcady. In that dainty land real country people, rustics, do
not belong,—unless admitted to be laughed at, like William
and Audrey in *As You Like It*. Silvius and Phebe are indeed
"Arcades ambo" imported into English Arden. In time,
Arcady—the pastoral Arcadia—came to be but a masquerade
name for the Court. In consequence, Jules de la Mesnardière
in his *Poétique* of 1640 holds it an insult to the "Court of
France" to introduce into "Arcadia" a shepherdess "coarse or
ill-nourished." He censures Guarini for the *Corisca* of the
Pastor Fido. His remarks indeed are illuminating for the
history of the pastoral. He says: "D'introduire en Arcadie
des bergères impudentes, grossières et mal nourries, c'est
mettre à la cour de France des dames laides et stupides; et
comme les poetes français meriteraient la censure s'ils don-
naient ces qualités aux dames de cette cour, ainsi les poetes
d'Italie meritent d'être blamés d'avoir donné ces sentiments
à des bergères d'Arcadie, puisque cette condition était la plus
avantageuse et la plus spirituelle de celle de ce pays-là durant
le siècle des fables." [1] And a century and a half later, Marie
Antoinette in her toy-village of the *Petit Trianon* was still

[1] Pp. 309-10. Cited from E. Rigal, *Alexandre Hardy*, etc., Paris, 1889, p. 506.
n. 3.

justifying De la Mesnardière's identification. From this land
of super-refinement, super-delicacy, of the quintessence of
courtliness, it is but a step to Mlle. de Scudéry's *Pays du
Tendre* with its allegorized topography handed down from
the *Roman de la Rose*. And with this the pastoral land of
Arcady evaporates into a cuckoo-cloudland of sentimental
inanity.[1]

It is a long way from Sannazaro's *Arcadia* to this extravagance of *preciosité*. Between, there intervene many pastoral
territories,—all colonized from Arcadia. I will mention only
as best known Jorge de Montemayor's *Diana*, Sir Philip Sidney's *Arcadia*, Honoré d'Urfé's *Astrée*. Although these romances incorporate other materials, their root-conception derives from the work of the young Spanish Neapolitan. This
not only affected subsequent pastoral in all its forms and
kinds, but also by its success gave a powerful impulse to the
pastoral vogue.

It would be unfair to leave the impression that Sannazaro's praise of nature and the natural is altogether a literary
pose. Indeed, even supposing he borrowed from other poets
of nature all the colours of his landscape, it was a landscape he
painted. And he was—for his own time and place—creating
a fashion, not following one. Admittedly later, in the full
vogue of the pastoral, imitation became too often merest
closet-echo without reality. There is no reason to doubt the
sincerity of Sannazaro's feeling for nature. Only, it was nature at her very very gentlest and most decorous that he
looked to and longed for,—a land of moral holiday from
hard reality,

"The worldes sweet In from paine and wearisome turmoyle."

[1] Jusserand in his *English Novel in the time of Shakespeare*, p. 359, reproduces
the allegorical map of the *Pays du Tendre*.

There, I think, is the fundamental and quite sincere appeal of the pastoral to the Renaissance. The times were strenuous; and more than one artist of delicate dreams was—like Perugino—a hard-bitten and hard-living man. It is *in principle* the same gospel as Wordsworth's—of "the healing power of nature." Only, we may believe that Wordsworth has painted a truer and more significant nature.

If Jacopo Sannazaro painted nature idyllically, glamorously, and human nature in childlike playfulness and ingenuous affection, a somewhat younger contemporary, Niccolò Machiavelli, shows another picture. In his delineation, men by nature would seem to be less gentle shepherds than rapacious wolves, and "only by compulsion are made good." And Machiavelli's lifelong study was to determine the best means and methods of such compulsion,—that is to say, the best *government*.

XI

MACHIAVELLI

B Y dramatic coincidence, in the same year 1498, Girolamo
Savonarola was burnt in the public square of Florence
and Niccolò Machiavelli became Secretary of the Republic.
Theocratic medievalism passed; opportunist modernism
emerged. Instead of Holy Scripture and the example of unworldly saints, common sense and the example of the Romans, masters of worldly success, are invoked to guide men.
Human experience, not divine dictation, is to be the test of
policy. Not the ideal right, but the practicable expedient, is
to be sought. Machiavelli declares in the *Prince*,—and it is
the key-note of his thought: "It being my intent to write
what may be useful to him that reads, I have felt it expedient to get down to the effectual truth of the matter, rather
than to indulge in imaginings about it; and many have
imagined to themselves republics and kingdoms that were
never actually seen or known, because it is so far from how
men live to how they ought to live that he who leaves what
is done for what ought to be done, prepares so his ruin rather
than his preservation; because a man that follows in all respects the profession of goodness is bound to go to ruin among
so many that are not good."

This is not the Florentine Secretary's most cynical utterance, but by itself is enough to account for the odium so long
attached to Machiavelli's name. But the utterance should not
be taken by itself, but in its context. It has been his misfor-

tune that, being a man of exceptional intelligence himself, Machiavelli assumed somewhat exceptional intelligence in his readers. He assumed that his utterances would be understood and judged in their context, not divorced from it, and made absolute and universal. Exactly the opposite has been the case, —even with a critic of the intelligence of Macaulay, whose celebrated essay on the *Prince* is a very masterpiece of misunderstanding.

The passage I have quoted from the *Prince* has a *political* context. And, to Machiavelli's thinking, the business of politics, of statecraft, is to attain ends of state. The State is an entity working for the good of all. Success in that is its sole virtue. The private virtue of individuals is altogether another story. Indeed, public and private virtue may be altogether incompatible. Who would deny a statesman or a diplomat the right—nay, the duty—to lie, if to tell the truth might, say, involve his country in a ruinous war? In any case, the thing is done by statesmen and diplomats of every country today.

The trouble with Machiavelli is his appalling frankness. He speaks out while we salve our collective consciences with a euphemism. No doubt, the *raison d'etat* covers for him more and worse private sins than we today would willingly allow. At the same time, it may be said that he never went as far as his contemporary, the saintly Sir Thomas More, who in his scheme of an ideal state in the *Utopia* advised, to the end of shortening a war, assassination of the enemy ruler and poisoning of the wells of the enemy country; also advised, in order to strip war of its glamour,—and to spare Utopians,— the debauching of a more primitive people, the Zapolets, for use as savage fighting-men, ready-to-hand cannon-fodder. Of course, the excuse for More is that he was an out-and-out pacifist, than which there is at times nothing more brutal.

Niccolò Machiavelli's appointment to a place in the Secretariat of Florence on June 19, 1498, and assignment on the following fourteenth of July to the Council of "Ten of Liberty and Peace," mark not only his first appearance in public life, but virtually the first we know of him individually. According indeed to the records he was born May 3, 1469 in Florence. His father, Bernardo, was a lawyer; his mother, Bartolommea, came of the family of the Nelli, prominent socially and politically. Niccolò was evidently well-educated along humanistic lines. He showed himself later a man of wide reading, in both Italian and Latin authors, especially the Roman historians. His entering into affairs as late as he did—at twenty-nine—has led to the supposition that his youth was more or less frivolous.

From 1498 on to his last days, however, he was indefatigably industrious. In addition to his secretarial duties at home, he was sent on various foreign missions,—four or five times to the King of France, Louis XII, to Cesare Borgia, to Pope Julius II, to the Emperor Maximilian. His business on these missions was chiefly to observe and report. So efficiently did he fulfil his duties at home and abroad that he came to be known everywhere as simply "The Florentine Secretary."

This busy official life lasted for fourteen years. Then, on November 7, 1512 he was deposed from office, and shortly after imprisoned and put to the torture on suspicion of conspiracy against the Medici, now returned to power.

It must be said that Machiavelli showed himself no Cato towards the new Caesars. He was anxious enough to make his peace with the Medici, but for long his overtures were without avail. For the next seven years he was left in poverty and neglect on his little farm at San Casciano outside of Florence. To this enforced retirement indeed, we owe the *Discourses on the first decade of Titus Livy* and the *Prince*.

At last, in 1519, the Medici Pope, Leo X, evidently placated and assured of Machiavelli's loyalty, commissioned him to draw up a plan for the political reform of the Florentine state. And in the following year, at the instance of Cardinal Giulio de'Medici, he was also commissioned to write a history of Florence. This he finished, and presented to Giulio, now Clement VII, in 1525. The Medici certainly had no occasion to complain of the position accorded to them by the historian.

During the next two years Machiavelli worked feverishly upon his favourite plan of developing a defensive militia for Florence. The situation was indeed perilous. In 1527 occurred the terrible sack of Rome by the Imperial mercenaries. Florence took advantage of this disaster to drive out the Medici again, and to proclaim the republic under Niccolò Capponi. Machiavelli paid the penalty of his submission to the Medici and his acceptance of their favours. He was ignored by the new government, proclaiming itself on May 16, 1527; and he survived the humiliation by little more than a month, dying on June 20th. At least he was spared seeing his militia melt away, and his beloved city taken, three years later, by the troops of Charles V, and with the treacherous connivance of his own patron, Giulio de'Medici, nephew of the great Lorenzo himself.

One is tempted, perhaps unjustly, to moralize on Machiavelli's life, and to reflect that, astute as he was in the affairs of men, he was assuredly not astute to his own advantage.

Machiavelli wrote voluminously: official reports bulking large in the sum; essays on government, the art of war, language and style; a history; a biography; a *novella*; two comedies; a verse-chronicle. Yet he really lives in one short book, —and chiefly for that reason has been misunderstood, or successfully misrepresented. His *Prince* has been read and judged out of the context both of his other writings and of his life. Thus Cesare Borgia has been called the hero of the *Prince,* and therefore a hero in Machiavelli's eyes. Yet in his *Decennali,* or verse-chronicle of events in Italy during the decade after 1494, Machiavelli calls the same Cesare a "basilisk," well meriting his harsh fate, and surrounds Cesare's father, Alexander VI, with a *cortège* of the Deadly Sins. The argument of the *Prince* appears to be a plea for despotic rule, —for more than a Prince, for a Dictator. Yet the conclusion of Machiavelli's most fully elaborated political treatise—the *Discourses on the first decade of Titus Livy*—is that the ideal form of government is the *republic,* though in the present state of human development a *constitutional monarchy,* which on the one hand checks the fickleness of democracies, and on the other curbs the caprices of kings, might be a happy compromise. Nor can either work be regarded as a recantation of the other, for both were written within the same time,—in the early years of the author's enforced retirement at San Casciano.

But we need not turn from the *Prince* to the other works to find discrepancies, even apparent contradictions, in Machiavelli's moods and thought. The last chapter of the *Prince* itself is, in spirit, totally opposed to the preceding ones. We have been listening to a cold-blooded analyst; suddenly an eager enthusiast calls to us. There has been discussion wholly of conscienceless policy, pure expediency; now there is appeal to patriotism, to sacrifice, to an ideal. We are invited, against the author's own warning, to "leave what is done for what ought to be done."

Readers of the *Prince* have not unnaturally been perplexed by this seeming inconsistency. The most surprising guesses have been offered to account for it. Some—probably most—have taken this last chapter as a mere rhetorical flourish, meant to gloze over Machiavelli's real "Machiavellian" purpose, which was to preach despotic rule, and so to curry favour with the Medici prince to whom the book was dedicated. Such is substantially Macaulay's conclusion, except that, in accordance with nineteenth century notions, a good part of the blame of Machiavellism is laid on "the times." An extreme and amusingly opposite point of view is taken by an anonymous writer in the English periodical, *The Craftsman* (No. 431) in 1731. This apologist hails Machiavelli as a "friend to the cause of liberty;" and explains away the apparent praise of tyranny in the *Prince* as bitter irony. The work then, is to be interpreted as a mock-encomium, a satirical portrait of a Tyrant. And the libertarian peroration gives away the trick!

And the real explanation is so simple. A German by the name of Christ first hinted at it in 1731. (Possibly it was his argument that inspired the article in the *Craftsman* of the same year.) But to Gervinus and Ranke in Germany, and to Tommasini and Villari in Italy, the definitive interpretation of Machiavelli is due. And the explanation of the *Prince* is that the last chapter, or peroration, presents the noble patriotic end which justifies the necessary, if perhaps sometimes ignoble, *means* recommended directly or by implication in the earlier chapters. Unscrupulous tyranny is neither defended nor held up to scorn. A ruthless dictatorship is advocated to meet an extreme emergency.

The dream of Lorenzo the Magnificent of the "prosperous success" of Florence and Italy was proved a dream, and an empty one. With his death in 1492 there slipped the cornerstone of that fragile federation of the five major Italian states which his astute diplomacy and financial power had precariously held together. His successor in Florence, Piero, weak, vain, vicious, was worse than a nullity. With no leader capable of holding her together, Italy was about to illustrate again the fable of the faggots.

Also in 1492, Spain, by the conquest of Granada, freed herself from a cramping enemy within her gates. In the same year, by the discovery of America she was to discover as well a rich source of revenue. Welded into national unity by the Catholic monarchs, Ferdinand and Isabella, she was free and able to pursue an ambitious expansionist policy. The virtually unresisted invasion of Italy by Charles VIII of France proved the helplessness of the regionally divided Italians. Italy was a ripe plum ready to drop into the hands of the first-comer.

But if Spain noted the opportunity and put forward a claim to the kingdom of Naples, France, also consolidated and enriched by the miserly but astute Louis XI, now under the ambitious Louis XII reached out, on the basis of another shadowy claim, for the duchy of Milan. After that, what delayed for three decades the subjection of Italy was less her resistance than the mutual rivalry and occasional stupidity of her invaders. Her most successful resistance, indeed, was not by arms but by the shrewd diplomacy of indomitable Julius II, who—far more Italian potentate than Christian pope—having first, in 1508, made himself predominant in Italy by the League of Cambray, then fomented jealousy between Spain and France, and played off one enemy against the other.

Thanks to this singularly belligerent priest, the French threat was averted. By the victory of Ravenna in 1512 Louis XII was decisively driven out of Lombardy. Possibly, had Julius II lived longer, or had Louis XII and Ferdinand had weak successors, there might still have been some faint hope for Italy. But Julius, dying in 1513, was succeeded by the frivolous *dilettante*, Leo X, and he by his still less dependable cousin, Clement VII, more concerned for Medici rule in

[183]

Florence than for the independence of Italy. In place of Louis and Ferdinand came Francis I and Charles V, the former energetic and valiant to rashness, the latter the outstanding political personality of the age, implacable, far-seeing, and uniting with the power of Spain that of the Empire—in his hands still a mighty reality. The virtual finish of the duel came in 1525, when in the battle of Pavia Francis was defeated and taken prisoner by Charles. France out of the way, the end for Italy came quickly. In 1527 Rome fell, and was most horribly sacked. In 1530 Florence, the last Italian stronghold, surrendered and was delivered over to Medici dukes, ruling effectively as Spanish viceroys. Italy as a political entity ceased to be; and the name of Italy became, as Metternich was to say, merely "a geographical expression."

The *Prince* was written, however, while valiant Julius was still living,—while there still seemed hope. Although not finally published until 1516, it was substantially completed by the end of 1513. Its author realized clearly the desperateness of the situation. There was no one anywhere in a better situation to know it. And the pamphlet was a desperate appeal to desperate remedies, the summons to a forlorn hope. If all but that last urgent chapter do not give this impression, but rather an impression of cool scientific detachment, there are two good reasons for it. First, the Florentine Secretary was much too experienced in men and affairs to rely, Shelley-like, upon any mere emotional appeal. There needed definite, very definite, practical and practicable plans and counsels. Secondly, it so happened that Machiavelli was engaged upon a broadly based investigation into political science—to result in the *Discorsi* of a few years later. And, disconcertingly, he begins his polemical pamphlet as if it were also to be a general and theoretic treatise on government, defining and discussing the several kinds thereof. We are mentally started along a wrong track; and when the real and sole subject of the argument emerges, we hardly recognize it for such. This subject is government by a *new prince*. And a vast amount of misunderstanding would have been avoided if the title of the book had been frankly *Il Principe Nuovo*.

Even the term "new prince" is too comprehensive. It would include a prince just come into his inheritance. Machiavelli is not concerned with such. He is concerned solely with a prince, or ruler, *new* in that he owes his dominion to his ability, *virtù*, and fortune alone. And the reason for this single concern of Machiavelli's is simple: *whoever unites Italy into one nation must of necessity be a New Prince to all regions save that of his birth.* It matters not whether or no he has any colour of right, or whether or no he is a self-made man. Regardless of these considerations,—and moral ones,—it was because Cesare Borgia had shown such extraordinary ability in uniting again under his control the recalcitrant states of the Church in the Romagna that Machiavelli, who had watched him at close range, presented him as a model of political behaviour for the hoped-for Liberator and Leader.

To be sure, Cesare Borgia had fallen, and his newly united dominion had crumbled. But, as Machiavelli points out, his fall was due to an unforeseeable conspiracy of fortune,—the mischance of both son and father being stricken down together, Cesare by grave illness and the pope by death, at a moment of crisis. Even then, Cesare's only error of policy,— always supposing he had any choice in the matter,—was permitting a personal enemy, the Cardinal della Rovere, to succeed his father as pope. On the other hand, continued evidence of Cesare's politic as well as strong government appeared in the fact that more than one of the cities he had conquered remained faithful to him for some time after his downfall.

As a counterfoil to Cesare Borgia's address as a "new prince" Machiavelli set the blundering policy of Louis XII, who, when his game in Italy was almost won, made five wrong moves in succession. Five! And Machiavelli tabulates them with the disgust of a chess-master. And even then, Louis might have won, but proceeded to a sixth error! So, if Cesare's exhibition of *virtù* makes a fit model for the New Prince, Louis's painful lack of it makes him a "horrible example."

Thus far the modern reader may without difficulty go along with Machiavelli. Repugnance begins when he specifies certain lines of conduct as justifiable for the New Prince,— deliberate cruelty when seemingly expedient, deceit, treachery, even murder, and appeal always to men's fear rather than to their love. In fine, the political end—the *raison d'état*— would seem to justify anything and everything.

I shall not venture upon the casuistry of this issue,—beyond remarking that it is still a live issue. Perhaps today political *virtù* is less completely divorced from private virtue than in the early sixteenth century. Perhaps we do not have enemies of the State assassinated—except under due process of law. Our statesmen do not *lie*, they merely deny or affirm *officially*—as may be expedient. I would make the point, however, that Machiavelli is condoning such practices *only* for a Prince, a *new* Prince, under dire necessity, and for the best of all possible political ends—the independence and security of a people. On the other hand, the distinguishing mark of what is still popularly known as *Machiavellism* is the unwarranted belief that the Florentine Secretary recommended conscienceless practices to any political, and even to any private, end and interest; that his idea of *virtù* means— in the vernacular of today—ability to "get there," to arrive, regardless; that any other kind of "virtue" would be, in Andrew Marvell's phrase,

"A faint green sickness of brave souls."

On this misunderstanding—or misrepresentation—is based the legend of Machiavelli as the Italian Mephistofeles, the Niccolò who, according to Samuel Butler, gave the Devil his name of "Old Nick." Marlowe made the shade of Machiavelli speak the prologue to *The Jew of Malta,* and sponsor the sly and villainous chicanery of the Jew Barabbas. In the early seventeenth century, Machiavelli, Rabelais and Pietro Aretino are declared the "Anti-Trinity" of Treachery, Lechery, Gluttony. These libels were due to misrepresentation as well as to misunderstanding. And one prolific source of libellous characterization was a work commonly known as *Contre-Machiavel* by a French Huguenot named Gentillet, which, published shortly after the Massacre of St. Bartholomew, put the whole burden of responsibility for that atrocity upon Machiavelli's shoulders, Catherine de'Medici appearing as his docile pupil. Gentillet used the convenient, and one might say *Machiavellian,* method of citing statements entirely out of their context,—and so open to wrong understanding or at least to wrong emphasis; and, when such distortion appeared insufficient for his purposes, he invented statements and maxims out of his own imagination. Thus he *quotes* Machiavelli as recommending the free use of poison against inconvenient adversaries, which is quite untrue—unless we are naïve enough to take as such the figurative recommendation for emergencies of "strong medicines," *medecine forti.* It is himself, not the Florentine, that Gentillet shows up as unscrupulous; but his book, specious and unfair as it was, nevertheless went far towards shaping the judgment of Machiavelli in Protestant opinion.[1]

Actually, Niccolò Machiavelli appears to have been a very human and lovable person, with traits almost childlike. In a letter which has become famous he unwittingly draws a vivid self-portrait. It was written on December 10, 1513, from his farm at San Casciano to his friend and former official colleague, Francesco Vettori. Little more than a year had passed since his deprivation of office and virtual exile. He tells how he now spends his days. In the morning he goes bird-hunting, talks with the woodcutters, meditates by the brookside over Dante or Petrarch or a Latin poet. In the afternoon he plays cards at the inn with his humble neighbours,—the miller, the butcher, the baker, and mine host,—all often becoming uproarious. But in the evening, he says, "taking off my everyday clothes, soiled and muddy, . . . I enter into the ancient courts of ancient men," and speak with them, and ask them the reasons for their actions. "And they in their humanity answer me; and for four hours of time I feel no tedium, forget every distress, fear not poverty, death itself terrifies me not: wholly I give myself to them." It is a charming gesture,—and one indicative of Machiavelli's dramatic imagination,—that he should dress up for the authors he held in reverence.

Indeed, if the author of the *Prince* had a scientific mind and training, he had also a strongly dramatic imagination. Without such, he could not have written distinctly the best comedy of the Italian Renaissance—the *Mandragola*. (I shall touch upon it later.) In fact, this dramatic imagination of his —together with an ardently emotional temperament—affected powerfully, and not always fortunately, his historical writing and his conception of history. Like Tacitus, Macaulay,

[1] Cf. Edward Meyer, *Machiavelli and the Elizabethan Drama.*

Froude, Carlyle, he saw history as drama, and never let literal fact spoil dramatic effect. His contemporary, Guicciardini, is far more impartially accurate, if for that very reason less interesting. Most of us like to take sides, to play favourites. Machiavelli's *Florentine History* progresses as inevitably and dramatically to the triumph of the Medici as Macaulay's *History of England* to the triumph of William of Orange. The biography of Castruccio Castracane, captain of adventure, *condottiere*, makes an appeal not wholly unlike Marlowe's *Tamburlane*,—being the "true tragedy" of a man who by his own *virtù*, fortune-aiding, rises to greatness, and as suddenly falls. It is the Renaissance tragic plot *par excellence*.

Again, the pure objectivity of Machiavelli's historical judgments, and of his political policies too, was affected by a theoretic philosophy as *aprioristic* as it is pessimistic. Machiavelli's opinion of human nature is depressing. *"Men,"* he says, *"are only by compulsion made good."* That opinion explains a lot of things in his doctrines; but it is, after all, only an opinion, unproved, unprovable,—unless indeed, recourse is had to theological arguments on "original sin." And the Florentine Secretary was hardly one, I think, to fall back on theology.

Another fundamental preconception is what has been called "cyclical regeneration" in history. The notion that history, cosmic and human, moves in recurrent cycles is of course ancient. Plato makes much of it; Virgil illustrates it; Dante approvingly transcribes the prophetic words of the Fourth Eclogue, which imply it:

"Secol si rinnova;
Torna giustizia e primo tempo umano."
[*Purg.* xxii, 70-1]

[189]

That is to say, "the age renews itself," or the cycle of time revolves *back* to the "Golden Age," when justice prevailed. For Virgil this Golden Age was when Saturn ruled; for Dante it was before Adam sinned. For Dante—symbolically and actually—the ideal of mankind was to get back to that first innocence, to regain Eden, to unwind time. Machiavelli applies the same idea to politics: "If we would that a sect or republic live long, it is necessary often to recall it to its beginnings." (*Discorsi* III, i.) This is of necessity the political cycle: anarchy, monarchy, oligarchy, democracy, anarchy— and so *da capo*. Machiavelli reasons the series. Primitive anarchy—*bellum omnium inter omnes*—is resolved by the Strong Man, who by *virtù* and fortune dominates; whence *monarchy*. But the Strong Man grows old, dies, and is succeeded by a weak heir,—so at least it is bound to happen sooner or later. The weak heir, unless brushed aside by another Strong Man, becomes the puppet of a group of ministers or favourites, who really rule; whence *oligarchy*. But the rule of several invites discord and jealousy; each seeks backing from the people, and pays for it by surrendering power and privilege, until gradually all power and privilege get into the hands of the many; whence *democracy*. But rule of the many is a leading in many directions at once,—which is the same as no leadership; whence *anarchy* again. (To the objection that there might be rule of the majority, Machiavelli could retort that this would be a rule of some,—that is, *oligarchy*.)

Now I hope I have not distorted Machiavelli's conception by this brief and schematic summary. At least I have indicated the cyclical notion. As a notion of political history it is ingenious,—just as Rousseau's notion of an original "social contract" is ingenious. And both notions have some degree of *a priori* truth, of imaginative plausibility. But against them and their like we may quote Machiavelli's own words: "It being my intent to write what may be useful to him who reads, I have felt it expedient to get down to the effectual truth of the matter, rather than to indulge in imaginings about it." The temptation is strong to make facts fit theories; and no doubt even Machiavelli too often yielded to it. More certainly than any depravity of mind or of character, more perhaps than any contagion from the unscrupulous statecraft practised in his day, are Machiavelli's theoretic low estimate of human nature and denial of the possibility of real progress accountable for many of the sinisterly cynical judgments which so long brought his name into disrepute. If men be by nature ignoble, if it be the nature of things that *plus ça change plus ça reste,* what use preaching noble motives or hope of human betterment?

Fortunately, as among other things the peroration of the *Prince* proves, Machiavelli was—for all his rigorous logic—inconsistent. His was not an ignoble nature, and he responded—with the "reasoning of the heart" at least—to faith in humanity and to hope for its betterment. Read *through,* his writings carry the antidote to any poison of cynicism in them.

Taken then in his wholeness, Machiavelli is today recognized as the founder of political science as it has come to be, and as one of the most patriotic and sagacious of statesmen. Like Dante, he stood resolutely for the separation of Church and State, and denounced the corrupting influence of temporal power upon the Church itself. And the truth of the charge has been courageously acknowledged by the present Pontiff in asking no more than the nominal temporal sovereignty of Vatican City. So are vindicated by the Papacy Dante, whose essay on *Monarchy,* and Machiavelli, all of whose works, the Papacy laid under its ban.

Another far-seeing policy of the Florentine Secretary was

his persistent advocacy of a citizen-militia as against mercenaries knowing no patriotism but that of pay. Furthermore, in
his *Art of War* he urged that military service should not be a
profession in a standing army, but a training-school for every
citizen capable of bearing arms in the national need. This is a
salutary plan which the nations are even now discussing, but
have not as yet the courage to put into operation.

To Italians, Machiavelli—along with Dante and Petrarch
—is a national hero, a prophet of their *Risorgimento*. The
peroration of the *Prince* belongs with Dante's open letter
To the Kings, Princes and Peoples of Italy, and with Petrarch's ode *Italia mia.* The mood of all three is summed in
Machiavelli's one bitter phrase: "To everyone stinks this
dominion of barbarians"—*A ognuno puzza questo barbaro
dominio.* And again, like Dante, he forewarned that the rival
temporal sovereignty of the Papacy must be the great inter-
nal obstacle to Italian unity,—an obstacle now happily and
harmoniously removed.

To Machiavelli's style applies—and is a sufficient comment—Horace's phrase *simplex munditiis*—"plain in its neat-
ness," as Milton translates. There is no ornament, no need of
ornament; or, limpid clarity, exact fit of word and thought,
is ornament enough. And this exquisite simplicity of prose is
the more notable when ornate Ciceronian periods, aggravated by the *morbo italico* of the adjective, were dominating
Italian prose.

Machiavelli plans the Renaissance State; Castiglione plans
the Social Life of that State. Next to the right *Prince* the
right *Courtier.*

XII

CASTIGLIONE

FROM Machiavelli we may construct in our minds the Renaissance state. If in ultimate ideal a *republic*, the state prescribed by Machiavelli for Italy and for the near and predictable future was *monarchical*,—later to become perhaps constitutional. In fact, the whole movement of the Renaissance was towards monarchical government, consolidated nationally in France, Spain and England, in Italy multiplied into petty duchies and principalities. The concentrated aristocratic oligarchy of Venice, for all that it preserved some form and semblance of a republic, is hardly an exception.

The gentleman of the *Cinquecento* is, therefore, naturally the courtier, companion and adviser of the Prince. The root of gentility is courtesy, and courtesy is of the Court. So Edmund Spenser:

> "Of Court, it seemes, men Courtesie doe call,
> For that it there most useth to abound;
> And well beseemeth that in Princes hall
> That vertue should be plentifully found,
> Which of all goodly manners is the ground,
> And roote of civill conversation."
>
> [*F. Q.* VI, i, 1]

So the Conte Baldassare Castiglione, himself a perfect courtier after his own noble pattern, in his *Cortegiano* portrays the "goodly manners" and "civill conversation" of the Court

[193]

of the Duchy of Urbino. Nay more: he is the *arbiter elegantiarum* for all Renaissance Europe.

Italian culture had become conscious of itself, interested to define itself to itself. The interest was not merely curious; it was the zeal of the artist to formulate for himself the methods and ends of his art so that he may be the better artist. For never perhaps so much as in the Italian Renaissance have human institutions, the state and society itself, been regarded as works of self-conscious art.[1] The idea was more completely possible then, before the formulation of theories of historical evolution, of slow complex growth, of the past living inevitably on into the present. As yet it seemed quite possible to wipe clean the slate, and to write on it altogether new figures. Petrarch could not see why Rienzi's shaky little republic at Rome should not legislate out of existence all that had happened since Julius Caesar, and so continue on where Caesar left off. For Dante language—at least, language fit for gentlemen and poets—was not a growth but an art, a "grammar." The Renaissance held to the notion, if at times modifying its terms. I take two illustrations at hazard; but the idea was everywhere. There were, however, special reasons why social life should be theorized about, as if it were potter's clay capable of being softened out of its existing forms, and remodelled at once on a new pattern.

As far back as Guinizelli and Dante, Italians were already calling in question the claims of blood-nobility so absolute in the feudal north. Revived influence of ancient writers gave further authority for the doubt in the fifteenth century; and the many mushroom despotisms springing up from the ruins of the communes naturally encouraged indifference to birth and family tradition. Most of the *Quattrocento* despots were

[1] This is the main thesis of Jacob Burckhardt's classic work, *Kultur der Renaiss. in Italien.*

self-made men, if not bastards. "But," as Burckhardt says, "in proportion as distinctions of birth ceased to confer any special privilege, was the individual himself compelled to make the most of his personal qualities, and society to find its worth and charm in itself. The demeanour of individuals, and all the higher forms of social intercourse, became ends pursued with a deliberate and artistic purpose." Cultivated Italians conceived, and within certain limited circles realized, social living as a fine art.

A large conception of a society so artistically ordered, and at the same time a remarkably brilliant picture of a social circle actual and actually so artistically ordered is given by a member of the circle itself, Count Baldassare Castiglione, in his dialogue *Il Cortegiano,* "The Courtier." The dialogue, or rather conversation,—for the term *dialogue* suggests something too bookish and set,—is carried on in the drawing-room of the gracious Duchess of Urbino, Elizabetta Gonzaga, where she, assisted by her vivacious and witty cousin, the lady Emilia Pia, entertains a group of some of the most distinguished men of the day—churchmen of high rank, diplomats, men-of-letters, artists, statesmen. The theme is the character of a right Courtier; this first, and then the portrait of a Court-Lady fit to match and inspire him. There is nothing dull or didactic in the talk: definitions, qualifications, applications emerge spontaneously from thrust and counter-thrust in the debate; there are sallies of wit, phrases of sentiment; the argument grows warm, but no one gets heated; all aspects of life are touched on from boudoir and drawing-room to cabinet and throne; there is no mincing but no indelicacy. For these people are consummate artists; they possess what is declared to be the essence of social refinement—grace, *grazia,* the trained instinct which can do or say difficult things with apparent ease. A word more specific to social intercourse itself would be *tact*. But for all that they take the amenities of life so seriously, neither are the men fops or dawdlers, nor the women unwomanly. Eighteenth century "Belinda" and "Sir Fopling Flutter" are still unborn. After all, as is concluded in the dialogue, the principal interest and profession of the Courtier is that of arms. Castiglione himself was one of the foremost diplomats and soldiers in Europe. It is reported that, on hearing of Castiglione's death, Charles V said: "I tell you there has died one of the knightliest men in the world." If Castiglione would have his perfect courtier of noble birth, it is only because he believed in—and himself lived up to—the maxim of *noblesse oblige*. The Duchess Elizabetta was a devoted wife and capable consort as well as a social leader and a highly educated woman. She was neither the meek *Quattrocento* housewife sketched with approval by Leo Battista Alberti in his essay *On the Family*, or illustrated in the flesh by Lorenzo de'Medici's Clarice, nor yet the mannish *virago*, the executive woman like Caterina Sforza who so long held Forlì against the terrible Cesare Borgia himself. Elizabetta is the modern woman of society—in the best sense.

In the Courtier—the *gentleman* of the Renaissance—Cicero's *humanitas* is almost perfectly revived, even to the courtier's supreme virtue as adviser of state. The connection is not mere coincidence, for Cicero is constantly quoted by Castiglione. But I say the revival of Ciceronian *humanitas* is *almost* perfect. The self-made Roman, a vain and weak man for all his intellectual genius, was incapable of feeling or inculcating the aristocratic Italian's chivalry, at once sensitive and courageous. There is another important difference. Castiglione's courtier has all the virtues that Cicero attributes to his gentle-man; all his faculties are likewise developed to the full; he is in his degree the "universal man"; [1] but the chief

[1] Cf. E. K. Rand, *supra*.

influence making him all this, drawing out the best in him, is an influence unknown to the gentleman of ancient Rome,—or at least unrecognized by his portrayer, Cicero. It is the influence of a beautiful woman.

When the company at Urbino have drawn the right courtier full-length and four-square, they raise the question—*What is he good for?* Well, of course he has many functions, being by definition a many-sided man; but his last and supreme function is to be counsellor of state, adviser to his Prince. To that end he must be much experienced, naturally; but he must be high-minded as well as broad-minded, and there is no real high-mindedness which is not based on religious faith.

Now so far Cicero might have spoken,—in fact, did so speak. And, curiously, for the religious faith, the creed, of his gentle-man, Cicero anticipates Castiglione in turning to Plato, a mysticized Plato,—but a Plato with no woman in the case.

The faith of Castiglione's courtier is in the Beautiful,—one might say in Fine Art, in the divine art which made the world beautiful, and all things in it, and more especially beautiful women. But his attitude towards these last is that we have heard prescribed by the Platonist Benivieni. Approach to perfection is by the "ladder of love." But to get started, the courtier must be in love. And here is where the court-lady comes in. Dante's angelic lady descends to earth to become a social force, an agent of spiritual development in the courtier, a refiner of the brutal sex. To her, as artist of the beautiful, the courtier will be able to say, as the poet-dean, Dr. John Donne, said to a great lady of the court of James I:

"Madam:
You have refined me, and to worthiest things."

Castiglione was well aware that in recommending love, however "platonic," for a beautiful woman as a medicine for the soul, he was dealing, as it were, with a high explosive. The Platonist defined his love as the friendship of souls. But if two souls have bodies of different sex, their friendship is also a little different. So Byron, for instance, notes:

"No doubt the secret influence of the sex
Will there . . .
An innocent predominance annex,
And tune the concord to a finer mood."

But that the concord may keep in tune, the man, though something more than a *friend*, must also be less than a *lover*. There is perhaps wisdom as well as flippancy in Byron's conclusion:

"No friend like to a woman earth discovers,
So that you have not been nor will be lovers."

In any case, it is the Platonist's conclusion. The balance between platonic and profane love is a nice one; and Castiglione puts it into the court-lady's keeping. She must accordingly, for her medication by love of the courtier, have developed *"una certa mediocrità difficile,"* "a certain golden mean of reserve,"—must be not a wanton, nor yet a prude. She must be gracious, but not too gracious; not "easy," and yet not *difficile*. In a word, she must have the *tact* to draw out the bashful, but to check the overbold. Edmund Spenser has drawn her allegorical portrait in his Medina. (*F.Q.* II, ii.) Medina has two sisters, Elissa and Perissa, who fail to appreciate her nicely balanced courtesy:

"One thought her cheare too little, th'other thought too much."

[198]

Elissa and the sour-faced Huddibras just sit stupidly star-
ing at each other. Perissa and "the bold Sansloy" overstep
all bounds of propriety. Medina plays the part of moderator:

"That forward paire she ever would asswage,
When they would strive dew reason to exceed:
But that same froward twaine would accorage,
And of her plenty adde unto their need:
So kept she them in order, and her selfe in heed."

Now while there are ladies like Elissa and Perissa, the
prude and the wanton, there will be lovers like Huddibras
and Sansloy, the precisian and the lawless. A Medina will
call to, and call forth, a Sir Guyon of knightly temperance.
And like Medina and Sir Guyon are Castiglione's court-lady
and courtier. Their loves will be gentle because they themselves are gentle-folk. "If," declares the *Magnifico* Giuliano
de'Medici at the last, "beauty, demeanour, wit, goodness,
knowledge, modesty, and all the other virtuous parts we have
allotted to our lady, shall be the occasion of the courtier's love
towards her, necessarily will the end of that love be also virtuous; and if nobility of soul, valour in arms, accomplishment
in arts and letters, in music,—if courtesy, charm of speech,
grace in conversation, shall be the means whereby the courtier
wins the love of that lady, it must needs be that the end of
his love is of the qualities through which it attains its end."

On these foundations—and who can doubt their sufficiency
if they are anywhere to be found?—the elegant churchman
and poet, later Cardinal Pietro Bembo raises again the six-
runged Ladder of Love. Castiglione's choice of him for the
spiritual guide of the courtier was not arbitrary. Already, in
1505, Bembo had published his dialogues *Gli Asolani*, a
Renaissance courtly imitation of Plato's *Symposium*. The
scene is laid in the residence of Caterina Cornaro, once Queen

of Cyprus, at Castello di Asolo. Three youths and three maidens debate upon the worth of Love, its evils and excellences, joys and sorrows, until finally one of the youths, supposedly reporting a wise hermit,—as Socrates reports the wise woman of Mantineia,—exalts as true love desire of eternal Beauty, of which earthly beauty is only a pale reflection.

These Platonic dialogues of Bembo were widely read, and certainly would be present to the minds of Castiglione's audience. It is also true that Bembo lent his counsel toward the composition of the *Courtier* itself. And his formulation in that work of the Platonic creed is then a virtual summary of his own dialogues. "True love leads the soul," he says, "from the particular beauty of one body to the universal beauty of all bodies, and so in the last grade of perfection from the particular mind to the universal mind. And thence the soul, kindling in the sacred fire of the love truly divine, soars to union with the angelic nature, and not only altogether leaves sense behind, but even no longer has need of the discoursings of reason; for, transformed into an angel, it comprehends all things intelligible, and through not any veil or cloud, beholds the wide sea of the pure divine beauty, and is filled with it, and enjoys that supreme felicity which to the senses is incomprehensible." And the orator thereupon bursts into an apostrophe to sacred Love of such pious fervency that he seems fairly transported and entranced. He comes down from the ecstatic vision he has himself evoked like a second Moses returned from Sinai. "He seemed," reports Castiglione, "as if transported and spellbound, and stood mute and immobile, as if he were distraught; until the Lady Emilia . . . took him by the hem of his garment, and plucking it gently, said: 'Have a care, Messer Pietro, lest with these thoughts your own spirit be reft away from the body.' 'Madam,' answered Messer Pietro, 'nor would that be the first miracle which Love hath wrought in me.' " In vain the company urges him to tell more of this wondrous Love. He has told, he protests, what the "fury divine" has dictated. The frenzy has passed: Love would not have his further secrets revealed. It will be remembered that Benivieni ended his ode of Love with the same enforced reticence.

Bembo's pious and mystic protestations do not—to my ear, at least—ring quite true. That gallant retort—"Madam, nor would that be the first miracle which Love hath wrought in me"!—betrays the pose, the make-believe, the play-acting in this courtly religion of Beauty. The genuine mystic, "the deep transported mind" that has "at Heaven's door look'd in," is not the next minute ready with a witty phrase, a *mot* of the *salon*. Bembo's mysticism, like all else in this ardent but artificial Renaissance society, is religion become a fine art of living, *savoir vivre*. The Platonist and Petrarchist who speaks is rather the new *arbiter elegantiarum* than the priest. I do not mean that Bembo or Castiglione was consciously insincere in professing a religion of Beauty, of living as a fine art. Even if the new Platonic piety were partly make-believe, the new Platonic homage to ladies partly pose, the make-believe and the pose might yet have a pragmatic value. Treated as true, the cult might be in its effect as good as true. By it womanhood might be exalted, manhood ennobled and refined, society enriched and purified. Had not the divine Plato commended just such "medicinal lies?"

In any case, not Italy alone, but all Europe listened to Castiglione, applauded, and followed. The *Courtier* was read, translated, imitated in every country. Austere Roger Ascham, tutor and secretary to two English Queens, he who found in Italian society itself only a "Circe's Court," and in nine days saw, he says, in one Italian city "more libertie to sinne, than ever I heard tell of in our noble city of London in nine

[201]

years,"—he who condemns "these bookes, made in Italie, and translated in England" for opening, "not fond and common wayes to vice, but such subtle, cunnyng, new, and diverse shiftes to carry yong willes to vanitie, and yong wittes to mischief . . . as the simple head of an Englishman is not hable to invent, nor never was hard of in England before," —yet this same censor of things Italian praises, and urges to be "advisedlie read, and diligentlie folowed" Castiglione's *Courtier*, "an excellent booke for a gentleman." Sir Philip Sidney, that very perfect gentleman, is said to have shaped his life upon it. Upon it Spenser modelled in principle his Knight of Courtesy. Meanwhile, great ladies, and small, were everywhere administering that "medicinal lie" of charming men into worthiness.

Let us consider—sketchily—the course of this religion of Beauty.

XIII

"THE NEW RELIGION IN LOVE"

Orsames: I had no sooner named love to her, but she
Began to talk of flames, and flames
Neither devouring nor devour'd, of air
And of chameleons.

I Courtier: O the Platonics!
II Courtier: Those of the new religion in love! your lordship's
merry,
Troth, how do you like the humor on't?

Orsames: As thou wouldst like red hair or leanness
In thy mistress, scurvily! 't does worse with hand-
someness
Than strong desire could do with impotence:
A mere trick to enhance the price of kisses.
[John Suckling, *Aglaura*, c. 1638]

With the sixteenth century women had emerged. It was no
longer the thing to regard them as the natural inferiors of
men. Occasionally indeed in the satirical and humorous writings of the period the old calumnies recur; but now satirists
and humourists write mostly with their tongues in their cheeks.
In Castiglione's *Courtier* itself there is introduced a self-
professed woman-hater. But he is manifestly a straw man to
be knocked down for greater effect. To his mild ironies the
Magnifico Giuliano de'Medici retorts: You say man is more

perfect than woman. But how? In physical strength? An argument of light weight truly; "for even among men themselves those who have more strength are not on that account more highly esteemed than others. Even in war, which offers the greatest scope for strength and endurance, the hardiest man is by no means the most valued one. And as for intelligence, I say that everything that men can understand women can understand also; and that whithersoever can penetrate the intelligence of the one, can equally well penetrate the intelligence of the other." So convinced of women's intellectual equality was the learned Professor of Law and eminent Rector of the University of Strassburg, Henri Estienne, that he seriously urged the establishment of a female senate to consult with the male senate of the land. To be sure, there was later in the Protestant north a Puritan reaction against this feminism, against any "monstrous regiment of women," as John Knox put it; but no such reaction took place in Italy.

There, before the end of the fifteenth century higher education for girls was already general among the upper classes. Dante had explained vernacular poetry as having in the first instance been written for ladies, who, as he avers, naturally would not understand Latin. But already there were misses in their teens whose Latinity was far more classically perfect than Dante's own. It was the fashion to be *literary;* and to appear—literally speaking—*high-brow*, the young Minervas of the period drew their hair back from their foreheads, even shaved these—as appears in the charming profile of a lady in the Poldi Museum at Milan, and ascribed to Verrocchio. And of all fashionably learned matters most in vogue were Plato's doctrines of Love and Beauty,—or at least what passed for such.

Consequently, the most "learned ladies," *femmes savantes,* of the Renaissance differed from some of their modern sisters-of-research in by no means disdaining adornment of their persons. They might pretend to masculine minds, but certainly not to mannish hair-cuts and trousers. They realized that wit and charm were more effective together than either separately. Perhaps more than ever before or even since, beauty was in demand; and in response to the demand numbers of books were printed, defining and prescribing for personal beauty. So far as I know, however, the commercial beauty-specialist and "beauty parlour" were not yet.

One such book on Beauty,—and also one bringing down to a popular level the Platonic warrant for beauty—was entitled *Dialogo delle Bellezze delle Donne* (Dialogue of the Beauties of Women). Its author, the versatile Agnolo Firenzuola, protégé of Pope Clement VII, dedicated it in 1541 to the "fair ladies of Prato." He ended his life indeed as Abbot of Vaiano in that territory, having resumed the monastic life after a period of withdrawal sanctioned by Pope Clement. Firenzuola anticipated the type of the French literary abbé of the eighteenth century, urbane and witty and with a smattering of philosophy. His cloth did not prevent his writing *novelle* and plays by no means edifying.

The Dialogue in question takes place in a convent-garden between the Platonically trained connoisseur Celso Selvaggio and four ladies. These "interview" him, one might say, on the subject of feminine beauty. And Celso dilates enthusiastically and with punctilious detail on the subject. I may summarize part of his prescription (using the English translation by Clara Bell, London, 1892): The hair, he says, should be a soft yellow, inclining to brown; the forehead just twice as broad as high (*not for him the physical high-brow*); the skin transparent, not dead white; eyebrows dark, silky, most strongly marked in the middle, and shading off towards the ears and nose; the white of the eye faintly touched with blue,

[205]

the iris not actually black, but deep soft brown; the lids white, and marked with almost invisible tiny red veins; the hollow round the eye of the same colour as the cheek; the ear of a medium size, with a stronger colour in the winding than in the even parts, with an edge of the transparent ruddiness of the pomegranate; the nose to recede gently and uniformly in the direction of the eyes; where the cartilage ceases, there may be a slight elevation, but not so marked as to make the nose aquiline; the lower part to be less strongly coloured than the ears (*surely desirable this!*), but still not of a chilly whiteness, and the middle partition above the lips to be slightly tinted with red; the mouth smallish, neither projecting to a point, nor quite flat, with lips not too thin, and fitting neatly together; except in speaking or laughing never more than six upper teeth should be displayed. As points of finesse may pass "a dimple in the upper lip," "a certain fulness of the lower lip," and a habit of "closing the mouth sometimes with a tender air and a certain grace of the right side of the face, while the left side of the mouth parts as with a stolen smile" (*which I suppose can be achieved with practice*). And so on; for our connoisseur pursues his analysis through other parts of the person, and with gravity, since for him there are sermons—in *looks*. Marvellous indeed for Messer Celso are the effects of beauty. "For beauty," he says later in the Dialogue, "we see a man forget himself; and on beholding a face graced with this celestial gift, his limbs will quake, his hair stand on end, and he will sweat and shiver at the same time; just as one who, seeing on a sudden some heavenly vision, is possessed by the divine frenzy; and when he is come to himself worships it in his thoughts and bows down to it in his heart, and acknowledging it as it were a god, gives himself up as a victim and a sacrifice on the altar of that fair lady's heart."

At this point it is asked why a fair woman is so much more

alluring to a man than any other fair thing. The question is significant; for it raises the point of difference between Platonism proper and its romantic Renaissance derivative. Plato had no thought of women as by their beauty spiritual uplifters of men. But Celso refers his questioner to Aristophanes' oration in Plato's *Symposium*, in which it is told how men and women, originally one, go seeking each his or her other half. The meaning is, as Celso informs his fair listener, that "you and we are one and the same, and of equal perfection; and that you have to seek us and love us, and that we have to seek you and love you; our completeness is in you, and yours in us . . . Forget not, it is of Plato; bind that well in your mind." And the real Plato hesitated whether to class women among rational animals!

Celso—and the Renaissance with him—has still more ecstatic thoughts about fair women. "How," he asks, "should man on earth ever convince his mind that our future bliss, which shall chiefly consist in contemplating for ever the omnipotent essence of God and rejoicing in His divine presence, could be a joy forever without a thought of weariness, were it not that to gaze on the graces of a fair woman, to rejoice in her charm and feast the eyes on her gracious person, are an incomprehensible delight, a supreme beatitude, a joy which when it is over we long for again, which makes a man so happy that he forgets himself entirely?" In other words, it takes a pretty woman to persuade us that the beatific vision of the blest may not really be a bore. Shades of St. Thomas!

It would seem that if the beauty of women is really so potent, it would be pity to let such a power go to waste. Lorenzo de'Medici had said that "without the Platonic discipline, no one can be either a good citizen, or a good Christian." Doubtless he did not intend that the Platonic discipline was to be administered by women; but such was the intention of Bembo and Castiglione and Firenzuola and innumerable others.

It may be permissible to call the Platonic cult a social movement as well as a literary fashion. (Maulde de la Clavière in *Les Femmes de la Renaissance* does so frankly.) Beauty itself unmoved, moves to love, and from love to virtue, and from virtue to holiness. And there is a hierarchy of such angelical and evangelical beauties—from "thrones and imperial powers" down to where mere "angels sit in order serviceable." Emulative of the courts of queens were the drawing-rooms of ladies of the realm, great and less great. These were given homage in their degree, but with care not to excite the jealousy of Majesty. Courtly Spenser praises his private lady deprecatingly:

> "Sunne of the world, great glory of the sky,
> That all the earth doest lighten with thy rayes,
> Great Gloriana, greatest Majesty,
> Pardon thy shepheard, mongst so many layes
> As he hath sung of thee in all his dayes,
> To make one minime of thy poor handmayd,
> And underneath thy feete to place her prayse."

Following Italy's lead, all over Europe literary drawing-rooms, luminous spheres of Platonic influence and homage, multiplied. A typical *salon* of the late Renaissance in England was that of Lucy Percy, Countess Carlisle. Intimate of the French Queen, Henrietta Maria, and co-*Platonique* with her, Lady Carlisle exercised an extraordinary influence upon the men of her time, from statesmen like Strafford and Pym to poets like Carew, Herrick, Suckling, Waller, D'Avenant. Of her "chamber,"—that is, her drawing-room,—Edmund Waller writes:

[208]

"They taste of death that do at heav'n arrive;
But we this paradise approach alive.
Instead of Death, the dart of Love does strike;
And renders all within these walls alike:
The high in titles, and the shepherd, here
Forgets his greatness, and forgets his fear . . .
The gay, the wise, the gallant, and the grave,
Subdu'd alike, all but one passion have:
No worthy mind, but finds in hers there is
Something proportioned to the rule of his:
While she with chearful, but impartial grace,
(Born for no one, but to delight the race
Of men) like Phoebus, so divides her light,
And warms us, that she stoops not from her height."

Moving unmoved, "impartial" in her "grace," Lady Carlisle
reminds us of Castiglione's ideal court-lady. And her "character" as drawn at full length by one of her cavaliers, Sir
Tobie Matthews, strengthens the reminder. She exhibits precisely that *"mediocrità difficile,"* that "golden mean of reserve," which Castiglione recommends. As Sir Tobie puts it,
she will "freely discourse of love, and hear both the fancies
and powers of it: but if you will needs bring it within knowledge, and boldly direct it to herself, she is likely to divert the
discourse; or, at least, seem not to understand it." So Castiglione's lady, as we are told, "should seem not to understand,
and should put another colour on the lover's words, seeking
modestly, with that tact and prudence with which we have
endowed her, to extricate herself. Or if the address be such,
that she cannot pretend not to understand it, she should take
the whole matter as a jest, making as if she recognized that
only a compliment had been intended." Thus after a whole
century, and in an alien land, Castiglione's prescriptions hold
exactly good.

Apparently, being "born," as Waller says, "to delight the race of men," Lady Carlisle will not waste herself upon her own sex. That is not the vocation of the *Platonique*. Sir Tobie remarks, with some malice, that she "more willingly allows of the conversation of men, than of women, . . . and is more esteem'd than belov'd by her own sex, in two respects; the one, for that her beauty far exceeds theirs; and the other, for that her wit doth the like . . . She hath certain high and elevated thoughts, in which she is pleased most, and they carry her mind above anything within her knowledge." In this last is almost insinuated the Platonic rapture.

A nobler type than the Countess of Carlisle was the Marchioness of Pescara, Vittoria Colonna. And a nobler homage than any was paid her in the verse of Michelangelo. Indeed, these two may be said to exemplify supremely, and almost alone, the high seriousness of Platonic love as the sage and sober author of the *Courtier* conceived it.

A brilliant and beautiful girl, a woman the centre of homage in the literary centre of Europe, Rome, then—barely past forty—a saintly penitent and recluse, Vittoria Colonna impressed herself deeply upon the imagination of her contemporaries. She was herself an exquisite poet in some things—grace, purity, delicacy. The religious lyrics of her later years, if they lack the mystical fervour of those of Marguerite of Navarre, show also something of the moral spirit of the Reformation. Her sonnet-sequence—an *In memoriam* to her husband—is, like all others of the time, in Petrarch's manner, but chastely beautiful in form and tone.

That this union in one person of great lady and beautiful woman, poet and saint, should draw the divine fire of platonizing poets is not surprising. The name of those who burned verbal incense before her shrine is legion. One poet and Platonist of note, Galeazzo da Tarsia, never ceased to celebrate her in mystical verses as the very incarnation of the divine Idea. Others stooped to baser conceits. It was her misfortune that her name, which translated means Victory Column, should so terribly invite puns. She is—how many times! —a *column* wreathed with palms of victory. She is a *column* of purest white, but cold cold marble,—nay, but rather of fire-enkindling flint. Her admirers are shameless. Even fastidious Bembo addresses her as

> "High *Column*, all unshaken by the blasts
> Of angry heaven,—to which bright honor bring
> Those graceful limbs enwrapped in sable garb,
> And holy thoughts, and conversation high,
> And verse so tender!"

Certainly, a *Column* of parts!

Many under the form of love celebrated Vittoria Colonna; but she lives in the praise of one. Michelangelo was a Platonist of another stamp than the courtly triflers about him. He grew up in Florence under the influence of the gentle and serious founder of the Platonic Academy, Marsilio Ficino; the preferred spiritual guides of his maturity were Dante and Savonarola. Ideal love was for him no affair of gallantry, but a leading kindly light. He has compressed the essence of romantic Platonism into a brief madrigal:

> "Mine eyes, desirous of all fairest things,
> And evenso my soul of her reward,
> In having these adored
> Win their one virtue, which to heaven wings.
> From the high stars there springs
> A splendor, hither flowing,
> Which thither desire brings,
> And men call Love, unknowing.
> Nor cometh Love, all-glowing,

Into the gentle heart, save from a face
Within whose eyes those stars have left their trace."

Within the eyes of Vittoria Colonna Michelangelo saw the trace of the high stars. As a lover, he satisfied Castiglione's prudent requirement of age. He was sixty-three when he first met Vittoria; she was forty-eight, and had already entered into the nun-like retirement of her later years. One thinks of the aged Cyrano with Roxane in the convent-garden. But it was not age, surely, but reverence that kept the still passionate artist's love passion-free. Hearing of her death, he exclaimed simply,—"I have lost a great friend," *grande amico*. He said *"amico"*—masculine, as if her soul were masculine, or beyond sex. Again and again he protests the pure spirituality of this love of his, which is perfected friendship:

> "I say for that which lives that which decays
> Cannot assuage desire; Eternity
> Waits not on Time, where man's hair whiteneth.
> Unbridled will is lust, not love, and slays
> The soul; on earth this love of me and thee
> Perfecteth friends,—and more in heaven through
>   death."

And so, as a friend, she perfects his nature as an artist his creation:

> "When noble and perfected art conceives
> The form and features of a subject, next
> A mere rude model, in base matter fixed,
> Is the first birth which ever art conceives;
> But in the second birth the hammer gives
> Fulfilment to the promise of that text,
> Whose sense now shines forth fair and unperplexed,
> Till none deny that it eternal lives:

[212]

So was I born, mere model of myself;
Now is that model of me born again
Fairer through thee, Lady august and good."

To her on earth, as Dante to Beatrice in heaven, he turns for spiritual guidance:

"A blank sheet here I spread
For thy dictation blest.
Nor should love spare, but pity truth indite;
So that my soul, safe-led,
May swerve not from the best
This little while, but mine eyes see the light."

She is his giver of life, for here and hereafter:

"In me is death; but life, O Love, in thee,
My span of life dost thou alone allot,
And measure short or longer by thy rod.
Blessed I hold me in thy courtesy;
But most for that thou, where time runneth not,
Fittest my spirit to contemplate God."

Michelangelo in his platonizing poetry expresses philosophical reality, not a pose, a pretence. One of his contemporaries so puts it to the fashionable poets of the moment:

"He speaketh things, you others only words."

Benivieni, Bembo, Castiglione, Michelangelo—these are the outstanding heralds of the Platonic cult in Italy,—authentic voices to which respond a thousand echoes, none really significant. Socially, Castiglione's medicament of a purely spiritual love and refining affinity degenerated at last into the pitiful travesty called *cicisbeismo,*—that singular amendment to matrimony which permitted to every woman of fashion, besides a husband, a *cavaliere servente,* or companion of the soul.

But, transplanted, the Platonic cult flourished in other soils, —especially of France and England. Marguerite of Navarre preached it in the framing conversations and in some of the tales of her *Heptameron,*—in singular juxtaposition to tales of ribaldry and licentiousness. Maurice Scêve paid mystical homage to his *Délie,* whose name reveals in anagram *l'Idée* —his Platonic Ideal. A century later, Honoré d'Urfé was to run the gamut of love from sensual to pure Platonic in the character-motives of his symbolic romance, *l'Astrée.* And the Hôtel de Rambouillet was to make Platonic love a *divertissement* in *le Pays du Tendre.*

In England, Sidney as *Astrophel,* "lover of the star," deepens his homage of *Stella* with implications of Platonic idealism. Walter Raleigh, celebrating Queen Elizabeth as *Cynthia,* declares her the very incarnation of the triune Idea of Beauty, Wisdom, Truth. Spenser, in close likeness to Benivieni, dramatizes upon a supposed personal love his doctrinal *Hymnes* to Love and Beauty, and then indoctrinates them with Calvinism. And in the third and fourth books of the *Faerie Queene,* not unmindful of Castiglione, he allegorizes in pairs of characters the rungs of the Ladder of Love from lowest to highest, from lust to love purely spiritual. Thus he parallels in principle d'Urfé, and inspires John Fletcher to make such a symbolic love-scale of the characters of *The Faithful Shepherdess*—from the lustful Satyr and Chloe to the paradoxically pure Thenot and his Clorin, Thenot loving Clorin only because, and so long as, she is true to the memory of another. With high platonic seriousness John Donne celebrates the beneficent beauty and virtue of Mistress Elizabeth Drury,—as to his own *love* of her saying "what he was not sure was quite truth, but the best he could conceive." And finally, the cult in England ends in comic-opera under the auspices of the sentimental *précieuse,* Queen Henrietta Maria. Court-wits such as D'Avenant and Suckling produce at command, but with covert mockery, plays and poems paying lip-homage to the "new religion in love," as Suckling calls it, while questioning if it be not just

> "A trick to enhance the price of kisses."

Elegant Lord Herbert of Cherbury, indeed, seems to take it seriously, and in a lengthy poem called *The Ecstasy, An Ode upon a question moved whether love should continue forever,* pictures two Platonic lovers lying together for so long in rapturous "silent moveless peace" that they seem dead,—and the reader hopes they are.

Naturally, when, outside Henrietta Maria's court, wit and satire were the order of the day in poetry, these serio-comic attempts at Platonic idealism were met with merciless irony or open jeers. *The Antiplatonic* by John Cleveland is but one of many gaily cynical attacks upon the sentimentalized cult. He protests—among other things:

> "For shame, thou everlasting wooer,
>   Still saying grace and never falling to her!
> Love that's in contemplation placed
> Is Venus drawn but to the waist . . .
>
> For shame, you pretty female elves,
> Cease thus to candy up your selves! . . .
>
> Virtue's no more in womankind
> But the green-sickness of the mind;
> Philosophy (their new delight)
> A kind of charcoal appetite. . . .

[215]

They are sickly pleasures keep a diet.
Give me a lover bold and free,
Not eunuched with formality!" . . .

Still, it is stupid to judge a thing by the abuse of it. The Renaissance gospel of Platonic love is not in itself—in the understanding of Castiglione or in the practice of Michelangelo—vapid or silly or perhaps vicious. It may have "refined" many others besides John Donne to "higher things." It certainly did on the whole increase respect for womanhood, leading towards Goethe's ideal of *das Ewigweibliche*. Incidentally, it made for better social manners. And, as a literary motive, it inspired a very large part of the imaginative prose and verse of the period.

XIV

PETRARCHISM

ONE literary concomitant of the Platonizing cult, for Italy first and for the rest of Europe after, was the enormous vogue of Petrarch's lyrics, especially his sonnets. They seemed as by preestablished harmony suited for the service of "the new religion in love," as the Platonics' hymnal. Petrarch's commoner mood had been just that mixture of mysticism and gallantry which appealed to the elegant Bembo, and which could without causing embarrassment be addressed to a lady in a drawing-room. Gabriel Harvey, as I said in dealing with Petrarch, bespoke marvellously well the sentiment of the *salon*-poets of the Renaissance when he wrote that "Petrarch was a delicate man, and with an elegant judgment graciously confined Love within the terms of civility." And Petrarch's love-lyric was a model for these *salon*-poets for being, as the Cambridge Don averred, "the grace of Art, a precious tablet of rare conceits, and a curious frame of exquisite workmanship; nothing but neat Wit, and refined elegance." In a phrase, nearly all the Petrarchistic lyric of the sixteenth century is *vers-de-société*. An amusing example of how the Petrarchan model was exploited appears in the journal of the Elizabethan courtier-poet and translator of Ariosto, Sir John Harington. "The Queene stoode up," he records, "and bade me reache forthe my arme to rest her thereon— oh, what swete burden to my nexte song!—Petrarke shall eke out good matter for this business." I know not if Sir John ever

[217]

wrote that particular "nexte song," but I am sure that if he did, it was "nothing but neat Wit, and refined elegance." I am sure also that the underlying motive of his courtierly homage is betrayed in an epigram to the Queene on another occasion:

"For ever deere, for ever dreaded Prince,
You read a verse of mine a little since,
And so pronounst each word, and every letter,
Your gracious reading grac't my verse the better.
Sith then your Highness doth by gift exceeding
Make what you read the better in your reading,
Let my poore Muse your paines thus far importune,
To leave to reade my verse, and read my fortune."

We are reminded of that climax of "worthiest things" to which John Donne says the Countess of Bedford has "refined" him,—"Virtue, art, beauty, fortune." Indeed, too many a poet of the Renaissance was a pilgrim to the shrine of his Lady Bountiful,—more importantly bountiful than even beautiful; and his patroness-saint received canonization chiefly in the degree of her good works. Poets had to live; a paying public did not—in any adequate sense—exist; so poets borrowed from patrons, and repaid with thanks keyed high to the pitch of Platonic love. At least that would be their most preferred payment. And especially adapted for such amorous note-of-hand was the sonnet as Petrarch, in his merely gallant vein, wrote it,—a form brief, ingenious, pointed, pithy, a style all tender, obsequious, yet within bounds, delicate, a passion which flattered without compromising, in fine, a strictly legal currency for all compliment.

Towards the close of the *Quattrocento*, and concomitant with the growth of feminism and the *salon*, Petrarchistic imitation became indeed "a precious tablet of rare conceits,"—

"precious" from *préciosité*. *Improvisatori* became a necessary furnishing of a drawing-room, and usually had Petrarch by heart—to eke out "swete matter for *their* next song." One such "improviser" is in the Duchess Elizabetta's *suite* at Urbino. He is known as *l'Unico Aretino*, "the unique Aretine." His real name is Bernardo Accolti. He had won fame and fortune by his improvisations—"nothing but neat Wit, and refined elegance." In the *Courtier* he forces the opportunity to expound the signification of the tiny golden S suspended by a chain on the Duchess's forehead. Castiglione remarks that there was some reserve of opinion as to whether a sonnet of such very "neat Wit" would be altogether *impromptu* in its play on the mystic letter.

> "Vouchsafe, O sea of truth and excellence,
> Thy servant from his painful doubt to free,
> Whether that S on thy brow's ivory
> His sorrow or his solace represents,
> If it betokens succor or suspense,
> Safety, suspicion, stealth, or sympathy,
> Soundness or sickness, strife, severity,
> If strait his shackles, or if stricken hence;
> For that it giveth sign he sooth must fear
> Of stony-heart, of sighs, of sauciness,
> Sobbings and sweatings, sentences severe.
> But if have place the simple truth, this S
> With not a little cunning maketh clear
> A Sun in splendour sole and pitiless."

More famous even than the "Unique Aretine" was Serafino d'Aquila. In translations by Sir Thomas Wyatt, he influenced the new Italianate style in far-off England. In Italy he was the pet—the *Trissotin*—of the drawing-room. He was a little stout man. It is said that when he rolled up his shining black eyes, and ran his fingers over his beribboned lute, not a woman in Rome could resist him; when he began to improvise, they dissolved into tears.

Improvisations or not, Serafino published his poems. They are interesting as symptoms of a literary disease sporadic throughout the Renaissance, though more pronounced at the very end of it. Indeed, Italians call it *Secentismo;* and Samuel Johnson for England called it "metaphysical poetry," and dated it from Donne. The common symptom of this international disease is an eruption of *conceits,* verbal or logical, or both. I speak of a literary *disease;* but one can be too serious about the matter. It is really not fair to subject such *legerdemain* of wit to the cold scrutiny of print. No doubt, it was a crime for an *extempore* entertainer like Serafino to publish his tricks.

He knew Petrarch by heart, and had set him to music. That was his reserve to be drawn on when inspiration—or rhymes—failed. Much of his poetry is therefore mere sentimentalized echo. The novelty of his appeal was a type of conceit which takes a figure-of-speech at its word, and makes a metaphor go on all fours. Petrarch is forever drawing analogies between subjective moods and objective phenomena. Serafino makes analogy identity. His tears at the hard-heartedness of his mistress water the grass, and relieve the thirsty cattle; his hot sighs at her cold looks scorch the birds as they fly past. Again, anything can be turned by him into a compliment. A lady has lost a front tooth. Is it a thing to be passed over in sympathetic silence? Not at all. He assures her tunefully that Cupid has had it removed to provide him with a porthole, through which, seated upon her tongue, he may shoot his arrows. Translated from figure into fact, the effects of love make the lover a useful person:

[220]

"Castle besieged by cruel enemies—
If water fail, let me therein be sent;
Whatever man is born to plough the seas—
If wind fill not his sail, let me be lent;
If you in drear and stormy winter freeze,
Fire lacking, call on me, and be content:
Rich in three things Love makes me by his art,—
Wind in mouth, water in eyes, and fire in heart."

Pyrotechnic effects may be got by mere verbal iteration. The trick is easier and more natural in Italian. But here is a roughly Englished example:

"Your eyes are shouting to my heart: fly fly!
The only defence is defences that are weak weak.
Up up, into the breach, the breach, die die!
It burns, burns hot—hot in cold cold. I speak,
Speak softly softly then—then by-and-by—
Come come to me, O death, death oh, quick, quick!
Now am I still still, now cry, cry higher higher:
Help help, oh water water, fire fire!"

Serafino had numerous disciples. One of these, Panfilo Sasso, whose poems went through five editions between 1500 and 1519, may illustrate another phase of the conceit of the figurative taken as fact. This time it is the lady who is valuable:

"She in her mouth bears pearls, on her bosom silver,
Gold in her hair, upon her forehead heaven,
In one eye lo! the moon, the sun in t'other:
She sweateth balsam . . ."

The conception of a mistress so richly but surprisingly endowed became popular. At least one artist drew her portrait according to specifications—with an alarming result. (Jusserand reproduces it in his *English Novel in the time of Shakespeare.*) Shakespeare derides the conceit in his sonnet—

"My mistress' eyes are nothing like the sun."

Pietro Bembo recalled the Italian lyric to sanity,—from this conceitful travesty of Petrarch back nearer to the real Petrarch, though more to the elegant stylist than to the deeply moving poet that Petrarch is at his best. Indeed, Bembo's example and influence went a long way towards justifying Gabriel Harvey's estimate of Petrarch as essentially a drawingroom poet. Incidentally, Bembo's fastidious concern with form is shown by his alleged habit of passing his own sonnets through sixteen portfolios to receive a progressive polish. In general, his verses are formally impeccable, but empty of substance—expression hungering for thought.

But he gave new impetus to the vogue of the sweet singer of Laura. Fine ladies carried about the *Canzoniere* in miniature volumes—*Petrarchini*—attached to their girdles by gold chains,—as their grandmothers had carried their missals. Pietro Aretino describes dandies in the public streets, "riding languidly, servant at stirrup and only tip of toe in it, humming sentimentally,"—Sir Andrew Aguecheek anticipated.

Everybody wrote his or her book of sonnets as today everybody his or her novel. For the most part, the results are indistinguishable,—whether produced by professional poets or by men-of-affairs in off moments, by court-ladies or by courtesans. Bembo's purism had led to an even if colourless elegance of phrase and diction, closely following Petrarch's own, set to a delicately if monotonously balanced verse,—perfect art of song without words of any significance. A Vittoria Colonna builds a sonnet-memorial to her revered husband, or a Bernardino Rota to his revered wife, in a tone and style hardly distinguishable from a Molza lamenting in sonnets one more

[222]

outlived mistress, or a Tullia of Aragon flattering a venal lover.

Petrarch's own lines, like Virgil's in the later Empire, were reshuffled into new combinations—*centos*—more or less meaningful. A certain Giulio Bidelli boasts of having made in this fashion "two hundred stanzas and two *capitoli*." It would seem that Laura too had not been idle. In 1552 appeared *"The sonnets, canzoni and triumphs of Madonna Laura in reply to Messer Francesco Petrarca for his verses during her life, and after her death come into the hands of the Magnifico Stephano Colonna."* Rhyming dictionaries of the *Canzoniere* —*rimarii del Canzoniere*—were compiled to expedite imitation.

Criticism and exegesis were as abundant as imitation. In ever new editions of the *Canzoniere* the text appeared as a small island in wide sea of annotation. Four generations of commentators quarrelled over a sonnet, a line, a phrase. Imitators added learned notes to their own imitations. So notably one Cittadini. The sonnets were *spiritualized,* a certain Malipieri, for example, achieving his effect by simply substituting throughout for the name of *Laura* that of *Maria*. From the sonnets preachers drew texts for their sermons. The Poet's cat, said to have saved her master's manuscript from predatory mice, shared in his apotheosis. In his *Secchia Rapita* Tassoni bears witness of her:

> "A thousand songs were her *Magnificat;*
> And the high monuments of haughty kings
> Pale by the glory of a tombless Cat."

A natural feature of Petrarchistic imitation was the stereotyping of epithets. Madonna's hair is always golden; her eyes of topaz; her neck and breasts milk-white; her lips coral; her teeth pearls; her mien humbly proud. One frequent burlesque of the extravagant fashion was to shuffle the epithets. Thus, for example, Francesco Berni praises his Lady:

> "Fine silver tresses in a tangled grove
> Artlessly shading a fair face of gold;
> A crispèd brow that makes my blood run cold,
> And dulls the arrow-points of Death and Love;
> Two eyes of pearl, twin lamps that glare above
> All things of other and of better mould;
> Eyebrows of snow, and—what my heart cajoled—
> Fingers and hands too thick for jealous glove;
> Two lips of milk; a mouth most heavenly ample;
> And ebon teeth, most rare and most unstable,—
> Harmony not to hear of, not to tell!
> Behavior bold and balmy: for ensample,
> O sacred servitors of Love, I fable
> Of charms that, blended, make my Lady's spell."

The same burlesque device is used by Bottom as Pyramus to praise Thisbe in *Midsummer Night's Dream;* and John Donne gives a salacious twist to it at the beginning of one of his *Elegies.*

There are of course saving exceptions to the general indictment, though modern praise is usually bestowed upon *Cinquecento* writers of sonnets and *canzoni* in the precise degree of their independence of Petrarch. Thus Richard Garnett says of a favourite of his own, Luigi Tansillo: "After Michael Angelo he stands farther aloof than any contemporary from Petrarch, a merit in an age when the study of Petrarch had degenerated into slavish imitation." (*The Love-Story of Tansillo* in *Essays of an Ex-Librarian.*) In similar mood John Addington Symonds found sincere and powerful the "somber rhymes" of Monsignore Giovanni della Casa, whose sonnet to Sleep—and some others—he translates. This sonnet has also another interest in being what has been called a "tournament" sonnet, written, that is, as if in deliberate competition on a set theme. Here is La Casa's sonnet in Symonds's translation:

"O Sleep, O tranquil son of noiseless Night,
Of humid, shadowy Night; O dear repose
For wearied men, forgetfulness of woes
Grievous enough the bloom of life to blight!
Succour this heart that hath outgrown delight,
And knows no rest; these tired limbs compose;
Fly to me, Sleep; thy dusky vans disclose
Over my languid eyes, then cease thy flight.
Where, where is Silence, that avoids the day?
Where the light dreams, that with a wavering tread
And unsubstantial footing follow thee?
Alas! in vain I call thee; and these gray,
These frigid shades flatter in vain. O bed,
How rough with thorns! O nights, how harsh to me!"

English readers will recall and compare Samuel Daniel's sonnet to Delia, beginning

"Care-charmer Sleep, son of the sable Night,
Brother to Death, in silent darkness born!"

The sonnet of Tansillo's, which Garnett thinks "one of the finest in Italian literature," has had a curious history. It is recited by Tansillo himself as principal interlocutor in Giordano Bruno's *Eroici Furori,* and there interpreted as the vaunt of one "arising and freeing himself from the body and sensual cognition." And the sonnet might be so understood. It was also long supposed to have been written by Bruno himself. Symonds properly accredits it to Tansillo, but, translating it under the title of "The Philosophic Flight," says that "it expresses in noble and impassioned verse the sense of danger, the audacity, and the exultation of those pioneers of modern thought for whom philosophy was a voyage of discovery into untravelled regions." And the sonnet might be so understood. But then comes Garnett with indubitable evidence that Tansillo's desperate flight was no such thing, but a love-flight, perilously high-flying because the lady to whom he aspired was Maria d'Aragona, whose husband was the Marquis del Vasto, Charles V's celebrated general, and whose grandfather had been King of Naples. No wonder the daring of the poet-lover, himself a poor retainer of the Neapolitan Viceroy's son, is not unmixed with trepidation. Here is Garnett's version of the sonnet:

> "Now that my wings are spread to my desire,
> The more vast height withdraws the dwindling land,
> Wider to wind these pinions I expand,
> And earth disdain, and higher mount and higher;
> Nor of the fate of Icarus inquire,
> Or cautious droop, or sway to either hand;
> Dead I shall fall, full well I understand;
> But who lives gloriously as I expire?
> Yet hear I mine own heart that pleading cries,
> Stay, madman! Whither art thou bound? Descend!
> Ruin is ready Rashness to chastise.
> But I, Fear not, though this indeed the end;
> Cleave we the clouds, and praise our destinies,
> If noble fall on noble flight attend."

The "noble flight" of this Italian Ruy Blas lasted—with ups and downs in fervency—sixteen years. Then despairing of the inaccessible goal of his desire, he came back to earth—and to a humbler but more responsive spouse, whom presently, remarks Garnett, "he instructs in a very elegant poem ("La Balia") how to bring up her infant children." It is fair to remember that, if Tansillo failed to live up to the Ruy Blas rôle, Ruy Blas enjoyed the favour of his regal mistress, reached the goal of his love-flight.

The Petrarchan influence was perhaps more fortunate for French and English poetry than for Italian. Fifteenth and sixteenth century Italian imitators of Petrarch never more than approached his excellence, and they struck off nothing significantly new or different. In France and England there was reaction of the national temperament to the Italianate moods and motives, and therefore spontaneous variation. In Ronsard's best love-sonnets there is a masculine tenderness, a wistful playfulness, an ironic humour quite foreign to the elegantly plaintive Italian. We may call it, if we like, the effect of *esprit gaulois*. Anglo-Saxon surely is the common tone of downrightness, of defiant indignation mingled with the homage in the more characteristically English sonnetteers of the late sixteenth century—Sidney, Drayton, Shakespeare. Such a sonnet as Drayton's, beginning

"Since there's no help, come, let us kiss and part—"

breaks entirely with the Petrarchan tradition; as do Shakespeare's sonnets to the Dark Lady. And yet, but for the Petrarchan tradition neither Drayton nor Shakespeare would have written their sonnets. And especially close to the Italian model in temper are the sonnets of Daniel and Spenser.

XV

ARIOSTO

POET laureate by universal acclaim to Castiglione's courtierly audience was Ludovico Ariosto. He was besides all
things to all tastes: a refashioner of classical theme and epic
story for the pupils of the humanists; a spirit of romance and
sensibility for the gentle reader, the gentler sex; an inimitable
teller of tales for the multitude; a wit and humourist for the
intellectuals; a voice of bitter appeal to the patriot.

The man and the artist are greater than his material. It is
with him,—though with a difference,—as with Edmund Spenser. Whoever called Spenser "the poets' poet" did not mean,
I think, that the poets who have loved the *Faerie Queene* did
so for the tales of chivalry it incorporates. These grow mo-
notonous and tiresome. The incessant combats, often motiveless
and almost always with the hero easily victor, the long procession of fair ladies colourlessly chaste and plaintively defence-
less, the total absence of any real business anywhere in the
world except loving or lusting or fighting about it—surely
such materials of themselves can hardly hold the serious attention of grown-up people. When Ariosto first presented his
poem to his patron, the Cardinal Ippolito, the latter is said to
have commented derisively: "Wherever in the world did you
get all these old wives' tales?"—or words to that effect. The
remark is usually quoted to the frivolous prelate's discredit,—
and no doubt it is,—but the just reason is that he could see
the tales only, and not the poetry and beauty and humanity

reflected in and beside them. It is these qualities emanating from the poet himself that, as I suspect, induced Sir Walter Scott—himself called "the Ariosto of the north"—to read through the *Orlando Furioso* once again every year. And these qualities in Spenser,—rather than his frigid and confused moral allegory,—were what led Milton to declare Spenser "a better teacher than Scotus or Aquinas."

At first glance, a close similarity appears between the careers of Boiardo and Ariosto. Both were courtiers of the House of Este at Ferrara. Both were in the civil and diplomatic service of the state, as well as court poets. Both were classically trained, and poetized also in Latin. Indeed, until he was twenty-five, Ariosto composed almost exclusively in the language and styles of Catullus, Tibullus and Horace, and by no means unworthily of them. And Boiardo and Ariosto were virtual collaborators in what Tasso, modestly ignoring his own rival masterpiece, called the one great narrative poem of the age. Ariosto himself, in a letter to the Marquis of Mantua, announced as his simple purpose "to continue the invention of the Count Matteo Maria Boiardo."

As we look more closely, however, striking differences show themselves between the personalities and lives of the two Ferrarese poets. Count Matteo Maria was to the manner born of the court and of its chivalry. His Duke, Ercole I, was capable of appreciating him, and richly rewarded him. In Reggio, he was Governor of a peaceful thriving city. Ludovico Ariosto was a son of the Captain of the Guard of the citadel of Ferrara, a soldier unacquainted with the court, and dependent on his pay. On his father's death in 1500, Ludovico at twenty-six had, as the eldest, to provide for the maintenance and education of his four brothers and five sisters. Of his service in the retinue of his first patron, Cardinal Ippolito, brother of the

[229]

Duke, he writes caustically later in one of his so-called *Satires,*
—rather verse-epistles in Horace's manner:

> "For this long-drawn-out servitude abhorred
>   Not from the Cardinal has come to me
>   Even the wherewithal to pay my board.
> And thanks to thee, Apollo,—thanks to ye,
>   O sacred band of Muses, I possess
>   Not yet enough to clothe me decently.
> 'Oh, but,' you say, 'His Eminence gave you . . .' Yes,
>   Enough indeed to buy me several cloaks;
>   But not for *your* sake gave he it, I guess,"—

rather, as the poet bitterly reflects, for postboy services, running errands . . . He was a stay-at-home sort of person, hating
the discomforts of travel in those days. And there were even
other risks. He was sent on a delicate mission to Pope
Julius II, and that irascible prelate threatened to have him
thrown into the Tiber. The sensitive poet had no heart for
such adventures.

So, after fourteen years of the Cardinal, Ariosto in 1517
shifted to the Duke,—only to illustrate again, he says, the
fable of the Frogs and King Log. At bottom, he hated court
life:

> "How quickly from the court I'd up and pack
>   If for once only Maia's son were kind.
> A single saddle fits not every back,
>   Nor yet a single load: one for an age
>   Bears what would break another like the rack.
> Not long the nightingale endures the cage;
>   Longer the finch; the linnet long, mayhap;
>   The swallow in one morning dies of rage.
> Let him who covets 'spur' or 'scarlet cap'
>   With king, duke, cardinal or pope be placed;

Not I, who care for either not a rap.
At mine own table better turnips taste
    I've cooked myself, and on a skewer pressed,
    And with a sauce of must and vinegar graced,
Than at another's board wild boar or breast
    Of partridge; and beneath a common spread
    As well as under silk or gold I rest.
I'd rather stretch my lazy legs abed
    Than brag how they among far Scythians,
    Indians, or Ethiopians were led."

What most disgusts him with courtiers is their sycophancy:

"Much would it pleasure me to learn from you,
    Sandro my brother, Bagno my good friend,
    Whether at court remember me some few;
If still His Highness scolds; if to defend
    My name one rises, and would reasons tell
    Why on your travels I could not attend;
Or if those who in flattery excel,—
    Art that among us seems to best to pay,—
    To please Milord do on my weakness dwell.
Mad is the man that dare his Lord gainsay,
    Should he remark that he had seen the sun
    To shine at midnight, or the stars by day.
Let him praise this, or damn that other one,
    And the accord of many voices presently
    Will all around like pleasant music run;
And who for bashfulness dare not make free
    His mouth to open, yet with look applauds,
    Seeming as he would say: 'I too agree.' "

No doubt there may be some literary convention in this
ironic picture of the insincerities and trucklings of court-life,
which was a favourite theme of satire during the later Middle
Ages and the whole Renaissance. But Ariosto's aversion seems

to have been quite sincere. One is not so sure of the poet Spenser, for instance, bitterly as he inveighs against the court in *Mother Hubberds Tale.* There may have been a taste of sour grapes in his case.

Ercole, in 1487, made Boiardo Governor of the thriving town of Reggio in the fertile valley of the Po. It was, by the way, Ariosto's birthplace. Alfonso, in 1522, made Ariosto Governor of Garfagnana, a remote and recently acquired mountain hamlet, virtually at the mercy of roving bands of banditry. Ariosto did his best to pacify the district, but the task was utterly repugnant to his gentle, rather easy-going temperament, and he was ill supported from Ferrara. After three distressful years he obtained recall.

Here is part of his own comment on the experience:

"This is a ditch I live in, dark and deep;
    I cannot move a foot unless to climb
    The wooded Apennine's horrific steep.
Whether I keep the Castle, or take the air,
    Nothing but squabbles, pleas, complaints I hear,—
    Feuds, murders, thefts, strife everywhere.
Now with bland smiles, now in pretence distressed,
    I needs must coax this man, and threaten that,
    Sentence another, and dismiss the rest;
And daily reams of messages write out—
    In vain—for aid and comfort from the Duke
    Against these bandits who are all about.
Assassins are so thick upon this crag
    That all those stationed here to capture them
    Dare not draw out the banner from its bag . . .
Think if Apollo, did he hear me calling,
    Would come, leaving his Delphi, leaving Cynthus,
    Among these caves, among this endless brawling!"

The episode is a good illustration of the absurdities of the patronage system. Imagine Queen Victoria sending Alfred Tennyson to pacify a disturbed district in Afghanistan.

Returned from Garfagnana, Ariosto bought with his savings a small house in the environs of Ferrara, and there spent the last seven years of his life in quiet domesticity, tending his garden. Over the lintel of his door he inscribed the Horatian motto:

"Parva, sed apta mihi: sed nulli obnoxia, sed non
Sordida, parta meo sed tamen aere domus,"—

which may be paraphrased:

"Small, but well suiting me; eyesore to none;
Not squalid; just a home, and all mine own."

Besides these differences of temperament and circumstance to separate the two poets, there was also the tragic change that had come over Italy since Boiardo's death in 1494. Ariosto lived until July 6, 1532. He so outlived the sack of Rome and the fall of Florence. He so lived through the whole slow agony of Italy's humiliation and alienation. A mere forehint of the catastrophe to come had abruptly shut off the *Orlando Innamorato,* but the poem as it stands was composed while the Magnificent Lorenzo could still dream of a "prosperous success" for Florence and for Italy. Although forty cantos of the *Orlando Furioso* had appeared by 1516, the complete edition of forty-six cantos came out only in 1532. Meanwhile the poet had never ceased to file and to revise his work; which may as a whole, therefore, be said to reflect the ultimate moods of his life.

Under such conditions, personal and national, Ariosto, proud, sensitive, patriotic, composed for the delectation of patrons who valued him more as a courier or commissary than as a poet, the in seeming most light-hearted of poetic tales. That he lived in and loved his art, found solace and serenity in it, may be granted; but it is hardly surprising that his laughter should ring a little hollow, and his gaiety mask a certain cynical bitterness—all the more poignant as set against his natural kindliness and good nature.

Torquato Tasso says in his essay on the "heroic poem": "The *Orlando Innamorato* and the *Furioso* are to be considered, not as two distinct works, but as a single poem, begun by the one, and with the same threads, though better knotted and better coloured, finished by the other poet; and, regarded in this manner, it will be a complete poem, lacking nothing for the understanding of its fables." And as we turn from the *Innamorato* to the *Furioso*, we may feel at first Tasso to be justified. Boiardo's heroes and heroines had slept for a generation; now, like the people in the enchanted palace in the old fairy-tale, at the touch of the Prince Charming they wake up without surprise or sense of change, and go about their various businesses just where they had left off. Angelica continues to urge on her steed, fleeing from enamoured Orlando, and only

> "the lightlier fleeted through the forest";

Marsilio and Agramante rub their eyes, and proceed with their review of the Saracen hosts besieging Paris; old knightly rivals, meeting again after three decades of oblivion, have at each other with only increased fury. Orlando's volcanic nature had sent forth flames and steam of love; now it erupts into madness from jealousy.

But as we read, we become conscious of a deeper *awakening*—from dream, from illusion. Ariosto's people are Boiardo's people *waked up*, disillusioned. They act from more sophisticated motives; they have more *savoir faire*. Orlando goes mad

with jealousy; but when his sense is returned to him, he is
not only cured of jealousy, he appears disillusioned with love
itself:

> "And her, who had so gentle seemed before,
> So fair, and whom he so had loved, he now
> Regarded—save for a vile thing—no more."

That is not a very chivalrous way of regarding a fair lady—
just because she had not returned his love. Boiardo's motto,
his inspiring motive, is denied. "Love conquers all things"—
except *good sense*. It is almost the "Enlightenment," the
Aufklärung, of the eighteenth century.

Also, at moments this great dual narrative poem of the
Renaissance reminds one of that other great dual narrative
poem of the Middle Ages,—the *Roman de la Rose* by Guil-
laume de Lorris and Jean de Meung. De Lorris glorifies
womanhood and chivalrous love; De Meung scoffs at both.
So more than once Ariosto would seem to scoff not only at
Boiardo's chivalry, but also at the ideal love and lady-homage
that his contemporaries Bembo and Castiglione were so earnestly preaching. The notorious twenty-eighth canto of the
Furioso might be dismissed as simply a *novella à la mode.* But
the apologetic stanza introducing it is in the deliberately
mocking and cynical *politesse* of a Voltaire or a Wycherley.
We can see the disillusioned poet declaiming it, hand on heart,
ironical smile on lip. He addresses the ladies,—and remember,
for all their wit and refinement, they could take publicly and
unblushingly the scabrous tale that follows.

> "Ignore this canto, gentles, for without it
> My story's so writ plain you can't mislay it.
> Since Turpin gives the canto, I'll not flout it,
> Nor yet in malice or in mischief say it:

The teller loves you ladies,—can you doubt it?
That he ne'er grudged his debt, or failed to pay it,
He's shown a thousand times, and now assures
He is, nor ever could be else than, yours."

Truly indeed, the *complaisant* poet of the court does not leave his gentle listeners defrauded of their romance. Why does enamoured Orlando become the mad Orlando? because Angelica, so scornful of the renowned paladin of France, of great kings and valiant princes, surrenders her love, herself, her kingdom to a pretty soldier-boy she finds wounded on a battlefield. It is an idyl worthy of the school of Jean-Jacques, of romantic equalitarianism and sensibility.

But Ariosto is more amused than moved by Angelica's romance. It is a pretty paradox of the heart,—"just like a woman." And Medoro has the soul of a tenor. No, Ariosto refuses to be serious—for long. It is as if he were afraid to be. Even in the most chivalrous, most tender moments in his poem, he will deliberately turn pathos into bathos, will *wake us up*. There is no more admired scene in the *Furioso* than that of the constant Isabella lamenting over the body of her dead lover. Critics have been unanimous in praising its romantic truth, its delicate and moving sentiment. And so it is—up to a point. But at last, as we are told, Isabella, having "abandoned herself" to the bloody corpse, and bathed it with her copious tears, then

"So shrieked that round about for miles and miles
Resounded wood and meadow."

"For miles and miles"—*a molte miglia!* It is too much. The lady's lungs are too strong. We perceive that the poet is mocking his own pathos—and his reader.

Subtler is the mockery of his nobler self in the episode of

Astolfo driving away the Harpies from the paladins at table. Ariosto thinks of those other Harpies devouring his country. For a moment he is serious and indignant:

> "Ye greedy Harpies, foul, ferocious, cold,
> That unto Italy, blinded and misled,
> Perchance to punish some wrong act of old,
> At every board bring retribution dread!
> Fond mothers and their innocent babes behold—
> Whilst they all helpless cry in vain for bread—
> These monsters gorging at one sole repast
> What for *their* lives would plentifully last."

Then he smiles at his own impotent fury. After all, once upon a time Astolfo, the puny braggart of the blatant horn, drove away the brutish Harpies with a big noise:

> "Il Paladin col suono orribil venne
> Le brute Arpie cacciando in fuga e in rotta."

And surely present-day Italians can make a big noise, are a "big noise!" That is the implication. This is not levity; it is an irony akin to despair.

Boiardo treats his chivalric material with indulgence faintly touched with humour. His world of knight-errantry may be a make-believe world, a land of faerie, but it is none the less one of ideal nobility, heroism, devotion, and deserves respect. On the other hand, many of Ariosto's incidents—even the central incident of Orlando's madness and cure—are pure *extravaganza*. Not Pulci, hardly Rabelais, can match the burlesque of the crazed paladin running amuck, naked, armed only with a tree-root, through France and Spain, spreading everywhere terror and desolation, and then, swimming the Strait of Gibraltar, to devastate likewise Africa. And unique in fantasticality is the account of little Astolfo carried on the hippogriff to the Earthly Paradise, and thence, together with St. John, in the Chariot of Elijah to the Moon, whence he brings back, safely corked up in a vial, the lost sense of the *moon*struck paladin. This is not the ingenuous exaggeration of medieval popular romance, but the sophisticated absurdity *pour rire* of Baron Munchausen.

And yet, all the while, Ariosto is constructing his epic according to classical precedent. Indeed, Pio Rajna regards the *Orlando Furioso* as inaugurating the age of classicism. The title of the poem is from the *Hercules Furens* of Seneca. Epic unity is given by the war between Charlemagne and Agramante, corresponding to that between Agamemnon and Priam for Homer, and to that between Aeneas and Turnus for Virgil. Directly or indirectly, the episodes of the *Furioso* derive from the war. Also, as the Trojan war was effectively ended by Achilles slaying Hector, and the Latin war by Aeneas slaying Turnus, so the war of the Saracens against the Christians was ended by Orlando slaying Agramante.

To become thus the Christian champion and saviour, Orlando must be cured of his mad passion for Angelica, which had so long—even before his actual madness—made him recreant to his duty as a paladin of France. So Achilles had to be cured of his infatuation for Briseis; so Aeneas must desert Dido. Mercury descends from heaven to bring Aeneas to his senses; Astolfo ascends to heaven to bring his sense back to Orlando.

Slaying Turnus, Aeneas more than ended a war, he began a dynasty. He won the bride, Lavinia, from whose union with him was to come the imperial house of Caesar, the *gens Julia*. For Turnus had opposed that union. Now Ariosto reproduces this situation in the slaying of Rodomonte by Ruggiero. For Rodomonte had challenged Ruggiero, the convert to Christianity, to mortal combat as a renegade. And from the

[238]

union of Ruggiero and Bradamante was to come—according indeed to Boiardo's original plan—the ducal house of Ferrara, *la gente Estense.* So by imitation, Spenser was to derive the royal house of England, the Tudors. From the union of Arthegall and Britomart,—whose name, while reminiscent of Bradamante, would signify the British Mars, *Britannia.*

In style, as in analogies of plan, the *Orlando Furioso* is classic,—that is, Tuscan graduated from Latin School. Ariosto perfects the process Dante had begun. In the last canto of the finally completed poem indeed, he hails as his master in language Pietro Bembo, champion of *toscanità*, the sovereignty of Tuscan unalloyed:

> "là veggio Pietro
> Bembo, che'l puro e dolce idioma nostro
> Levato fuor del volgar uso tetro
> Qual esser dee ci ha col suo esempio mostro."

> (I see Pietro Bembo here,
> Him who our pure and dulcet speech set free
> From the base vulgar usage, and made clear
> By his example what it ought to be.)

It is interesting to remember that the same Bembo had urged the young Ariosto to follow up his early successes in Latin poetry, and that Ariosto had replied that he would rather be first in Italian than second in Latin. In him is declared the definitive triumph of the vernacular.

Following Bembo, Ariosto commends indeed not a mere local idiom, an unstudied mother-tongue, but a language of calculated art, following the very opposite, one might say, of Wordsworth's precept. For Ariosto's diction is a "poetic diction," emphatically not of everyday or of the plain people. And his vernacular so ennobled, *illustré*, realized to the highest degree the common ideal of the Renaissance. According to

Drummond, Ben Jonson said carpingly that "affecting the Ancients, Spenser writ no language." The charge is true enough, if by "language" is meant the idiom used by the poet himself and his contemporaries in everyday discourse. And of course, one might perhaps question on artistic grounds Spenser's precise eclectic blend of poetic speech, might perhaps find the ingredient of the archaic, for instance, to be in excess; but that is another story. Besides, *would* we wish the language of the *Faerie Queene* different? A poem is not a conversation-manual. Wordsworth's protest—as his own style at its best shows—was not really against "poetic diction" itself, but against the stilted and mouthing eighteenth century variety of it.

The Renaissance classicism of Ariosto's style, however, goes deeper than language, or diction, or any decorative accessories of rhetoric. He was himself saturated with the spirit of the ancient Roman *humanitas*,—of a humanity wise, humorous, tolerant, but by no means indifferent or *blasé*. He is sardonically contemptuous only of the unworthy or insincere. Doubtless, like his cured Orlando, he was man of good sense rather than of idealistic enthusiasms. Assuredly he loved beauty, but I am confident that he—like his contemporary Rabelais—had no patience with the sentimental cult of it by the "Platonics." Perhaps, in mood and temper he was nearest to Horace,—as also in his *curiosa felicitas* of phrase; but it must be said that Horace never produced any such long-sustained imaginative work as the *Orlando Furioso*,—to the making of which went —besides Boiardo and medieval romance—the influence of Homer and Virgil, the taste of the Ferrarese court, and the Italian comic spirit.

If the poet was ill-rewarded in life, the posthumous success of his poem was immediate and enormous. Within the sixteenth century it went through one hundred and eighty editions, many of them magnificently illustrated. It was translated into all languages, imitated in every literature. In Italy there was a veritable flood of encomium, comment, criticism, reaching its height in the famous controversy that raged after the publication of Tasso's *Gerusalemme Liberata* as to the poetic supremacy of the one or the other work. Italian imitations, sequels, developments of this or that episode, this or that character, were countless, but mostly valueless. The only significant serious narrative poem of chivalresque character in Italian after Ariosto's was indeed Tasso's.

Besides the exploitation of a literary success, besides the somewhat doubtfully persistent interest in tales of chivalry for their own sake, there was for the attention focussed upon the *Orlando Furioso* another, and very vital reason. I mean the existence of a real and increasing "eastern peril." Ariosto's make-believe war between Christian and Saracen was more and more being translated into real war, and for Christendom disastrous war. Already Ariosto felt the threat, and perhaps the most bitterly caustic passages in the poem are those in which he arraigns the European Powers, the Pope himself, for their cynically blind indifference to the danger and to their duty. Tasso's crusading epic is response to a concern far more pressing by his time, but his ornate words carry no such weight of stern warning.

The major characteristic of the *Orlando Furioso* is irony; and irony may be defined as a balance of seriousness and levity. No Italian narrative poet following Ariosto maintained, or perhaps attempted, this balance. There is a striving towards epic seriousness. There is frank travesty and burlesque. We may glance—and for a special reason—at an exponent of each kind.

XVI

FOLENGO—TRISSINO—CRITICAL THEORIES AND TENDENCIES

TEOFILO FOLENGO is the Italian Rabelais. Unfortunately, his masterpiece and literary lifework, *Baldus*, asks a very special—indeed, a highly specialized—audience. To say that it is written in "macaronic" verse,—though true enough, since the term derives from it,—is nevertheless misleading. The *Macaronicae*—"macaronic" books—of *Baldus* are written in correct classical Latin hexameters which every little while lapse into provincial Italian with Latin endings. It is as if a person who has been carefully, but newly, coached in social deportment, should now and then, all unaware of it, make a vulgar break. And the satire is manifestly directed against the pretentious purists of the day,—whether in Latin or in the vernacular,—who, without being to the manner born, affect an extreme fastidiousness in language and style. Folengo manages the huge academic jest with amazing verve and skill; but since full appreciation of it calls for familiarity both with Latin and with certain local Italian dialects, I suspect the masterpiece to have been more often taken on hearsay than read. At least it was read with profit by Rabelais.

Like Rabelais and Erasmus, Folengo was—for some years at least—a defrocked monk. His story is variously told. Some say he was a young rake who in a fit of remorse turned monk,

and then ran away from the cloister with a girl. Others say
he was disgusted by the ignorance, hypocrisy and immoral-
ity of the monks themselves. Colour for this view is certainly
to be found in his writings, which scourge the existing monastic life as mercilessly as Erasmus or Rabelais. But then, of
course, so did Dante—and how many others since. In any
case,—and whether or not driven to beg reinstatement by
poverty,—some ten years later, in 1534, he was again accepted into the Benedictine Order. He was then about thirty-
eight. He lived ten years longer, writing only pious works,—
yet could never renounce polishing and amplifying his *Baldus*. Thus the seventeen *Macaronicae* of the first edition of
1517 grew at last to twenty-five.

Shortly after leaving the cloister, Folengo composed two
works, *Orlandino* and *Chaos del Triperuno*. The former is a
Pulci-like burlesque, in rough Italian octaves, of chivalric
adventure, and with much anti-clerical satire. The *Chaos* is a
Dantesque allegorical voyage of the author from the port of
Innocence through the seven seas of Sin to the haven of Redemption. Divine Grace and Holy Scripture have been his
sole guides,—a suggestion of Protestant heresy.

In the *Chaos* Folengo is shaping his macaronic style. At
times in it he merely—like John Skelton, for instance, in
Speke Parrot—mixes in Latin words and phrases with the
vernacular. This is what is usually understood by macaronic
style, but is no invention of Folengo's. Also in the *Chaos*,
however, appears the subtler method of the *Baldus*,—not a
mere mingling of Latin and Italian, but a *mangling*, as it
were, of Latin by Italian. The effect is, as I have intimated,
of a would-be Latinist in straits, and reduced to making a
vulgar Italian word look or sound something like good
Latin.

If such a style be rather a jest for the learned, the story it tells is popular enough. Baldus is the son of a descendant of the renowned Rinaldo. But as his mother—a princess of France—dies in giving birth to him, and his grief-stricken father immediately retires to a hermitage in the desert, young Baldus is brought up by peasants in the hamlet of Cipada. But blood will tell; and the scion of the valiant paladin, though ignorant of his noble descent, so repeats the ancestral prowess that he reduces the whole countryside to desperation. He is, so to speak, a Don Quixote with power, but without scruple. At length, shut up by a trick inside the walls of Mantua, he becomes head bully of a band of ruffians, terrorizing the town; until, escaping with three strange mates, he and they go through fantastic adventures by land and sea, and finally land in hell,—where they belong, and where the poet leaves them.

In this burlesque of chivalric adventure the knight-errant has degenerated into a rascally nuisance,—which if translated literally from medieval romance into modern reality he might well be. By the same token, in Folengo's handling, the chivalric romance becomes in effect a *picaresque* novel full of sardonic and realistic satire on every phase of human society.

The common aim of the serious narrative poets of the Renaissance was to emulate the epics of Homer and Virgil. Dante starts the line, calling the poet of the *Aeneid* "my master and author." Petrarch attributed his laurel to his epic *Africa*, celebrating Scipio *Africanus* as the *Aeneid* celebrates Aeneas. During the two following centuries nearly every serious poet of every country aspired to be the Virgil of his age. Outside Italy, Ronsard, Spenser, Camoens are only the more outstanding names. And sometimes the ambitious aspirant looked behind Virgil to Virgil's own master, to Homer.

The methods of the imitators could be naïvely simple.

The not undistinguished poet Luigi Alamanni,—whose satires
on the Court were freely translated by Sir Thomas Wyatt,—
conceived the ingenious notion of making another *Iliad* by
rewriting the old one under new names. The siege of Troy
by King Agamemnon becomes the siege of Avarco by King
Arthur. The wrath of Achilles becomes the wrath of Lancelot—in love with Arthur's Queen. All the Homeric personages but one have their Arthurian counterparts. Only Helen
is passed over,—Helen, pivot of the whole Homeric plot!

Naïve in another way is the conscientious effort of Gian-
giorgio Trissino in his epic *Italia Liberata dai Goti*. Trissino
was a man-of-letters prominent in many fields. He was the
first editor of Dante's *De Vulgari Eloquentia*, took conspicu-
ous part in the later controversies on the issues raised by
Dante, and wrote the first tragedy according to the Rules.
But he himself regarded as his masterpiece the epic on which
he spent twenty laborious years. Yet—outside of Italy at any
rate—the *Italy Liberated from the Goths*, like Folengo's
Baldus, has been more often referred to than read. Because
its blank verse has been thought—probably without justification—to be Surrey's model in translating Virgil, the poem is
mentioned by most historians of English literature. And the
common impression they give is that Trissino's epic is, if
blank in interest as in verse, also coldly and classically correct,—a progenitor of Addison's *Cato*. The impression is untrue. The work is not "faultily faultless," nor is it "icily
fair." It is constantly at fault in taste—indeed to an amusing
degree. Its appeal is the opposite of austere. Indeed it fluc-
tuates between the melodramatic and the operatic. It is also
a most perfect illustration of the working, at its extreme, of a
theory of literary composition which was coming more and
more to dominate in Italy, and to spread from there into
other countries, especially France. I mean the theory of com-

position according to *rules* formulated—after Aristotle, Horace, Quintilian, Seneca and other classical authorities—from the supposed practice of the ancients. These rules assembled in the form of a legal digest constituted a so-called *classic canon* by which literature was to be regulated and judged. There resulted—or might result—not imitation of the classics themselves, but observance of certain abstract rules. This academic doctrine of the later Renaissance well deserves the name of *pseudo*-classicism.

Trissino, coming early, deduced his own rules. Homer's epic was his source. And the supreme rule to be deduced from Homer's practice is, as explained in the preface to the *Italia Liberata,—be specific*. It is in his specific touch, his particularity and abundance of detail, that Homer surpasses his Roman imitators, even Virgil, who, "to give elevation (*fare altezza*) to their verse, avoided telling diligently all the circumstances and particularities of their actions, as things which make vulgarity (*fanno bassezza*)." Be specific then; give plenty of true-to-life detail. No doubt, Trissino is right—in principle. Homer is graphically specific, whereas Virgil tends to the elegantly abstract and general. Now a good example of Homeric particularity, specific detail, is the arming of Agamemnon at the beginning of the eleventh book of the *Iliad*—in Andrew Lang's translation:

"Then the son of Atreus cried aloud, and bade the Argives arm them, and himself amid them did on the flashing bronze. First he fastened fair greaves about his legs, fitted with ankle-clasps of silver; next again he did his breastplate about his breast, the breastplate that in time past Kinyras gave him for a guest-gift . . . Now therein were ten courses of black cyanus, and twelve of gold, and twenty of tin, and dark bluesnakes writhed up towards the neck, three on either side, like rainbows that the son of Kronos hath set in the clouds, a marvel of the mortal tribes of men. And round his shoulders he cast his sword, wherein shone studs of gold, but the scabbard about it was silver, fitted with golden chains. And he took the richly dight shield of his valour that covereth all the body of a man, a fair shield, and round about it were ten circles of bronze, and thereon were twenty white bosses of tin, and one in the midst of black cyanus. And thereon was embossed the Gorgon fell of aspect glaring terribly, and about her were Dread and Terror. And on his head Agamemnon set a studded helm with a fourfold crest, and plume of horse-hair, and terribly the crest nodded from above. And he grasped two strong spears, shod with bronze and keen, and far forth from him into the heaven shone the bronze, and thereon Hera and Athene thundered, honouring the king of Mykene rich in gold."

Here is indeed true-to-life detail; but the life is heroic, and the detail is carefully chosen to bring out the dignity, power, beauty of the hero. Least of all are we made to think of a gentleman dressing with the aid of a solicitous valet.

Now armed with his rule *Be specific!* and unafraid of *bassezza*, Trissino admits us to the dressing of *his* great King, the Emperor Justinian. The occasion is solemn, rather—momentous. For an Angel has come in a dream to Justinian, bidding him deliver Italy from the Goths. And Justinian is anxious to get to work. So, although it is not yet daylight, he summons his chamberlain. But does he, like the mighty Agamemnon, arm himself for combat? He does not. We witness rather the valeting of an exquisite, a royal dandy. But judge for yourselves:

> "The mighty King awoke; and well he knew
> An Angel of the Lord had been with him.
> Hence unto true Pilades, who so long
> Had waited on his person, he called out:
> 'Pilades, sleep no more. Arise, and quick

[247]

Fetch me my garments, for I would get up:
Not long it can be from the break of day.'
Up rose the Chamberlain; and first he took
An undershirt of linen, fine and white,
And drew it o'er the honourable shoulders;
And over this again a jerkin drew,
Which was of cloth of gold; then stocking'd him
With pink and silken hose; then on his feet
Sandals of rosy-coloured velvet laced.
When he had done these things, he offered him
Water for washing in a basin rare
Of clearest crystal, and beneath that held
A larger basin of the purest gold.
And therewithin He washed his hands and face,
Drying them with a towel clean and white
And fringed around with fine embroidery,
Held out by Filocardio the Squire.
And this one combed for him his tresses blond
And soft and wavy, and fitted thereupon
The cap imperial, and the diadem
Variegate with jewels rich and gold.
Over the jerkin draped he then a gown
Of crimson silk, which round about the neck,
And eke the skirt, showed choice embroideries.
With honourable girdle this he girt;
Then over all he cast the sumptuous robe
Of cloth-of-gold, magnificent, superb,
Trailing along the floor for three palms' length.
This to the dexter shoulder he affixed
With a round pearl which was of greater size
Than any nut that is, and quite as smooth,
And all so white and lustrous in its tint
That a whole province would not pay its price,—
Truly, of Nature 'twas a flower unique."

Homer is indeed far far away!

Trissino is evidently interested in fine clothes,—or "honourable garments," as he would be likely to call them. Later he admits us to a *grande toilette intime* of the Empress Theodora on an occasion when she particularly wished to impress "the Emperor of the mundane peoples," as she appropriately calls him. Perhaps Trissino remembered that the real Theodora had been an actress. Anyhow, to win over her majestic consort to a match between her son Justin and the lovely Sophia, she has the happy thought—the mundane, or *demimondaine*, thought—of seducing him by her beauty fully adorned.

"Wherefore within her bower she withdrew,
And there her clothes of everyday took off.
Her limbs, lissome and delicate, she laved
With essence called 'of angels,' and with myrrh;
And after they were cleansed, anointed them
With oil of Zederben and other scents.
Then a chemise of white and woven silk
She donned, and a bright golden petticoat
Put over that; and stockings then of pink
Drew on, binding them just above the knee
With garters dainty . . .
Then combed she her blond tresses, fine and curled,
And over them a perfume sprinkled such
It seemed ambrosia out of paradise;
And then she plaited them in two fair braids,
And on them set a coif of woven gold,
Adorned with many a choice and lovely gem.
Then over that most dainty underskirt
She draped a robe of purest damask white,
Patterned in squares, and all the squares were joined
By pearls of price in pretty knots of gold,
And central in each square were diamonds set,

[249]

> So lucent that they seemed like little flames
> Enkindled deep within transparent glass."

There are further *boudoir* particularities, but these will do.

The "Homeric" poet now introduces another kind of true-to-life detail. The Emperor responds to the allurements of his lady—to an embarrassing degree. She demurs:

> "Suppose somebody were to come this way,
> And see us—really, I should be so shamed
> That never could I show my face again!"

However, she gains her point. But alas! young Justin, sailing home to wed his Sophia, is shipwrecked. When the "Angel" Neptune—for Trissino so admits the pagan deities into the Christian hierarchy, and his epic machinery,—the "Angel" Neptune sustains and guides the unconscious youth ashore to the very feet of his beloved as she gazes seaward. Seeing her dear one apparently drowned, Sophia snatches from her maid a bottle of cosmetic, and swallows its contents. But a "kind doctor," *medico gentil*, opportunely at hand, stands Justin on his head to let the water run out; and for Sophia he

> "Oil mixed with tepid water, and gave it her;
> And drank it she, and vomited the poison."

So all ends happily.

Now all this may sound like deliberate burlesque. But it is not so. Trissino is in deadly earnest. Nor was he a fool. On the contrary, in his other literary activities he passed for a man of talent. Besides, Alamanni's epic *Avarchide* was in its own way quite as inane a performance. So was the *Franciade* of Ronsard, supreme lyricist of the French Renaissance.

The common explanation for such dismal failures is blind

subservience to *rules*. We shall find the truth of this explanation demonstrated again—and tragically—in the case of
Tasso. And to repeat, the trouble was not *imitation*—even
slavish imitation—of the classics. It is impossible to conceive
Trissino—however lacking in humour—as imitating Homer's
arming of Agamemnon in his dressing of Justinian. He had
not Homer's picture in mind at all, I think. He had in mind
only the deduced rule *Be specific, do not spare true-to-life
detail for fear of vulgarity*. And Trissino stands by his rule
with the spirit of a martyr, willing to be damned for its
greater glory and rightness.

Trissino's case was an extreme one. Still, it was symptom-
atic. Subservience to rules was the characteristic of the decline of the Renaissance in Italy. The rules—and indeed the
principle of rules—had behind them the warrant of a great
authority, of "the master of them that know," of Aristotle.
Moreover, in addition to the compelling authority of the
great Stagyrite, there was for Italians after 1530 an increasing habit of subservience to authority,—a habit enforced by
an inquisitorial spiritual, and a tyrannical and alien temporal,
power, the Roman Church and the Spanish suzerainty.

To make the situation clearer, however, it may be well at
this point to trace in brief outline the course of Renaissance
literary theory and criticism.

The first stage was, as we have seen, that of humanism as
a literary revival—an attempted resuscitation or reliving,
Wiederbelebung—of Roman antiquity. Classical Latin was
declared to be—with partial and later exception of Greek—
the one enduring medium of culture and letters. When the
national vernaculars reasserted themselves,—as we can see
now they were bound to do,—the first activity of literary
critics and theorists was naturally defensive of the mother-

tongue. Even before the temporary triumph of humanism, Latinizing all culture, Dante and Boccaccio had written eloquent defences of Italian. Lorenzo de'Medici—or Poliziano at his bidding—started the Italian revival with a defence even more patriotic. So Joachim du Bellay defended the literary potentialities of the French language; Roger Ascham those of the English language.

From the start, however, a second line of defence was called for,—defence of poetry, of imaginative literature, itself. We have heard Petrarch encouraging the worried Boccaccio not to yield to any monkish ban upon secular letters. And Boccaccio, reassured, devoted two books—the fourteenth and fifteenth—of his *De Genealogia Deorum* to the defence of poetry,—though indeed he rested his case more on the truths allegorically presented in poetry than on what we should regard as its *poetic* value. Savonarola included in his "Bonfire of Vanities" literary works. The Catholic *Index* increasingly during the sixteenth century extended its ban upon all writings counter to papal opinion. Extremist reformers in Germany, France and England were as dictatorially hostile to profane letters as lay in their power to be. It was against the unmeasured attacks of the Puritan Stephen Gosson that Sir Philip Sidney wrote his *Defence of Poetry*.

But there was a more disturbing antagonism to poetry than from ecclesiastical obscurantism or moralistic bigotry. Humanists—in the broader sense of lovers of humane letters —found themselves confronted by an enemy within their own camp. It might not matter so much to anyone of culture and enlightenment that a strait-laced, narrow-minded "Precisian" like Gosson should libellously call poets "catterpillars of the commonwealth." It became serious, however, when he is heard citing the divine Plato as his witness and authority for the indictment. And Plato did exclude poets from his

ideal Commonwealth. Not Sidney, not any Renaissance apologist could deny it,—nor tried to. The Renaissance apology
for poetry as against the author of the *Republic* proceeded
by two steps. First, the Plato of the *Republic* was confronted
by the Plato of the *Ion* and the *Phaedrus*, for whom the
poet—the true poet—is an inspired prophet, a revealer by
"reminiscence" of Ideas but faintly reflected in things of sense.
The poet as conceived in the *Republic*, on the contrary, does
the opposite; his appeal is to the senses, deceiving and titillat-
ing them. Obviously, then, the second step of the apology is
to distinguish between the two kinds of poets. Let those be
condemned and banned whose art of words but conjure up
illusions to stir men's appetites. But let those be honoured who
—through images of sense indeed, for there is no other
human avenue of approach—inspiredly recall to the mind
ideas and truths beyond the reach of sense or experience.

Accordingly, in theory at least, the Renaissance rests its
apology for poets on faith in *inspiration,—furor divinus*,
Shakespeare's "divine frenzy." The favourite saying of the
period is the Latin poet's:

"Est deus in nobis, agitante calescimus illo."

Consequently, the true poet builds better than he knows; and
Dante, after all, might be justified in saying to Virgil's shade:

"Thou didst like one who, going by night, displays
A light behind him, and helps not himself,
But makes them wise that follow in his ways."

Furthermore, since in true poetry more is meant than meets
the eye, *allegory* continues to be given right and warrant.
By allegory the poet is *deliberately* transmitting ideas of the
mind through images of sense.

[253]

In Platonic theory, inspiration is tantamount to *reminiscence* of the intelligible or real world from which the soul has descended to dwell among shadows. Simply more than others, the true poet *remembers* the lost homeland of truth, and in his rapture would tell of it; but—and here is the all important point for Renaissance poetic doctrine—he must himself find modes of expression, words and forms, for his memories beyond words, his intimations of immortal things. He is in the position of Paul *after* coming down from the third heaven where "secret words," *verba arcana,* have been spoken to him: he must find, as best he can, for these "unspeakable words" human words. He must decode, as it were, the divine message into another language. And to do this aptly, he must labour and learn. *Poeta nascitur non fit;* he must *fit* himself. The whole doctrine is effectively summed in the "argument" to the "October" eclogue of Spenser's *Shepheardes Calendar.* Poetry is "rather no arte, but a divine gift and heavenly instinct, not to bee gotten by laboure and learning, but adorned with both, and poured into the witte by a certain ἐνφουσιασμὸς and celestiall inspiration."

To direct the "laboure and learning" by which this "celestiall inspiration" sponsored by Plato is to be given adorned expression the Renaissance with unanimity elected Aristotle, —the Aristotle of the *Poetics.* Someone has said of Machiavelli and his *Prince* that "rarely has a man walked down the aisles of time with so small a book under his arm." At least a good second would be Aristotle with his *Poetics.* Recovered only in 1498, and first formally expounded by Robortello in 1548, the small book became the literary Bible of the Renaissance—and after. And like the Bible, its meaning was confounded in a babel of interpreting tongues. But in 1561 Julius Caesar Scaliger published his *Poetices Libri Septem;*

which the Renaissance accepted—wisely or not—as its *Summa Poetica* according to Aristotle.

Professor Francis Bowen of Harvard University used to deride J. C. Scaliger as "a man who could talk like a fool in forty languages." I cannot undertake to confirm or to dispute this judgment, but it is safe to affirm that Scaliger talked foolishly of the *Poetics*—though no doubt he was not foolish alone. The foundation of his fond and foolish interpretation was the unwarranted assumption that Aristotle, instead of merely analyzing and noting the literary methods of certain representative ancient poets, was deducing rules of composition to be applied with rigour of law for ever and ever. There could be just so many poetic forms, and each form must satisfy just such and such requirements. "Celestiall inspiration" was to be put into a straitjacket.

Now it is of course possible to imitate, and even so to create, within rules. The French classicists of *le grand siècle*, themselves obedient to Julius Caesar Scaliger through their own Malesherbes and Boileau, proved this. Goethe reaffirmed it in his old age. But Corneille, Racine, Molière, Goethe himself, even while observing the rules, kept their eyes on their great models. They did not, like unfortunate Trissino, observe the rule, but forget the model.

While the *Cinquecento* recognized *in principle* this regulative sovereignty of Aristotle, it never wholeheartedly accepted its academic results. Trissino's epic fell flat. Tasso's readjustment of his *Gerusalemme Liberata* to rule in the *Gerusalemme Conquistata* was ignored. Spicy action ruled out of plays as against decorum was given back in interludes. Perhaps the most popular of all forms of literary expression was outside the rules, and in prose. I mean the *novella,*—at which we may now glance.

XVII

NOVELLA

THE *novella* remained singularly static in Italy after the *Decameron*. The most notable difference between that master-model and the horde of imitations is the inferiority of these. No one approached Boccaccio's deft and finished technique, or showed his tolerant humanity and humour. And this statement holds good also for imitations outside of Italy.

The only quality of the *Decameron* which does not fall off is its occasional lubricity. And to lubricity many of the later *novelle* add a veritable sadistic riot of cruelty and horror. It was indubitably *novelle* that sturdy Roger Ascham had in mind when he spoke of "these bookes, made in Italie, and translated in England," that "open, not fond and common wayes to vice, but such subtle, cunnyng, new, and diverse shiftes to carry yong willes to vanitie, and yong wittes to mischief . . . as the simple head of an Englishman is not hable to invent, nor was ever hard of in England before." The judgment may be a little insular,—like Matthew Arnold's three centuries later on the "lubricity" of the French novel,—but it is just. And the English translators decidedly tempered their tone, too.

At least highly exaggerated, on the other hand, is the inference drawn by John Addington Symonds and others that the society in which and for which the *novella* was written must be bankrupt in morals. Bandello, declares Symonds, "paints a society in dissolution." But the same society as painted not long before by Castiglione appears as cultivated and refined as our own. Why not look on this picture rather than on that?

In point of fact, fiction—even realistic fiction—rarely presents life in true perspective. Zola, most rigorous of realists, admits *"un but,"* an *"end."* He meant a moral end. And to that end, inevitably, all the lines of his picture of life converge. Inevitably, the moralist darkens the shadows, and dims the lights. If he is to warn us by a horrible example, should he not make it as horrible as possible? To show a sufficiently horrible example of New York social depravity Mr. Upton Sinclair attributes to a single family in the smart set the authentic misdeeds scattered through a number of years of a dozen families. The effect of such *focussing* of evils is not unlike that of focussing the sun's rays through a burning-glass: what was harmless—or may have been—is made to hurt, becomes a burning shame. Again, Mr. Hutcheson disapproves of a woman combining business with marriage; and proves his thesis by a novel in which all the children of such a woman go to the dogs. I should say this was playing with stacked cards.

I do not impugn the sincerity of these novelists, and am willing to believe that they drew life as they saw it. Let us say they looked through glasses coloured by moral or social prejudice. The same is true of many of the writers of fiction, the *novellieri,* of the Renaissance. And these wrote before the triumph of Science had exalted the importance of the exact fact. But many other—perhaps most—*novellieri* are not concerned with fact at all, but only with diverting or exciting *fiction.*

To a large extent, the materials of their fiction were not taken from contemporary life, but from previous literature.

Especially, in this time of belief in *fixed* forms, the *novella* was very much a thing of convention and tradition. Plots and personages had been handed on, and had become stereotyped. Tales were expected of dissolute monks and frail nuns, wives whose one purpose in life is to make cuckolds of silly and pompous husbands, or of incredibly innocent and super-resolutely chaste virgins, of amusing knaves and rustic morons, of panders and pedants, of courtiers and courtesans. Some of these characters have been passed on from the *Decameron,* though originating rather in the medieval sources of that work; some are taken over from the Roman comedy or from the Greek romances. They may or not belong in a true picture of sixteenth century Italian life. What does it matter? They are perennially amusing inventions—like the thrifty Scotchman in *Punch.* Indeed, a large part of the appeal of these fictitious types is due to their *being* traditional, and *being* exaggerated. We are expected to take them as caricatures of reality. And the plots in which these personages move and act are as largely conventional. The mood of any reading public is not so very different from that of the child who clamours: "Tell it again!" It is so today; but the foreigner shows himself merely ignorant who from the constant repetition of the triangle in French fiction deduces a triangle in the average French household.

Still, the vogue of the *novella* as it was does reveal something of the taste of its public,—just as the vogue of the detective story reveals something of the taste of its public today. Only, it should be borne in mind that the taste for sensational fiction, for "thrillers," was only one taste among many of a complex time, and that it was a taste for relaxation and escape. Writers on the Renaissance like Gobineau, Stendhal, Symonds, taking the supposed revelations of the *novella* at their full face value, melodramatize the period.

The first considerable collection of *novelle* after the *Decameron* was that of the Florentine Franco Sacchetti. Some two hundred and twenty are extant of the three hundred written by him between 1388 and 1395. They are rather anecdotes than full-length *novelle*,—gossipy items of Florentine life. Many of the persons introduced are well-known. The greater number of the tales are of practical jokes, *burle*, a species of humour of which Renaissance Italians, especially Florentines, appear to have been inordinately fond. A long section of Castiglione's *Courtier* is given over to a consideration of such jests and jokes,—of their kinds, their permissibility, their limits and control. The term *burla*, indeed, covers a wide variety of humour—from a witty retort to a spicy bit of scandal, from harmless practical joking to grinning sadistic cruelty. Under the title of *La Cena delle Beffe*—Englished as "The Jest"—the modern Florentine dramatist Sem Benelli has vividly illustrated the last named type. It motivates many *novelle* of the *Cinquecento*,—especially those of Grazzini, "Il Lasca." Sacchetti is not guilty of it. Early Renaissance Florence physically was a small town. Its life was small-town life. Everybody familiarly knew everybody. And the people lived as much as possible out-of-doors, in the public street. George Eliot gives a good picture of this communal life at the beginning of *Romola*.

One day, records Sacchetti, the illustrious poet Dante overhears a teamster humming some of his verses. Suddenly the fellow breaks into a verse with a loud *Arri*—"Ged-up"—to his horse; and the indignant poet, taking it for a corruption of his line, boxes the teamster's ears. Another day Giotto the painter is upset by a stray pig. He only laughs. After all, the pig was merely getting even. "I've made in my day," remarked the good Giotto, "thousands of *lire* with pigs' bristles, and never gave one of 'em as much as a spoonful of broth."

A merry wag makes Messer Dolcibene eat, without knowing it, roast cat. Very well, the victim says nothing, but presently feeds the joker with roast mice. *The Taming of the Shrew* is anticipated in miniature. Messer Porcella has a scold of a landlady. He prays to God: "Good Lord, if thou wilt do me the grace to let my wife die, and Ugolino [*her husband*] die, truly it will be my pleasure to take this woman to wife, and to punish her for her mad quirks." And so it happens. Apprentice Bonamico, to get even for being waked so early in the morning, sets loose in his master's bedchamber a lot of cockroaches with lighted tapers on their backs. The master takes them for devils, and repents him of his harsh treatment of Bonamico. The humble "Don Quixote", old Agnolo, pores over romances of chivalry, and dreams of tourneys and jousting. One day a wag sticks a thistle under the tail of Agnolo's nag. Run away with, shaken to bits, jeered at by the townsfolk, scolded by his goodwife, "Agnolo no longer wants to go a-jousting."

Sacchetti's *burle* are mostly like these,—generally good-natured, if not always in the most refined taste, good *bourgeois* fun. About a century later appeared another *burla*, told anonymously, also set in Florence, and also introducing well-known people. It is a tale much longer and more dramatically elaborated than any of Sacchetti's, yet working more or less the same vein of humour. Only the practical joke is carried to cruel extremes. But in execution, the *novella* of "The Fat Cabinet-maker," *Il Grasso Legnaiuolo*, as it is called, is a work of fine art. We are transported into the very quick of the life of Medicean Florence. The narrative is rapid, and yet realistically detailed. The Florentine idiom, at once racy and urbane, is admirably fitted to carry the solemn levity of the situation.

By a conspiracy of wits,—among whom we are surprised to

find the great architect Brunelleschi, the fastidious humanist and dramatist Rucellai, the sculptor Donatello,—a worthy if simpleminded craftsman known as *il Grasso*, "Fatty," is by a series of carefully worked-up deceptions driven to doubt his own identity. Grave and weighty citizens accost him as one Matteo, with whom they profess to have business. In vain he expostulates. They dismiss his denials with a smile and a wave of the hand,—as if to express appreciation of his joking. He begins to get bewildered. There are more serious misunderstandings. He is thrown into jail for Matteo's debts. More and more confused, he begins to believe he *must* be Matteo. All these great people cannot be mistaken. But though their victim is plainly going mad, the jokers do not let up. It was not considered at all unseemly to bait an insane person. And even when at last wearied of the long drawn out game, they tell the poor man the truth, they make such a town laughing-stock of him that finally in despair, abandoning everything, he runs away to Germany.

Now if this tale of a man persecuted *pour rire* be based on fact, if men like Brunelleschi, Rucellai, Donatello really lent themselves to the heartless jest, we might perhaps draw conclusions on the cynical cruelty of the time. So it may be. But there is risk that the joke may be on us, and that the whole thing is just a pleasant invention—*pour rire*. Remember the good people in Sir Thomas More's time who wanted to have missionaries sent to Utopia.

In one respect at least, there is no doubt about the *novelle* of Masuccio of Salerno. They are certainly not pleasant inventions, but highly "unpleasant" ones—in Bernard Shaw's sense of the word. Masuccio's collection, called *Il Novellino* and published at Naples in 1476, was dedicated to Ippolita Sforza, consort of Alfonso, Duke of Calabria. For her delectation and edification, ostensibly, these unsavoury tales are told and moralized. For Masuccio is as relentlessly repulsive and moral as Zola. He follows each tale with a little sermon against the vice just graphically exemplified. His fifty *novelle* so fall into moral categories. The first category, *hypocrisy*, applies almost entirely to monks, against whom Masuccio is more than usually scathing. The category of *incontinence* is naturally given over to women. Fifth and last category is of *generosity*, advisedly of princes,—an idea the author may well have desired to leave in the mind of his regal patroness.

Perhaps because of its author's unmeasured denunciation upon monks the Church put the Novellino upon the *Index*.

Careful differentiation of the *Cinquecento novellieri* would be a task hardly, I think, worth the pains. They are numerous; they all imitate—without in the least rivalling—Boccaccio. And, as I have already said at some length, their value as a mirror of the times has been much overrated. The greater importance of these Italian tales is as transmuted into other literary kinds,—especially drama. Supplementing the greater tales of the *Decameron*, they provided European playwrights for generations to come with a seemingly inexhaustible plot-book. Without them, we should not have *Romeo and Juliet* or *Othello*. That fact alone would justify their existence.

Giambattista Giraldi Cinzio has little besides moral seriousness to recommend him as a writer of fiction. Published in 1565, his *Ecatommithi*, "Hundred Tales,"—actually one hundred and twelve,—show the influence of the Catholic Reaction. In them Virtue always wins, and Vice is punished. Boccaccio's gay wantonness is not tolerated. The holy state of matrimony is no longer mocked. But the tales are dull things dully told. Giraldi was a learned professor, and proves it. He was prominent in the critical controversies of the period, and to illustrate his notion of a right tragedy, wrote half a dozen tragedies. The frame-story of his *Ecatommithi* is a rather ingenious variant upon that of the *Decameron*. Instead of fugitives from the Plague at Florence, Giraldi presents fugitives from the Sack of Rome, who by story-telling kill time on shipboard.

From early youth Matteo Bandello was a Dominican monk, but his life was anything but monastic or ascetic. As secretary to his uncle, General of the Order, he travelled throughout Italy, and became familiar with all classes of Italian society,—especially with the monastic orders whose abuses he was later to show up so mercilessly in his tales. Milan was his ostensible home; but for various reasons he was continually being obliged to leave it. From about 1506 he made trips beyond the Alps for his patrons of the Bentivoglio family. When in 1515 the French took Milan, he passed to Mantua, and there was in attendance upon Isabella Gonzaga, paying her platonic court. In 1521 the Sforza regaining power in Milan permitted his return there; but five years later, apparently for implication in a political conspiracy, he had to flee from Milan for good and all. Two years afterward he turns up in the train of the *condottiere* Cesare Fregoso. Then, after a decade of varied and adventurous experiences, he followed Costanza, Fregoso's widow, to France, where she was given hospitality by the French King, her late husband's employer. Bandello now divided his time between revising and publishing his *novelle*, and celebrating in Petrarchistic verses his third platonic mistress, Lucrezia Gonzaga. Apparently as a reward for this not very ecclesiastical labour, he was made in 1550 titular Bishop of Agen,—a sinecure he enjoyed four years, then making way for a son of Costanza's. He died in 1561.

It was a restless, much-experienced life,—one that might have sated Ulysses'

> "zeal to have experience of the world,
> And of the vices and the worth of men."

It was an ideal life, one would suppose, for a novelist. And Bandello did write down—as in a chronicle in fragments—the more striking incidents he had himself witnessed or heard tell of,—or indeed read of. He has the zeal and industry of an historiographer, but little dramatic imagination or psychological insight or artistic skill. He has drawn no memorable character. His French translators—Boistuau and Belleforest—stress the badness of his style. Perhaps the very colourlessness of his treatment made his tales the more available as *scenarii* for dramatists, whose own imaginations were left free to clothe the bare bones of plot.

I may overstate the case. Now and then Bandello may feel, and to some extent convey, the poetry of a romantic situation. John Addington Symonds, indeed, prefers his *dénouement* of the tragedy of Romeo and Juliet to Shakespeare's own. Bandello allows his heroine to revive in her tomb, and to rejoice at finding her lover there. She does not know that, supposing her dead, he has already swallowed poison. "What Shakespeare would have done with that situation!" comments the English critic. Still, what *would* Shakespeare have done with it? Lengthen out the agony? Make a death-scene *à la* Tristan and Isolde? No, that is a theme for music, but not for conversation,—at least not much of it. Shakespeare probably knew what he was about.

Nevertheless, Bandello appears at his best in this story,—as in his romantic stories generally; and his more lasting literary influence has come from these. A large proportion of his two hundred and fourteen tales, however, are satirical.

Like Masuccio, he directed his bitterest satire against the Church, vowed servant of it though he was. And Masuccio appears at least to be honestly indignant at clerical abuses; Bandello's tone is that of the cynical man-of-the-world, which indeed he was. For that very reason he gave, though no reformer himself, a strong handle of attack for the reformers of the north.

Some of his *novelle* cater also to that strong-nerved zest for horror that is so insatiable in the period, and that in England finds expression in the later chapters of Thomas Nash's *picaresque Jack Wilton* and in the so-called "tragedy of blood" of Webster and Tourneur. (It must be said, however, that the same *macabre* taste has never been more fully fed to than at the *Théâtre du Grand Guignol* in contemporary Paris.) A typical specimen of this sinister sensationalism in Bandello is the story of Violante cutting up into little pieces, bit by bit, her unfaithful husband,—and with *scizzors*. The domesticity of the weapon seems to add to the atrocity. (The ghastly description is deprecated, yet retailed at length in the *Edinburgh Review*, No. 380.)

One of the tales in *Le Cene* of Antonfrancesco Grazzini fairly matches Violante's revenge. In this pleasant tale a husband surprises his wife and son in incestuous union. He cuts off their hands and feet, and cuts out their eyes and tongues, and so leaves them. The story is told with an air of quiet refinement, even of piety. The husband and father is only acting as a gentleman of honour.

Grazzini was a Florentine druggist and a noted wit. He is better known as *il Lasca*, the "Roach," his *sobriquet* in the *Accademia degli Umidi*, of which he was one of the twelve founders. The mood of this Academy was—to start with— anti-academic, against purism and classicism. Certainly, it was outside of academic precincts that *il Lasca* won his own literary fame. He was the leading exponent—after Berni himself—of the so-called *poesia bernesca,*—satirical, burlesque and facetious verse. He was also a successful comic playwright. His *Cene,* or "Repasts,"—so called because the included tales are told before and after dinner in carnival time by a set of gay young men and women,—were not printed until the eighteenth century. The pornographic reputation of the work is indicated in the dating as from "Stambul, dell' egira 122" of the London edition of 1756.

Only two or three of the twenty-two extant tales are of the grisly kind. Most illustrate again the Florentine love of the *burla,* the practical joke. One such is attributed to Lorenzo the Magnificent himself. At his order, a certain Messer Manente—an unoffending person—is made drunk, carried into the Medici palace, and locked up there. Meanwhile, it is given out that Manente has died of the plague; and a real corpse is buried in his name. In due time the true Manente is let out. All unsuspecting, he goes home,—to be driven off by his terrified wife, who takes him for a ghost. After a variety of misadventures, Manente is given a hint to lay his hard case before the great Lorenzo, who gravely decides that black magic has been at work. It is the cow-boy idea of fun, —the kind that used to make a tenderfoot dance to bullets.

Also in carnival time, but on the island of Murano in the Venetian lagoons, is the setting of Giovanfrancesco Straparola's *Tredici Notte Piacevoli* of 1550. The main interest of Straparola's *novelle* is the appearance among them of folktales destined to become international—such as Puss-in-Boots. But also differentiating them is a note of the eerie and bizarre not heard elsewhere in the Italian *novella.* One of the seventy-three belongs to a satirical group in which figure Machiavelli's *Belphegor* and the English trio—John Wilson's *Belphegor,* Dekker's *If it be not good, the Devil is in it,* Ben

Jonson's *The Devil is an Ass*. All play with the supernatural, and the common target is Woman: the Devil can stand hell, but not a wife.

Although I doubt if the *novella* in its brutality and lewdness is a true mirror of Italian society, there nevertheless were developed in that society of the period individuals who were living *novelle*, the truth of whose careers is almost as startling as sensational fiction itself. There were many such, but two stand in direct connection with literature; and the masterpiece of one—Benvenuto Cellini's autobiography—might almost be classed as an extended *novella*. At least there may be as much fiction as fact in it. The other individual is Pietro Aretino.

XVIII

BENVENUTO CELLINI—
PIETRO ARETINO

BENVENUTO—*"Welcome"*—Cellini was born in Florence in 1500. He died there in 1571. But during considerable periods of this long life he was rarely *welcome* long in any one place. The story is largely one of escapes and flights. Thanks to the protection of two Popes, he could stay longest in Rome; Francis I gave him asylum for five years in Paris; and Duke Cosimo made his later years secure in Florence. But he was ever and everywhere in hot water.

An American poet has said of himself:

"Within this earthly temple there's a crowd."

Within Cellini's "earthly temple" there was everything from an *apache* to an Apollo. He can stab an enemy in the dark, and is an artist so exquisite that Kings and Popes contend for him; he can brutally beat up his mistress, and can believe that the Holy Virgin visited him in a vision to give him comfort; with his arquebus he kills the Constable of Bourbon, who is besieging Rome; he practises black wizardry in the Coliseum at midnight; thanks to the malevolence of the Pope's nephew, he is jailed for a year for stealing the Pope's jewels; he escapes from the Castel Sant'Angelo with the address and daring of a Monte Cristo; an enemy gives him powdered glass to swallow, and he recovers; in his sixties, while working at

[268]

his art, he dictates—at least mostly—these experiences and more to a fourteen-year-old apprentice, and makes the dictation itself a work of imperishable art.

In a book on *The Victorian Masters*, W. C. Brownell controverts Ruskin's dictum that a great artist must be a good man. Brownell reminds us that Benvenuto Cellini was a great artist—and a great rascal. I wonder, however, if a distinction may not, in some measure, justify both Brownell and Ruskin,—and Shelley also, calling poetry product of "the best moments of the best and happiest minds." I mean, putting it simply, a *time* distinction. I doubt if Cellini was a great artist and a great rascal in one and the same moment.

> "Within this earthly temple there's a crowd:
> There's one us that's humble, one that's proud . . ."

Whatever he may have been in other ways, Benvenuto Cellini was "humble" before Art. In its moments of artistic creation his was among "the best and happiest minds."

Read the graphic account of the moulding of the Perseus. The mood of the artist is that of a martyr ready to sacrifice anything. The child of his imagination *must* be born, not for the profit it may bring, or the fame, but for its own right to be. Infernal powers seem to be allied against him. He is shaken with a sudden fever,—and ignores it. His furnace cools for want of fuel,—and he feeds to it all his household furniture. Fantastic accidents happen,—his workhouse catches fire, it is unroofed by a sudden tempest, his furnace itself explodes. Only God can save! And finally, when the end is in sight, Benvenuto cries aloud: "O God! Thou that by thine immeasurable power didst rise from the dead, and in thy glory didst ascend into heaven!" "Even thus," he concludes, "in a moment my mould was filled; and seeing my work finished, I fell upon my knees, and with all my heart gave thanks to God."

Is this just histrionic? I do not see that anyone has the right to say so. Why believe Benvenuto only when he paints himself as a rascal?

Besides, the Perseus does not look like the conception of a rascally mind. The young hero is curiously innocent and boyish in his triumph, meditative rather than glorying or gloating. It is a charming conception, even if as sculpture not quite as perfect as it once was thought to be.

By rare good fortune, the autobiography—although rashly submitted to a literary friend for correction, and also not printed until 1728—has come down virtually as its author partly wrote, partly dictated, it. The literary friend, Benedetto Varchi, was a man of sense and taste, and returned the manuscript untampered with; and the eighteenth century editor was at once discreet and bold,—for it took some courage to print some passages of the book. But as it is, the spontaneity of the style exactly matches and expresses the amazing spontaneity for good and bad of the man. *Le style c'est l'homme*—as almost nowhere else in literature.

And the autobiography is to the Renaissance what the *Confessions* of St. Augustine are to the earlier Middle Ages, and what the *Confessions* of Rousseau are to later modern times. Each reveals not merely an individual experience, a temperament, a soul,—but the spirit of its age, focussed and concentrated. In and through Cellini's frank self-portrait we may see the composite photograph, as it were, of Renaissance Italy,—its serene self-confidence now and then extending and descending to *bravado* and *braggadochio*, its unaffected passion for the beautifully right a little regardless of the morally right, its elegance and chivalry, its callous cruelty.

Cellini appears, I say, altogether spontaneous. He appears

to live in the moment for the moment. At any rate, only in his art does he show consistency and plan. Quite an opposite type was his senior by eight years, Pietro Aretino. Aretino— so-called from his birthplace Arezzo—early resolved to "live resolutely," *vivere risolutamente*. And he meant by this not to let *virtue* stand in the way of *virtù*, "efficiency." He would have subscribed heartily to Andrew Marvell's saying:

"Virtue's a faint green sickness of brave souls."

His attitude is an extreme intensification of the individualism of the age, which found its first frank expression in the egoistic hedonism of Lorenzo Valla. Ben Jonson sums and condemns it in a pithy couplet in *Cynthia's Revels:*

"Humour is now the test we try things in: All power is just; nought that delights is sin."

On its better side, this conception of *resolute* living underlies Luther's injunction: *"Pecca forte!* that is, of course, if you must sin at all. The most shameful vice is moral tepidness, as Dante had said, or of the "ungirt loin," as Robert Browning was to say.

Pietro Aretino also formulated a plan of resolute living. He resolved to live, as he characteristically put it, "by the sweat of my ink." Writers in the sixteenth century—indeed, until the eighteenth century [1]—were dependent upon patrons. They had to please them to live. So we have heard Ariosto protesting bitterly in his satires. Michelangelo alternately defied and flattered Julius II; they were equally irascible, but Julius held the purse. Cellini shows the constant strain between his violent self-will and bread-and-butter compromise. The time was not yet when a paying Public could permit an Alexander Pope to declare with pride:

[1] Cf. Alexandre Beljame, *Le public et les hommes de lettres en Angleterre.*

[271]

"(thanks to Homer) . . . I live and thrive,
Indebted to no Prince or Peer alive."

Nor would it do to snub an offensively condescending patron,
—as did Dr. Johnson Lord Chesterfield. No, Aretino had to
stick to the Patron; but—*pocketed* him. On the title-pages of
his books he calls himself *"Per la grazia di Dio uomo libero."*
"A free man" he perhaps was,—in a somewhat dubious sense,
—but "the grace of God" had very little to do with his
being so. To speak quite plainly, he was a blackmailer. He
first effectively employed the methods of *Town Topics* and
similar yellow journalism. It was—and is—the choice: Your
money or your secrets told. If the money was forthcoming,
the victim was lauded in fulsome letters or verses. If not, he
would find libellous epigrams circulated about him, or "open
letters" unpleasantly allusive to scandals personal or family.
Another favourite terroristic device was an almanac-like bro-
chure—a prognostic or *giudizio*—which, under colour of pre-
dictions for the year, made discreditable revelations. Still
further, Aretino probably invented, and certainly made ample use of the *pasquinade*—an anonymous epigram attached on
St. Mark's day to an antique and dilapidated marble torso
set up in one of the streets of Rome. These *pasquinades* came
to attack indiscriminately all people of prominence in church
or state,—and Aretino's were the bitterest of all.

However successful financially, and for the gaining of
power, such literary methods might be, they obviously in-
volved personal risk for their exponent. Twice Aretino was
stabbed by hired *bravi*. The second time was in 1525. Thoroughly frightened, he took refuge first at Mantua with the
brilliant *condottiere*, Giovanni delle Bande Nere, who a
year later died in his arms. Then, in 1527, he found permanent asylum in Venice, ever hospitable to all refugees in

memory of her own beginnings. Aretino was safe there, and he wisely refused the most flattering invitations to go elsewhere even for a night.

Pietro Aretino's name has been until this century superfluously blackened. In 1901 it was brought out [1] that modern accounts of him had all been based on a scurrilously false life written by one of his numerous enemies. Truly, the buccaneer of letters had been hoist by his own petard! Still, all libels expunged, Aretino's career was scurvy enough. Yet more deplorable than his own means of success is the astonishing success itself. It is a sad commentary on human cowardice. Of nameless origin, poor, boastfully ignorant, this provincial from Arezzo made himself one of the most noted and feared men in Europe. His weapon was the at that time unfamiliar weapon of journalistic *publicity*. At one time, the two greatest princes of Christendom, Francis I and Charles V disputed for his favour; and after Francis's defeat at Peschiera in 1543, Charles received him royally as an ally. Ariosto, doubtless with a side-thought of another "Hun," called Aretino "the scourge of princes," *il flagello dei principi*. And Aretino printed the appellation, as if it were an honourary degree, on the title-pages of his books. English Gabriel Harvey repeats the compliment in another form. In a letter to Edmund Spenser, he asks: "Who but knowes Aretyne, was he not halfe-prince to the Princes?" Aretino admits his pre-eminence. He writes: "Without place-hunting, court-serving, indeed without stirring a foot, have I made all dukes, princes and kings tributary to virtue; I am the dispenser of Fame for the whole world; in Persia and the Indies is my portrait recognized and my name honoured." One might incline to substitute *virtù* for "virtue"; but not so his contemporaries, —at least not publicly. It was due to his stern sense of pro-

[1] Carlo Bertani, *Pietro Aretino e le sue opere*, Sondrio.

priety(!) that loin-cloths were painted upon the naked dead in Michelangelo's *Last Judgment*. In 1550, the Holy Father named him Knight of St. Peter; in 1553, embraced and kissed him. In 1556, he died in the odour of sanctity. (In 1559, his works were put on the *Index*, and mention of his name forbidden.)

Here is a specimen of the praise of the laity. A Venetian admirer (*or victim?*) writes to him: "I say that thou art the Son of God, indeed,—lest the droning monks get after me, —with this qualification only, that God is the highest Truth in heaven, and thou art such on earth. No other city than Venice is worthy to offer you hospitality, for thou art the jewel of the earth, the treasure of the sea, and the glory of the heavens. Thou art the golden jewel-encrusted vessel which should be laid upon the high altar of St. Mark's on Ascension Day." I might match this with a monkish tribute, but more would be too much. Meanwhile, it is said that this curious Saint dare not cross his threshold for fear of the cudgels and daggers of past victims, and was scarred from head to foot with retaliatory mementos.

Outside Italy, there was similarly extravagant praise and censure. An industrious German has counted five hundred references to him in Elizabethan writings. Thomas Nash said of him in *Jack Wilton:* "Aretine as long as the world lives shalt thou live. Tully, Virgil, Ovid, Seneca were never such ornaments to Italy as thou hast been." Later, in the early seventeenth century, his name was telescoped with Machiavelli's into "Mach-Aretine" to signify the vicious man complete.

Still, Nash's panegyric was not forced by fear. Aretino was long dead. Neither as man-of-letters nor as man was Pietro Aretino all bad. It seems he could not have been, and been the intimate friend he was with Titian, whose magnificent portrait of him hangs in the Palazzo Chigi at Rome. He made his money often vilely, but spent it generously and charitably. He was always ready to help the needy, especially struggling artists. His private life was dissolute; but it is said that, before discarding his mistresses, he married them off well, and saw to it that their husbands were faithful. He was a tender father to at least two of his illegitimate children,—daughters whom he named, as became his international importance, Adria and Austria. Once he really loved,— a young girl who deserted him for a younger lover, was herself deserted, and returned to die in Aretino's arms.

Similar contradictions appear in his writings. Himself unlearned, and proud of it, he ridiculed the purism and academicism of the day. He hated Luther as a good Catholic, but even more for his pedantries,—*"Lutero pedantissimo!"* he exclaimed. He would have no books in his study, only pen, paper and ink. Yet by common consent of critics, he wrote in his *Orazio* the best regular tragedy of the age, the only one with life in it. His comedies, too,—of which Gabriel Harvey spoke so highly to Edmund Spenser,—followed, though with certain licences, the prescribed formula of the Roman comedy—as indeed Harvey remarked.

The last irony of Aretino's singular career and reputation is the fact that, although he wrote much and in many kinds and sometimes well, the one of his works to survive today— outside of classrooms and literary histories—is the most infamous one, the so-called *Ragionamenti*. It is, conservatively speaking, the nastiest book ever written, and still fetches, for that reason, a high price among pornographic collectors.

XIX

DRAMA

MORE than any other literary kind the Italian Renaissance drama was dominated by rules supposedly laid down by the ancients. And nowhere else was there an enforcement of them so pedantically after the letter. Cramped by the so-called Aristotelian *unities* and gagged by Horatian *decorum*, Italian plays of the sixteenth century had small chance of life. And few indeed have lived; few did live even for their contemporaries.

The situation was similar in sixteenth century France. How amazingly rich and vital, on the other hand, were the dramas of England and Spain, where—as Lope de Vega was to say—the only constraint acknowledged by the playwright was to please his immediate audience!

The natural inference would seem to be that what ailed the *Cinquecento* drama was the constraint of rule. But then the fact calls for explanation that Corneille and Racine, and even Molière, wrote under fullest rigour of the rules. Genius can, as Goethe said. And the trouble may be that no real dramatic genius appeared in sixteenth century Italy,—none comparable to Ariosto or Tasso in the epic.

If sterile of masterpieces, the Italian Renaissance theatre was, on the other hand, an invaluable *laboratory*-theatre,— especially if we do not limit it to the so-called regular or "learned drama," *dramma erudito*. And even though the dramaturgical discussions of the age may have proceeded

[276]

from false premises to pedantic conclusions, they led toward the canon of a classic drama which was to hold the European stage,—or at least to dispute it with romantic rivals,—for many generations.

Ordinarily, I believe, the regular drama is understood to comprise only tragedy and comedy; but the French historian of literature, Gustave Lanson, seems to have found classical sanction, from the Renaissance point of view, for admitting as a third regular dramatic genre the pastoral play. Thus the classic or learned drama would consist, he says, of "Tragédie, Comédie, et, à distance égal des deux, la Pastorale, qui, entre les horreurs pitoyables des grands sujets heroiques et la gaiété facétieuse des sujets bas et familiers, introduit sa douceur sentimentale et un amour dont les torments n'ont rien d'atroce, ni les joies rien de lascif." (*Note sur un passage de Vitruve et sur l'origine de la distinction des genres dans le théâtre de la renaissance, Revue de la Renaissance* V, 72-84 (1904).)

Lanson notes that Vitruvius in his *De Architectura* describes stage-sets as of three kinds,—tragic, comic and satyric. The tragic set (*scena*) is a colonnaded royal court; the comic a city street; the satyric is among "trees, caves, hills and other rural features." By satyric play Vitruvius—like Horace in his *Art of Poetry*—means the type uniquely preserved in the *Cyclops* of Euripides. Shelley translated it; and Dryden long ago defined it as a mixture of "farce and tragedy," and said of it in his *Discourse on Satire:* "The adventures of Ulysses was to entertain the judging part of the audience, and the uncouth persons of Silenus and the Satyrs to divert the common people with their gross railleries."

This is not pastoral,—not arcadian pastoral of the Renaissance,—but when in 1485 Leo Battista Alberti wrote his *De re aedificatoria,* closely following Vitruvius, he was led, apparently by the similarity of setting, to identify the "satyric" with the arcadian pastoral type. "Since three kinds of poets," he says, "affect the theatre, the tragic who recite the miseries of tyrants, the comic who set forth the cares and troubles of family-men (*patresfamilias*), the satyric who sing the amenities of the countryside and the cares of shepherds (*ruris amoenitates pastorumque curas*)," their appropriate settings are "court or house or woodland (*seu attrium seu casa, seu etiam sylva*)."

So, amusingly, by a kind of false passport, the "low-flying pastoral" won entry into the company of learned and classic dramatic kinds. One can only hope that Renaissance critics, as well as M. Lanson, noticed its credentials.

In the later years of the fifteenth century Seneca's tragedies were frequently acted, both in Latin and in Italian, and especially at Rome and Ferrara. Poliziano's secularized "mystery," *Orfeo*, was reshaped, at the turning of the century, into a regular Senecan tragedy, but, in this like the "satyric play," incorporating pastoral elements. Before 1494 Boiardo produced an extraordinary hybrid of "morality" and Senecan tragedy. It is the tragedy of Timon of Athens, and taken from Lucian, who therefore speaks the prologue. It is in five acts, and in *terza rima*. "Decorum" is carried to extremes. During most of the first three acts Timon soliloquizes, or converses only with mythological and allegorical personages —Jupiter, Mercury, Wealth, Poverty. The final catastrophe is related by one called "the Auxiliary," *lo Ausilio*. Certainly, the very bare and abstract bones of a tragedy! Compare Shakespeare's handling,—even though *Timon of Athens* is one of his poorer plays.

After these, and other, experiments, the first regular

tragedy, in the Renaissance sense, is generally allowed to be the *Sofonisba* by Trissino—the same whose epic *Italia Liberata dai Goti* we have already considered. *Sofonisba* was finished in 1515, though publicly presented for the first time at Vicenza, the poet's birthplace, in 1562, twelve years after his death. There is record of a tragedy of *Sofonisba* by one Galeotto del Carretto as acted in 1502.

If frequent treatment proves dramatic availability, Trissino chose excellent material in this tale from Livy of the unfortunate Carthaginian princess, daughter of Hasdrubal, whom her lover and husband Masinissa saves from Roman slavery by sending her a cup of poison, which she obediently drinks, and dies. It was by coincidence theme of also the first regular tragedy in France—by Mairet in 1634. It was dramatized six times more in France,—by Corneille and Voltaire among the rest. In England Marston, Lee, James Thomson used it. It was Thomson's piece that contained the famous infamous line—

"O Sophonisba! Sophonisba O!"

Mellin de St. Gelais translated Trissino's version into French in 1553. The last time, I imagine, Sophonisba has appeared on the stage was in 1914 in the "movie" *Cabiria* by Gabriele d'Annunzio.

Trissino's version is "splendidly regular, icily *dull*." Unities of time and action are scrupulously observed, but the scene shifts from Cirta to Scipio's camp. Within twelve hours Sophonisba learns of the defeat and death of her first husband, Syphax; goes into mourning; meets, and is wooed by and wed by Prince Masinissa; is sent, a captive of war, to Scipio's camp; receives by messenger the poisoned bowl; drinks, and so dies. A full day!

The author fulfils the promise he was to make in his

Poetica of 1549: "I shall not depart from the rules and precepts of the Ancients, and especially Aristotle." The action of *Sofonisba* is broken only by choruses in the Greek manner; and they frequently intervene in the action itself. Blank verse is used to reproduce Greek tragic metre. Only the tragic spirit is wanting. Sophonisba is a puppet. Even in the dumb show of a silent "movie," D'Annunzio presents a proud and stormy Queen, a fascinating and moving woman. Masinissa's main preoccupation on hearing of his beloved's stoic death is, according to Trissino, that she may have a fine funeral. Strange that Tennyson should end his *Enoch Arden* with the same bathos!

Trissino's imitation of Greek tragedy had some immediate following, but an apparently more responsive chord was struck by Giraldi Cinzio, also critic and novelist, in preferring before the Greek, the Roman tragedy of Seneca. He justified his views by a series of nine Senecan tragedies, beginning with the *Orbecche* presented at Ferrara in 1541. And for the rest of the epoch the Senecan model triumphed.

It would be hard to make a less fortunate choice. Seneca is a moralist—Dante's "Seneca *morale*"—and a rhetorician, not in any vital sense a dramatist. His tragedies are rather exercises in declamatory and sententious style, and—to modify Harvey's description of Petrarch's sonnets, "nothing but neat wit and refined *eloquence*." Whatever little their arid formula might have left of really tragic action was dried up by the so-called rule of *decorum* of Horace.

The logic of the regular tragedy, *tragedia erudita*, then, is summarily thus. Tragedy is a reversal of fortune. To be significant the fall must be from a height,—preferably the fall of a prince. Now violence of any kind would be against the dignity of a prince. *Decorum* demands, therefore, that the "fall"—the catastrophe—be not actually witnessed, be not *"coram populo,"* but merely heard tell of. Moreover, the spectator is not to be admitted to the intimacies of the great, —that is, the principal characters. He sees and hears these conversing only with anonymous and insignificant counsellors, nurses, messengers, or perhaps personages allegorical or mythological.

In consequence, the most lurid plots—and most *Cinquecento* tragedies have lurid plots—are made *decorously* dull and tame. Only, the final messenger makes up in some part by particularizing in his report every atrocity and horror excluded from the scene itself. And sometimes the gruesome details were enacted in dumb show between the acts.

The full rigour of the Seneca-Horatian prescription was not indeed always observed; and it may be said that in proportion to the non-observance the play improved. The most freely handled tragedy still classifying as "regular" is Pietro Aretino's *Orazio,* and it is admittedly the best. The story—from Livy—is itself a good one. Celia, beloved of one of the slain Curatii, is also sister of the sole survivor of the three Horatii. Mortified by her grief at the loss of her lover, Horatius, even while Rome is fêting his victory, kills her. He is sentenced to be scourged and hanged as a murderer; but the people, appealed to by him, absolve him for his high motive and heroic services. Dramatizing the story through to this half-happy ending, Aretino in so far violates the formula of tragedy, but makes a play not without power and poignancy. Some infusion of comic relief into the action brings *Orazio* still closer to the free tragedy of Shakespeare and the Elizabethans. A greater than Aretino might have come nearer still.

In the *Marianna* (1565) of the Venetian Lodovico Dolce, an industrious if uninspired man-of-all-letters, there shows also a certain independence. Principals are brought face to face, and *decorum* is violated to the point of producing rather melodrama than high tragedy. Still, the tragic story of Mariamne and Herod, as told by Josephus, cannot altogether be spoiled, and Dolce's play is, in spite of its crudities, at least one of the most readable of the period.

For various good reasons the story has attracted playwrights of every stripe and of every country from Hans Sachs in 1550 to Stephen Phillips in our own time. Marvellously varied are the dramatic readings of the story. Dolce sees it only as a drama of domestic jealousy—a pale foreshadowing of *Othello*; Calderon makes it a strange piece of the "cloak-and-sword" type, in which Herod and Augustus Caesar appear as rival lovers, and a fated dagger plays a prominent part; Friedrich Hebbel turns it into a subtle psychological study; Phillips, into a brooding play of dark symbols and of cosmic destiny. There are more than a score of other treatments.

Dolce sets the story in the Senecan frame. There are two prologues and five acts. One prologue is spoken by Tragedy in person, who defines and deprecates herself; the second is a dialogue between Pluto, God of Hell, and his messenger against Herod—Jealousy. Fearful at being summoned to Rome, Herod has left the order with Sohemus, Mariamne's uncle and his trusted officer, to slay her if he, Herod, should not return. Sohemus is persuaded to reveal the provisional death-warrant to Mariamne, already suspicious of her husband because of his murder of her brother, the young high priest Aristobulus. Outraged by this new cruelty, she, when Herod does return, is cold to him. This gives Herod's sister, Salome, who is jealous of Mariamne, her chance. She accuses Mariamne of infidelity, and with Sohemus. Herod, who has already been informed of Sohemus's betrayal of the secret death-warrant, kills him; and then personally presents Mariamne with a bowl containing her supposed paramour's head, heart and hands. (And this, assuredly, was a breach of *decorum* on the playwright's part,—and on Herod's too.) Herod then has his wife strangled. But this, the technical catastrophe, is only told by a Messenger.

It is needless to analyze further *Cinquecento* tragedies. They offer the curious spectacle of a strong-nerved, sensation-loving people (consider the *novella*) defrauding itself on theory of what it really liked on the stage. If it could but have had its Lope de Vega to pay lip-service to the Rules, and then to forget them, the story of the serious Italian drama might have been different.

The story of *Cinquecento* comedy *is* different. If the comedies of the time show little of that profound and humane humour which marks the "comic spirit" as Meredith defines it, at least many of them are vivacious and entertaining, at least one—Machiavelli's *Mandragola*—brilliantly witty in its satire.

Virtually the one model was the Roman comedy of Plautus and Terence. During the later fifteenth century their plays were given in Latin at courts and universities and private palaces,—especially in Rome at the Vatican, in the mausoleum of Hadrian, even in public squares, and in Ferrara at the court of Ercole I (1471–1505). Vernacular imitations followed.

The real beginning of Italian Renaissance comedy was made by Ariosto with a piece called *Cassaria* acted with sumptuous accessories at Ferrara during the carnival time of 1508. Its success led to the production of *I Suppositi* in the following year. But Ariosto's third and fourth comedies—*Il Negromante* and *La Lena* did not come until 1520 and 1529 respectively; and his fifth—*Gli Studenti*—was never finished by him. If the poet's interest in the drama remained secondary, at least it manifested itself intermittently throughout his life. It is said indeed that he composed a *Thisbe* at twelve, and acted in it with his four brothers.

The first two of the five comedies are but close adaptations of Roman comedy. Their main importance lay in setting the type for Italy, and in some degree for England. At least, *I Suppositi* was translated by George Gascoigne under the title of *The Supposes*, and acted at Grays Inn in 1566— with the boast of being the first *regular* comedy in English. (The curious rendering of *Suppositi*, "Substitutes," as "Supposes" would suggest a French intermediary.)

Ariosto's last three comedies, written in his full maturity, show a great advance. The Plautian-Terentian mould is kept, but there is shaped in it a matter, relatively speaking, hot from contemporary Ferrarese life. There is keen wit and audacious satire. The ingenious *imbroglio* of trickery and disguise and "recognition" was still novel. There is indeed insistent play around loose and lewd situations,—for which the Roman comedy gave model and sanction,—but with Ariosto the indecency is never gross or brutal, and is antiseptized by wit.

Apology must be strained in this respect for *La Calandria* of Bernardo Dovizi, presented at Urbino in 1513. Adapted from the *Menaechmi* of Plautus, it challenges comparison with Shakespeare's *Comedy of Errors*. Only instead of twin brothers, Dovizi makes his twins brother and sister. From their mutual resemblance and the stupidity of the titular character, Boccaccio's Calandro, derives a series of "errors" sometimes amusing, but always indecent. There is no pretence of any motive but entertainment. Yet a few years later the author became *Cardinal* Bibbiena. His unsavoury piece was repeated before His Holiness, the Pope; and later, in 1548, before Henri II and Catherine de'Medici at Lyons.

No doubt no small part of the appeal of these and other Renaissance comedies was due to the magnificence of their presentation. When Ariosto's *Suppositi* was repeated at the Vatican in 1519, Raphael Sanzio did the scene-painting. The setting of the *Calandria* at Urbino in 1513 was designed— and in an extant letter described—by Count Baldassare Castiglione. The scene represented a city-street with real houses. Castiglione also provided *intermezzi*—ballet and mythological pageantry.

In the letter in which Gabriel Harvey reproaches his friend Spenser for not emulating Ariosto's comedies rather than his *Orlando Furioso*,—which last Harvey evidently felt to be beyond Spenser's powers,—he gives a glowing eulogy of the Italian classical comedy, and names as its chief masters "Those three notorious dyscoursing heads, *Bibiena, Machiavel,* and *Aretino* . . . (to let *Bembo* and *Ariosto* pass)." Why Bembo, I do not know; but the rest do today as in 1580 stand as representative.

The quality of Pietro Aretino's five comedies, composed within the second quarter of the century, is, like that of his tragedy, due to relative defiance of rule,—though perhaps also in some degree to limitations of scholarship. They depend less on literary sources than on observation of life,—an observation directed indeed by the Roman comedy to a seamy side of life, an underworld of bawds, pimps, blackmailers, ruffians, sycophants, harlots, spying lackeys, debauched old men and raffish young ones, and predatory women, young and old. It is by anticipation Hogarth out-Hogarthed. As satire it is "strong," but it takes a strong stomach to digest it pleasurably.

Perhaps the most interesting of Aretino's comedies is *La*

[285]

Cortigiana, which I am tempted to render as "The Female Courtier," to keep the allusion to Castiglione's *The Courtier.* For the piece is a satirical travesty, in effect, upon Castiglione's ideal high society.

A small-town person, one Messer Maco of Siena, comes into an inheritance, and decides to visit Rome. There, like Bob Acres in London, he is taken in hand by a plausible acquaintance, who promises to induct him, after proper grooming, into polite Society. Messer Maco is then made fit for that by being made at home in the lowest dives of the city!

The title-rôle of Aretino's *Ippocrito,* the "Hypocrite," is said to have been Molière's model for Tartuffe. But if so, the difference is as between a plaster-cast and a living figure. Indeed the fundamental defect of the comedy, as of the tragedy, of the Italian Renaissance is that it produced no outstanding or memorable character. The eye of the comic playwright was almost entirely on his plot, his *imbroglio,* his facetious situations, his epigrams and *mots.*

The nearest to an exception to this generalization is offered by the *Mandragola* (or *Mandragora*) of Niccolò Machiavelli. He wrote another comedy, *La Clizia,* but this is relatively negligible. The *Mandragola,* however, is classed by Voltaire above Aristophanes, and only second to Molière. This is perhaps not so surprising—coming from Voltaire. But moral Macaulay echoes by calling it "superior to the best of Goldoni, and inferior only to the best of Molière."

According to the prologue the piece was written as an antidote to melancholy in the first years of Machiavelli's rustication at San Casciano. Paolo Giovio, the biographer, says the story is based on fact, and the characters were well known in Florence; but modern critics dispute this. In any case, the characters have the stamp of real life.

The plot turns on the gradual seduction of an innocent

young wife by a city gallant, aided by an unscrupulous friend and a bribed confessor. The wife is young, but the husband is elderly—senile indeed—and most desirous of an heir. The trick is turned by playing on the old man's credulous belief in the magical properties of the mandrake-root. But though the husband is won over, Lucrezia the wife still has scruples. To overcome these becomes, for a consideration, Fra Timoteo's affair. With amusing if immoral astuteness, he finally succeeds. And the lovers are consoled spiritually as well as otherwise. After all, reflects Callimaco the gallant, "what is the worst that can happen? To die, and go to hell? Still, so many excellent people have died, and gone to hell!" And Lucrezia assures herself that she would never have yielded, had there not been at work some "influence of the heavens," *celeste disposizione*. So with a clear conscience, quite ignoring that her lover is virtually her husband's murderer, she joyfully assures Callimaco that "as it is, I take thee as my lord, my master and my guide." They are Dante's words to Virgil!

It is said that Leo X had a theatre erected in Rome to enable the people to witness the piece. It is also said that when *La Mandragola* was revived in Milan over three centuries later, the ladies in the audience wore masks. Whether the fact shows an improvement in morals I will not undertake to say.

Regular tragedy and comedy were both ever straining against the rules,—especially that of *decorum*, which denied the prevailing taste for thrills. By spurning the rules Giammaria Cecchi of Florence made himself the most genuinely popular playwright of his day. He composed genially in all kinds from sacred mystery to profanest farce, even occasionally penetrating into the academic camp, and adapting, after his own fashion, from the Roman comedy. Again, a little more of genius, and the independence and gay wit of

Cecchi might have given Italian comedy its place in the sun. But as it was, he wrote no notable piece. He did, however,—as Symonds pointed out,—presciently foredefine the emancipated comedy—or tragicomedy—that was to be—in England with Shakespeare and his fellows, in Spain with Lope de Vega and his. Cecchi is speaking of the *farsa*, "farce," but the name does not matter. I quote Symonds's translation: "the *Farsa* is a new third species between tragedy and comedy. It enjoys the liberties of both, and shuns their limitations; for it receives into its ample boundaries great lords and princes, which comedy does not, and, like a hospital or inn, welcomes the vilest and most plebeian of the people, to whom Dame Tragedy has never stooped. It is not restricted to certain motives; for it accepts all subjects—grave and gay, profane and sacred, urbane and rude, sad and pleasant. It does not care for time or place. The scene may be laid in a church, or a public square, or where you will; and if one day is not long enough, two or three may be employed. What, indeed, does it matter to the *Farsa?* In a word, this modern mistress of the stage is the most amusing, prettiest country-lass that can be found upon our earth." Cecchi created no *farsa* that resembles this vibrant portrait, but the word-sketch itself deserves to stand beside the famous pronouncement on his art of Lope de Vega. Cecchi's notion that the "modern mistress of the stage" was to be born into a third estate between tragedy and comedy is also interesting in connection with the development of modern social drama from the pastoral, another third between tragedy and comedy. I shall speak of this development in its place.

Actually the farce, even with Cecchi, was a far humbler form of entertainment. The word farce means, derivatively, *stuffing*. Goose *farci* still means *stuffed* goose. Originally a "farce" was a spicy episode introduced—or *stuffed*—into a solemn mystery for comic relief. Later it was—to continue the implied figure—served by itself as a separate course. As Cecchi says, it was without rules or restrictions. Most commonly it was slap-stick stuff, and between country bumpkins.

A company of actors from Siena specialized in this kind, mixing in, however, pastoral and mythological elements, and also what have been called "genre" characters—the pedant, the braggart, etc. This troupe was known as *I Rozzi*—probably from their rough and boorish rôles. Leo X summoned them often to Rome. Their type of farce is of interest to English readers, for it is precisely the same mixture as Sir Philip Sidney served up to Queen Elizabeth on her Progress through Kenilworth in his *Lady of the May*. That piece combines rustics with Arcadian shepherds, and introduces the pedant in the schoolmaster Rhombus, mouthing and mangling his Latin. Also, it has the typically Italian *dubbio,* or question of love, decided by the Lady. A more famous mingling of real rustics and arcadians, together with the genre characters of "melancholy" Jacques and Autolycus, appears in Shakespeare's *As You Like It.*

By far the most important dramatic entertainment outside the regular drama, and in international influence upon the theatre almost rivalling the regular drama, was the so-called *commedia dell'arte all'improviso.* As its name implies— "comedy of the craft," or guild,—it was the production of professional actors (and before long, actresses) in what would today be called stock-companies. In so far, these companies were like those in England that made a Shakespeare an actor-manager as well as a playwright. But although the Italian companies produced actors, and at least one actress—Isabella Andreini,—of European reputation, they produced no playwright of importance. The method itself of their acting in-

[289]

deed called for no play-*writing*. For in general, the dialogue—that is, the really literary part—of their pieces was improvised in the performance itself. Only a *scenario*, or plot-outline, was hung up in the wings. In time, indeed, an individual company would acquire a greater or smaller stock of written aids and accessories—type dialogues, rhymed tags for ending scenes, tried-out jokes and word-play, and so on. And an individual actor might repeat so many times a particular stock-part that it became second-nature with him, and he identified with it,—as in recent times Joe Jefferson with Rip van Winkle, the elder Sothern with Lord Dundreary.

The plots of the *commedianti* were gathered from everywhere and anywhere, but the favourite stage-devices and highly stereotyped cast of characters are so like those of the *commedia erudita* that the *commedia dell'arte* has been defined as a popular travesty of the former. Thus, for example, *Pantalone* (Pantaloons) is clearly after the *Senex* of the Roman comedy; the various *Zanni*, or clown-servants, from the Roman *Servi*; *il Capitano*, the braggart soldier, from the Roman *Miles Gloriosus*; and so on.

An original feature of the *commedia dell'arte*, however, was the gradual investing of these stock-characters from the old comedy with satirical local traits of new Italy. Thus *Pantalone* appears commonly as a philistine tradesman, a "Babbitt" from commercial Venice; *Graziano Dottore* is a pedant from the university town of Bologna,—a "Holofernes" mouthing big meaningless words; *il Capitano*—usually given a mouthful of a title like *Capitano Spavento da Valle Inferno* (Captain Horrific of Hell-valley)—hails from militaristic Naples, and often speaks Spanish, or at least uses portentous Spanish oaths. He is a devil with the ladies. Sometimes—not always—he is a coward, a Falstaff indeed, under his bluster.

Most famous differentiation was made in the *Zanni*. Nearest to the clever but rascally *Servo*, or valet, was *Pedrolino* (Peterkin). Favourite became the joyous simpleton and everybody's butt, *Arlecchino* (Harlequin). Only later, and especially in the numerous *Harlequinades* of the eighteenth century did he become the masked and acrobatic lover of Columbine, and his original rags were transformed into the familiar spangled and lozenge-patterned tights. He and his ballet-skirted little lady appeared regularly in Christmas pantomimes of the last generation.

Another as famous and—in a sense—longer lived was the luckless knave of hearts, *Pulcinella*, created by a Neapolitan actor at the beginning of the seventeenth century. We hear his woes still, and made truly tragic, in the opera of *Pagliacci;* and Mr. Punch is his lineal descendant, if somewhat transmogrified. The original *Pulcinella* wore a big false nose.

The vogue of the *commedia dell'arte* was in the later decades of the sixteenth century, and continued on until the middle of the next. Indeed, in mid-eighteenth century it was given a temporary new lease of life in modified form by Carlo Gozzi. Moreover, as I have said, derivative forms, like the *Harlequinade*, have flourished down to our own times—even in England and America. And one remembers the delightful French *L'Enfant Prodigue* of two decades ago,—a tragic *Harlequinade* in dumb-show.

For nearly two centuries the *commedianti dell'arte* visited, or were in residence at, all European capitals. A troupe of them accompanied Queen Elizabeth on her Progresses. Some of their stock-companies became world-famous, especially the Andreini family and *I Gelosi*. If they produced—partly, no doubt, by the very nature of their improvised dialogue—no great, or even notable, playwright, their character-types, dramatic methods and stage-business influenced most powerfully European drama and theatre alike. Lope de Vega's valets and swashbucklers, Shakespeare's clowns and clownage, not a little of Ben Jonson, and a great deal of Molière, show this influence. Ironical that the least literary *literary* output of the most literary age of a nation should be its perhaps widest known export!

The Ferrarese Agostino Beccari, presenting in 1554 *Il Sacrificio,* announced it in one of the two prologues as the first pastoral drama. The claim may perhaps be allowed to the extent that is allowed the similar claim of Bishop Hall to have written the "first English satire." Limiting satire in English to the strictly classical type imitated from the Roman satirists, *maybe* Hall was justified. Limiting pastoral drama to its definitive form, which—as perfected by Tasso and Guarini —spread throughout Europe, *maybe* Beccari was justified. He *is* justified by Guarini. In that case, the many and varied pastoral pieces *acted* before 1554 must be regarded as merely tentative approaches to the genre. In fact, such is the implication of Beccari's own historical *résumé* of the developments of and from the classical eclogue in the same prologue,— which so is, by the way, a rather interesting anticipation in principle of evolutionary criticism.

The most remote progenitor of *acted* pastoral—of course, the *Idyls* of Theocritus were *actable*—was the *Satyric* play, that third species of drama recognized by Vitruvius, as quoted at the beginning of this chapter. Indeed, the affinity between satyric, and pastoral, drama appears in a piece entitled *Egle* and presented in 1545 by another Ferrarese, the versatile Giraldi Cinzio. This is based on the one extant *Satyric* play, the *Cyclops,* but confines itself to the sylvan part. Ovid is also called on.

Advised by Egle, mistress of Silene, the fauns and satyrs in Arcadia try to capture Diana's nymphs by a trick. They pretend to abandon their children in the woods. And the nymphs, coming upon the lonely baby fauns and satyrs, do take pity on them, and play with them. But as the wood-gods rush in upon her votaries, Diana saves them by transforming them into trees, streams and other unmanageable objects. This disappointing outcome is narrated by the "messenger" Pan, who enters with a reed—all that is left of his beloved Syrinx.

Giraldi's play has the full Senecan form—five acts, scene-division, lyric choruses, dénouement by messenger, blank verse. It has the setting and all the earmarks of full Renaissance pastoral, or shepherd-play—except indeed *shepherds*.

But for the matter of that, for a real shepherd-play anticipating anything in Italy, and delightfully mingling the rustic and arcadian motives of the *pastourelle*, we may go back to the twelfth century *Robin et Marion* of Adam de la Halle. But it is unlikely that Beccari would know of this.

In Italy Poliziano's *Orfeo* seems first to have demonstrated the effectiveness of classic pastoral—here, as so generally later, blended with mythology—for courtly entertainment. It was quickly imitated at Ferrara in the Ovidian *Cefalo* of Niccolò da Correggio. Both of these were festival pieces, and were given elaborate presentation. For more ordinary occasions simple eclogues—or eclogues with more characters and more plot—sufficed. For instance, in 1506 Castiglione provided an elegant eclogue in which the shepherd *Tirsi* avers—like Tityrus in Virgil's first eclogue of Rome—that he has been drawn to Urbino by its renown, and finds rumour all inadequate. He then compliments the Duchess as *Galatea*, and the ladies of her court in their degrees. It anticipates the vein of Spenser's *Colin Clout's Come Home Againe*.

Or an eclogue may be enriched by a simple plot, as in one presented before Lodovico *il Moro*, in which two shepherds debate a question of love, and invite Lodovico to decide—as in Sidney's *Lady of the May* Queen Elizabeth herself is invited to decide the issue between the *forester* Espilus and the *shepherd* Therion. Or again, the eclogue may be pointed by satire, as in one presented by Serafino d'Aquila before Pope Innocent VIII covertly attacking corruption in the *Curia* itself—as in Spenser's *Shepheardes Calendar* Anglican abuses are attacked, or in Barnaby Googe's *Eclogues* Queen Mary and Bishop Bonner. These last were not acted, so far as I know; but they could have been. Sidney represents the eclogues of his *Arcadia* as acted; and we know that Garcilasso de la Vega's actually were.

Increasingly during the later fifteenth century, and earlier sixteenth, such pastoral entertainments multiplied, and became more dramatically varied and elaborate. Their experimental variation, and—after many false births—gradual approach to fixed genre—all this development interestingly supports Ferdinand Brunetière's theory of the "evolution of literary genres." In the case of pastoral drama the biological analogy works surprisingly well.

The preferred theme of pastoral drama—as of all *arcadian* pastoral—is Love, and especially the casuistry of Love. Thus one of the common issues of Renaissance debate is between the claims of Love and Friendship. An *Ecloga di Amicizia* by one Bastiano, a linen-draper of Siena, written in the early fifteen twenties, amusingly presents this issue.

The shepherd Cerfidio falls in love with Ippodamia, sweetheart of his friend Largio; but rather than wrong his friend, Cerfidio offers to kill himself. Largio, not to be outdone in generosity, counters by offering to give up the girl. Cerfidio, however, declines with thanks,—

> "E lei domanda in dono il terzo loco.
> Così tre cori avvampa un solo foco."

(And asks of her the guerdon of third place.
One flame so kindles three hearts unto grace.)

Here is hint of the superfine "point of honour" of the Spanish seventeenth century.

Beccari in his *Sacrifizio*, however, may be said to have fixated for Italy and Europe the typical love-tangle I have already referred to, in which the wrong people love the wrong people, and have to be unsnarled. Thus in the *Sacrifizio* Turico loves Stellinia loves Erasto loves Callinome loves only Diana.

But the pastoral dramatic genre itself was virtually once for all fixated in two antithetical types by the *Aminta* of Torquato Tasso and the *Pastor Fido* of Battista Guarini. They were the models ever after, so long as the pastoral drama lasted, for all Europe. They represent respectively, as types, classic simplicity and romantic variety. By such deliberate variation indeed, Guarini set out to emulate his friend's little masterpiece, which Guarini, I think, would have been the first to admit unapproachable in its own kind.

Tasso composed the *Aminta*—almost in one breath, it is said—for a midsummer festival at Ferrara. As first presented at the island-villa of *il Belvedere* on July thirty-first, 1573, it was the simplest of idyls. The choruses, interludes and episode of *Mopso* were added for the sumptuous repetition at Pesaro during the carnival of the following year. The pastoral was first printed in 1574.

The poet's immediate reward was appointment to the Chair of Geometry and the Sphere in the *Studio* of Ferrara!

The original plot of the piece is naïvely symmetrical. *Aminta* loves Silvia, once child-playmate, now huntress in Diana's train.

Act I, Scene 1

Dafne, Silvia's bosom-friend, would persuade her to love, urging that

> "il mondo invecchia
> E invecchiando intristisce."
> (the world ages
> And aging saddens.)

But Silvia is obdurate.

Scene 2

Tirsi, Aminta's bosom-friend, urges the forlorn and lamenting swain to boldness. Aye,—but how?

Act II, Scene 1

Enter the lascivious Satyr, prowling, and avowing his evil purpose.

Scene 2

Dafne and Tirsi put their heads together. Tirsi is to advise Aminta boldly to approach Silvia as she bathes at the spring.

Act III, Scene 1

Aminta comes to the spring just in time to save Silvia, bound to a tree by the Satyr. But, released, she scorns her rescuer, and rushes off.

Act IV

We are told how Aminta, despairing, has thrown himself from a cliff, and how Silvia, penitent, bewails him.

Act V

We are told how Aminta's fall has been broken by a bush, and—how all's well.

But the appeal of the *Aminta* is not from plot, nor from the purely stock-characters in the ingenuous plot. They are but pegs on which to hang a dainty garment of poetry. Set to music as it was, the piece was really an exquisite *operetta*. A pastoral "in porcelain," it introduced Europe to *"le Pays du Tendre."*

As in the case of the Alexandrian pastoral romance of *Daphnis and Chloe*, the ingenuousness of the *Aminta* appealed because its audience was sophisticated,—though it is fair to add that Tasso does not, like Longus, cater to the prurience of his patrons. On the other hand, he did slip into his arcadian idyl a bit of Ferrarese court-scandal. The added episode in which the sage Elpino woos in vain the fair Licori (I, i, 181 ff.) alludes to the Malvolio-like platonic wooing by the Duke's Minister, Pigna, of the court *belle*, Lucrezia Bendidio. The situation was quaint. Tasso—and his friend Guarini as well—had also been be-sonnetting the lady, but when the Minister became ardent, they not only conceived it the part of prudence to desist, but also took occasion to win favour by editing and annotating Pigna's own *canzoni* to his ideal mistress. Meanwhile, she was the real mistress of Cardinal Luigi d'Este, and was writing to him disrespectfully of "the bridegroom of the white beard," *lo sposo della barba bianca,* as she called her elderly admirer.

One may be sure the Ferrarese court knew about all this, and found amusement in Tasso's sly allusions.

Among the spectators at the original performance of *Aminta* was Guarini, who tells later of the delight he took from the piece, and of his own resolve then and there to emulate, and if possible to outdo, it. One may say that as against genius Guarini brought talent and industry. He laboured nine years at his rival piece, meanwhile submitting it to leading critics for advice. Later, when a puristic clerical critic objected to Guarini's term "pastoral tragi-comedy" as being twice over self-contradictory, there ensued a controversy filling two large volumes of the four of the poet's works. Guarini adduces unexpected evidence to support his thesis. For instance, that pastoral may rightly claim blood-kinship with royal tragedy, is evident when we remember that the Patriarchs of the Old Testament were also keepers of flocks. The whole argument is worth reading for the light it throws on the critical (?) habits of mind of the period. Also, from the resultant definition of "pastoral tragi-comedy" appears to be derived John Fletcher's definition of that mixed genre in the preface to his own *Faithful Shepherdess*, itself an imitation of the *Pastor Fido*.

The *Pastor Fido* has affiliation with Greek tragedy in that its action is the working out of an ambiguous Oracle, according to which an Andromeda-like sacrifice exacted of the Arcadians must continue until two of divine descent are joined in marriage. Thus hero and heroine are of even more than "tragic" stature. Silvio and Amarilli are judged to be the fated pair. But alas! there opposes the typical pastoral dilemma of misfit loves. Silvio loves only the chase; Amarilli loves Mirtillo, who loves her, but is also loved by the wicked and crafty Corisca, who is loved by the lustful Satyr, while to complete the vicious circle, unloved Dorinda loves loveless Silvio. We are brought "near to deaths,"—as also Fletcher allows to tragi-comedy,—when Amarilli, tricked by Corisca into a compromising situation, is condemned to die. But Mirtillo offers to die in her place, and so shows himself to be the "faithful shepherd" of the Oracle. And then, at the eleventh hour, it is revealed that Silvio and Mirtillo had been exchanged as babies; so that Mirtillo is really the fated seed of the divine Hercules. Thus by the familiar device of "recognition," tragedy becomes comedy. And the happy ending is made complete by Silvio, like Tasso's Silvia, finally being moved to love by pity,—when he unwittingly thrusts his hunting-spear into the constant Dorinda, who to be near him has disguised herself in a wolf-skin. Even the wicked Corisca repents, and is forgiven.

Guarini has worked in almost every known stage-trick, and with clever craftsmanship. And in fairness, it must be remembered that these theatrical devices of ambiguous oracle, substitution and recognition, tangled love-chain and the rest, had, relatively speaking, not yet been staled by frequence. If Guarini's poetic style has not Tasso's limpid sweetness, it is nevertheless finished with all the conscious art of the late Renaissance. In spite of their conventional pastoral labels, the characters of the *Pastor Fido* are much nearer to real life than are the graceful shadows of *Aminta*. Indeed the Machiavellian Corisca is as vital a creation as any in the drama of the period. Her scenes with the Satyr have a broad Elizabethan humour,—as when the brutal wood-god seizes her by her luxuriant hair, *and it comes off in his hands!* It was such grossness as this that made fastidious De la Mesnardière adjudge a "shepherdess" like Corisca unfit to be in courtly "Arcadia."

Guarini is at pains to emphasize his rivalry with Tasso. His fourth chorus for instance, exactly—rhyme for rhyme— matches Tasso's first; and celebrates, instead of the *freedom*, the *fidelity*, of the Golden Age.

The *Pastor Fido* was given a sumptuous first performance at Crema in 1596. It was published in 1590, but in definitive edition in 1602. Its success was immediate and enormous. It went through forty editions in the seventeenth century, forty more in the eighteenth,—and many of these were printed outside of Italy. It was translated into all principal European languages. Imitations were countless.

According to the interesting thesis of Jules Marsan in his comprehensive study of the pastoral drama Alexandre Hardy, by following farther along the lines started by Guarini, ended by transforming pastoral tragi-comedy into modern social comedy or comedy of manners,—"mistress of the modern stage," to borrow Cecchi's phrase. At the end, Hardy had only to alter names and setting.

In general, I think it may be said that the astonishing appeal—astonishing to us who merely *read* the sentimentally jejune texts—of the acted pastoral during full three centuries, —Crabbe is still protesting against them at the beginning of the nineteenth,—that this appeal was due less to text than to accessories. During the Renaissance itself, not only were pastoral plays given sumptuous settings, and enlivened by music and ballet and spectacular interlude, but also were presented out of doors among real trees, arbours, glades and grottoes. In recent years there have been presented in such a natural setting several of the more notable English Renaissance pastoral dramas at Wellesley College. I am sure that none who saw these would account them dull or insipid.

Still, as *literature*, the passing of the pastoral is not to be regretted.

XX

TORQUATO TASSO

NO poet has ever had as romantically poetic a legend as Torquato Tasso,—not Greek Sappho, nor Spanish Macias, nor English Sidney, nor German Heine. These sang a hopeless love, were

> "Most musical, most melancholy."

But Tasso was the veritable "Ruy Blas," loving above his station, and beloved,—caged as a madman by the jealous tyrant, her brother,—tortured,—escaping at last, only to die, poor and broken-hearted, among strangers,—and yet not before having enshrined in imperishable verse his love and his beloved. 'Tis in good sooth a moving tale! Goethe told it in a tragedy; Byron sang it as the *Lament of Tasso;* Victor Cherbuliez made it the theme of his novel *Le Prince Vitale.* And of course the poet's biographers made the most of it.

Naturally, Tasso's writings were interpreted in the light of this romantic legend. It was taken as the key to his many love-sonnets. It was made to explain the plot of his *Aminta.* He is Aminta; Leonora d'Este proud Silvia, won at last to love by pity. Even the sinister motive of his tragedy *Torrismondo*—unwitting incest—has been actually supposed to shadow forth darkly the almost equally illicit passion of vassal for high-born lady. Confession of the whole affair has been sensed again in the conspicuously placed episode at the very beginning of the *Gerusalemme Liberata*—of Olindo and Sofronia eager to suffer, each for the other, the punishment of a cruel tyrant.

When poetry so vividly reflects life, and life so romantically glosses poetry, it is almost a pity to consider too curiously the facts. But in 1895, in a monumental biography of Tasso, Angelo Solerti remorselessly and finally destroyed the legend. Tasso's story remains indeed a tragic one, but not a tragic love-story. He was a victim and martyr—but of no tyranny other than his own distempered imagination. Most of his sonnets—supposedly keys unlocking his secret heart— are addressed to other ladies, numbers of them; and most are but courtierly compliments in the Petrarchistic manner in vogue. The few to the Lady Leonora need have no more amorous significance than those so plentifully bestowed upon Queen Elizabeth by her gentlemen-poets. The *Aminta* presents the stereotyped pastoral convention, old as Theocritus, of faithful shepherd and heart-free shepherdess. As to the episode of Olindo and Sofronia, suffice it to say that Duke Alfonso himself, the alleged jealous tyrant, warmly defended it against academic critics who thought it out of place.

An excess of evidence proves that the poet's enemy was within himself. And the real key to his tragedy is in the words he put—all unwittingly—into the mouth of his Tancred:

> "Temerò me medesmo e da me stesso
> Sempre fuggendo avrò me sempre appresso."

> (I fear myself, and from myself shall hide me
> Ever, and ever have myself beside me.)

Obsessed by *idées fixes*, both of persecution and of damnation, he showed at length dangerous, even homicidal tendencies, and was of necessity confined.

By the grace of God and to the good fortune of posterity, Tasso finished his great poem, virtually as we have it, in the spring of 1575. For soon after this the débâcle began. Self-distrustful and indecisive like his father, Tasso, before publishing his work, sought approval, literary and ecclesiastical. He appealed to his princely friend Scipio Gonzaga, always his refuge in time of trouble. Gonzaga nominally accepted the task, but in reality turned it over to four others, learned and well-meaning men, but three of them sticklers for the classic rules, and the fourth a strait-laced ecclesiastical reactionary. Given their premises, it is not surprising that they found the poem no proper "epic" and certainly not a pious one, but a vain and amatorious romance. Tasso argued and pleaded on for two long weary years, and—capitulated. It was inevitable. For by the very tests he himself proposed, he had no case. The real struggle was within himself—between the instinct of his genius and his habit of obedience to authority. It was this last that won—after the man was exhausted physically and spiritually.

His first act of reparation was ingenuous. To save his poem, he declared it a moral allegory,—a thing quite unsuspected before. (To be sure, he might have pleaded the precedent of Dante and his "misunderstood" *canzoni!*) At least, he persuaded Edmund Spenser, who found "that part (*of a gentleman or noble person*) which they in Philosophy call Ethice, or vertues of a private man, coloured in his Rinaldo; the other named Politice in his Godfredo." This *ex post facto* moralization was made in the summer of '76. It proved insufficient to quiet his conscience. A year later he had determined upon radical revision of the poem itself . . . when the storm of nerves broke.

During the next three years he went from bad to worse. Trying in vain to escape from himself, restlessly he wandered from city to city, from court to court, to the retirement of a convent, to the home of his sister at Sorrento; but ever came back, as if fascinated, to familiar Ferrara,—and was ever there sympathetically welcomed. Duke Alfonso was long-suffering. The neurotic poet's constant suspicions and complaints, even an attack with a dagger upon a servant he supposed to be spying, were passed over. But finally, in March '79, there came an access of madness so violent, so abusive and threatening, that by the Duke's order the maniac—for the time being Tasso was that—was shackled and locked up in the *Spedale,* or "Hospital," of Santa Anna. This rigorous confinement lasted a year; after which he was treated gently, provided with books to read and encouraged to write, visited daily by courtiers and court-ladies and foreign guests, permitted to walk out—under charge. In fine, he was petted and made much of, but—was for seven years a prisoner.

This was not cruel treatment,—not after that terrible first year. It was exceptionally enlightened for the sixteenth century, when madmen were frequently chained and baited like bears. It was fortunate for poor Tasso, I suspect, that Duke Alfonso was a sincere lover of poetry. But naturally, the imprisoned poet himself could not appreciate his relatively good fortune. He overflowed with complaints.

During the twenty remaining years of his life after 1575, Tasso by no means lost his literary fertility. It was, if anything, greater after his break-down. He left nearly two thousand lyrics of all types and moods, the greater number composed after his incarceration. He completely reshaped and rewrote his *Gerusalemme;* he composed an "Oedipean" tragedy—*Torrismondo;* a religious narrative poem—*Il Mondo Creato*—Catholic analogue to the *Semaines* of Du Bartas. He wrote also copiously in prose—funeral orations, critical and philosophical essays and dialogues, innumerable letters. But this large miscellaneous output has added little or nothing to the fame of the poet of the *Aminta* and the *Gerusalemme Liberata*. His delicate genius was blighted. Now and then it flashed again in a lyric. But his life as a greatly creative poet ended in 1575, when he was barely over thirty.

On the other hand, his literary life began early. He was but eighteen when, in 1562, he published his first considerable poem, *Rinaldo*.

According to Tasso's own declaration many years later in an *apologia* for his father's ill-fated epic, *Amadigi*, the composition of the *Rinaldo* was in part an act of filial loyalty. The son would justify the father's thwarted plan,—would harmonize Trissino and Ariosto, epicize according to the rules popular romance. In the preface to *Rinaldo*, the young poet had exhorted his readers: "Let it not then displease you to see my *Rinaldo* composed in imitation partly of the ancients, partly of the moderns." The poem will present "one complete action of one man." It will not interweave, like the *Orlando Furioso*, various threads of action, but proceed by a "continuous and unbroken thread."

To make clearer Tasso's motives, however, and also for the light thrown on the period, I shall digress to consider the *Amadigi* itself, and its vicissitudes, briefly.

Bernardo Tasso illustrates again how precarious was the situation of a man-of-letters in the Italy of the Renaissance, especially after 1530. Not only political independence, but the individual spirit of independence, was lost. In its place grew a habit of obedience, of subservience. A poet had no recourse except to wealthy patrons, who in their turn were increasingly subject to tyrannical Spanish viceroys. The poet was no longer a citizen; he must be a courtier,—and was, in general, a servile one.

By nature and endowment, Bernardo Tasso was a man of

character and ability. He was far from the servile type, but he knew no way of livelihood but court-service. For twenty years from 1532 he served Ferrante Sanseverino, Prince of Salerno. The loyalty of the poet speaks also well for the patron. But when Sanseverino broke with the intolerable Spanish viceroy, and took refuge in France, Bernardo—despite his sixty years and a family—loyally followed his patron, though it meant confiscation of his property and exile from his beloved wife and children. Sannazaro's sacrifice for Federigo was a small thing in comparison.

The remaining years of Bernardo's long life—he lived to be seventy-six—were spent, after his return from France in 1554, in painful wandering from court to court, seeking meagre maintenance.

In 1542, in his prosperous days under Sanseverino, Bernardo had started to realize that common aspiration of Renaissance poets—to achieve an epic. Although still under the spell of Ariosto's prestige, still holding as of necessity to the materials of chivalry and romance, he sought novelty by turning to the unworked vein of the Spanish *Amadis de Gaula*. I say *Spanish*, for whatever the ultimate sources of the story, it was the early sixteenth century version of it by Garci de Montalvo to which the elder Tasso turned.

The story of the knightly Amadis of Wales and his difficult winning of the hand of Oriana, daughter of the King of Britain, was indeed a novelty for Italians,—too much of a novelty. These people from Britain, but of Spanish speech and manners, were complete strangers. Charlemagne's paladins and Arthur's knights were familiar, indeed almost naturalized Italians. Was not Orlando a *Senatore del Regno*?

Moreover, whatever appeal the adventures of Amadis might have had was lost when, in conscientious obedience to "Aristotle," Bernardo attempted to reduce their rich variety to the naked unity of "one complete action of one man," and for the flowing music of the octave stanza substituted the sluggish monotony of Trissino's blank verse—painfully hypothetical equivalent of the stately hexameter.

Bernardo's first rebuff came from Sanseverino, commanding Ariosto's metre. The courtier-poet must needs comply. Next, as his son tells, having begun reading a canto of his *correct* epic to a crowded hall, the unhappy poet finished it to an empty one. In consternation, he abandoned his academic gods, denied his Aristotle. All the variety taken out of the story was put back in. Again, "many actions of many men" were interwoven in Ariostean fashion.

It may be that Bernardo found prop and solace for this abrupt recantation in new authority. Opportunely, in 1549 appeared Giraldi Cinzio's sensible *Discorsi al comporre dei Romanzi*, distinguishing the Italian *romanzo*, or "romantic epic," from the classic epic, and defending the former as an independent genre of its own. Essentially, Giraldi's argument anticipated Bishop Hurd's defence of the "Gothic" *Faerie Queene* two centuries later.

Unfortunately, as is the tendency of converts, Bernardo went to extremes. His *Amadigi*, revised, ran three romantic "actions," and of different people, abreast,—of Amadis and Oriana, of Floridante and Filidora, of Alidoro and Mirinda, —which so continually interweave in and out that all but the very attentive reader loses the thread altogether. (Curious that one day the younger Tasso was to make precisely reverse recantation—from romantic to classic.)

Bernardo's poem appeared in 1560, and apparently fell flat. Whereupon, almost immediately young Torquato, with the intrepidity of youth and the zeal of affection, rushed in to prove his father right in the first instance,—at least in all but metre. Torquato preferred *ottava rima*.

Also, instead of the winning of Oriana by Amadis de Gaula, aliens both, the son sings in twelve cantos the winning of Clarice, sister of the King of Gascony, by the well-loved hero, Rinaldo da Montalbano. (Since Rinaldo is also winning his spurs, the poem belongs to the medieval type of *Enfances*.) Marvellous are the young hero's exploits. From the start he is resourceful. To capture the redoubtable Bayart for his charger, he interposes his own person between the infuriated animal and a tree. Bayart kicks; Rinaldo dodges; Bayart's hoofs sink deeply into the wood, and he—a humbler Ariel— is made "captive in the cloven pine." Many other incidents are as fantastic. The poet shows himself very young indeed. Yet there are forehints of the future. Rinaldo's most perilous adventure—as for a while seducing his heart from his true lady —is with the alluring Floriana, Queen of Media. Anticipated is the seduction of the other Rinaldo of the *Gerusalemme Liberata* by Armida,—only in fainter colours of drama, imagery, style. Also in the idyllic episodes of the poem is audible the note of wistful brooding melancholy most intimately characteristic of Tasso always. But as a whole, the work can hardly be said to justify appreciably the epic formula announced, or to attain epic dignity.

Even while finishing *Rinaldo,* as it would seem, Tasso wrote what is marked simply "Canto I." There are one hundred and sixteen octave stanzas, many of which recur substantially in the first three books of the *Gerusalemme Liberata.*

The mid-century was ripe for a crusading epic. A number were written—a *Liberazione di Terra Santa,* a *Siriade,* a *Malteide,* a *Croce Racquistata,* and others—but now remembered only by bibliographers. Already Ariosto, already Dante, had reproached the Pope for allowing the Holy Sepulchre to remain in the hands of the infidel. And certainly, such pious enterprise was wholly congenial to the mood of the Catholic reaction setting in with and after the Council of Trent.

Unfortunately, the boot was rather on the other foot. The pressing question now was not of attacking the infidel in Palestine but of keeping the infidel out of Europe. The Turks had invaded Hungary, besieged Malta, Nicosia, Famagosta; Biserta, La Coletta, Tunis had been won back, and again lost; with more and more difficulty Venice defended her wide-flung dominions; the very coasts of Italy were being raided. There had, indeed, been heroic defence; and Lepanto was a "famous victory," even if made sterile by the cowardice of Philip II. Italian independence might be lost; but there was imperative call to a larger patriotism—for imperilled Christendom itself. There would be inspiration in the memory of the triumphant first Crusade.

To these larger influences there were added, for young Tasso, personal ones. Kindly Don Angeluzzo, preceptor of his boyhood, had filled his imagination with tales of the Crusaders, and with legends associated with the tomb of Pope Urban in his own monastery at Cava dei Terreni. And imaginings had been translated into dread reality when, in 1558, his sister, with other girls of Sorrento, was all but carried off into captivity by Turkish raiders.

By 1570 the brief *Libro I* had developed into several cantos of the *Gerusalemme Liberata*. Meanwhile, Tasso's life and activities had been richly varied. Most importantly, he had entered the service of Cardinal Luigi d'Este, brother of the Duke; but, since his duties were largely nominal, residence at Ferrara did not preclude frequent visits to other Italian courts. Also, in 1570 he went in the train of the Cardinal to Paris, where he met Ronsard. Then, suddenly, for reasons unknown, he left the Cardinal's service to enter the household of the Duke,—by singular coincidence so repeating the experience of his great rival, Ariosto. In '73 came the great success of the *Aminta*. In '75 the *Gerusalemme Liberata* was completed, and dedicated to the Duke, in whose service he had spent the three happiest years of his life. In spite of his terrible temperament, his thin-skinned touchiness, he had prospered, and had been even popular at court. If later, he scolded at court life, it was not—as with Ariosto—because of a manly independence disgusted with subservience and insincerity. Tasso's weakness—aggravated indeed into a mental disease far beyond his control—was like that of a spoiled, unhappy child.

But in the year 1575 he seemed altogether favoured of fortune. His genius was at its noon. And then, when all seemed assured, those dangerous symptoms of morbid self-distrust, of vacillating will, of impotent exasperation which, as I have already related, left him defeated in the two year battle with pedantry and bigotry!

But the fire of his genius was saved to the world by what may be called a *Promethean* theft. In 1580, while the poet was helpless in his imprisonment, a certain Celio Malespini at Venice pirated the poem under the title of *Il Goffredo*. Also piratically, but with relatively greater care, Angelo Ingegneri had two editions made at Parma and Casalmaggiore from a more nearly correct text. To Ingegneri is due the credit of the title *Gerusalemme Liberata*. In the same year, 1581, consent was extorted from Tasso himself for a Ferrarese edition, embodying his own corrections; but later, the cowed poet insisted that only the "bowdlerized" *Conquistata* had ever received his sanction.

In the years before 1575, when Tasso was composing his epic, he had also been entering into the grand theoretical issue of the age in criticism,—as to what were the real doctrines of Aristotle concerning poetry. No one disputed Aristotle's authority; the difficulty was to agree upon just what he prescribed. The academic tyranny in letters, corresponding to the ecclesiastical tyranny in beliefs, was, as a modern Italian critic puts it, of "the commentators of the commentators of Aristotle." In the *Discourses on poetic art* of 1567, Tasso at least takes a broader, more philosophical point of view than most. His former Professor at Padua, Sperone Speroni, accused him indeed of plagiarism. The charge appears to have been without foundation; but, as one of the four Job's comforters invited to pass upon the *Gerusalemme,* Speroni had at least ample opportunity to pay off an old score.

In any case, Tasso, in his oft-quoted definition of the epic poem, rejects the current *arithmetical* notion of unity,—mere *oneness,*—substituting for it *organic wholeness.* By this richer formula he professed to build his own epic. It is of interest to English readers as being apparently the basis of Ben Jonson's definition of the genre.[1]

To use a favourite word of the period, Tasso conceives the epic poem as a *microcosm,* or world in miniature, reflecting the real world as a drop of water might reflect the surrounding landscape. Its unity, therefore, does not depend upon there being just "one complete action of one man," as the author of the *Rinaldo* had urged, but upon a *causal correlation into one whole*—a little universe—of as many actions as you like. The true epic poet, declares Tasso, will create his little world even as God has created *His* great world. The epic poem will be one "in which, as in a little world, there would be read here arrays of armies, here battles on land and on sea, here stormings of cities, skirmishes and single combats, here joustings, here descriptions of hunger and of thirst, here storms, conflagrations, prodigies; there

---

[1] *Discoveries,* ed. Schelling, p. 83.

would be found councils celestial and infernal; there would be seen seditions, discords, errors, adventures, spells; there deeds of cruelty, of audacity, of courtesy, of generosity; there experiences of love, now happy now unhappy, now joyous now pathetic." And all this variety must be so correlated as cause and effect that "if a single part be either removed or moved to another place, the whole would go to ruin."

Now I would not say that this last requirement is satisfied by the *Gerusalemme Liberata*—or by any narrative poem whatever. It is an ideal to which the human artist can only approximate. But certainly, Tasso's hypothetical list of incidents reads like a summary of his own narrative.

Virgil begins:

> *"Arma virumque cano."*

Tasso begins:

> "Canto l'armi pietose, e il Capitano."

But Godfrey of Boulogne, the "Captain" whose "pious arms" delivered Jerusalem, is modelled rather upon Homer's Agamemnon than upon Virgil's Aeneas. Rinaldo, on the other hand, while also the Achilles of the titular action, as importantly reflects, with Armida, Aeneas with Dido. Thus Tasso interweaves the motives of the two epics of Greece and Rome much as Boiardo those of the two "matters" of France and Britain. In Tasso himself, however, there is far more of Virgil's elegiac sensibility than of Homer's serene virility.

The poem has an additional appeal. Rinaldo, namesake of the famous paladin of France and fated champion of the Crusaders, is Rinaldo d'Este, whose descendants—predicts Peter the Hermit—will be of such prowess that

> "One day shall Este's mighty Eagle run
> Along a higher pathway than the Sun."

And thus again—no less than Ariosto—Tasso conjoins with heroic poetry courtierly tribute.

And after all, history was not so flagrantly violated. Godfrey was *as good as* "Captain" of the first Crusade, and *was* elected to govern the liberated city; and a Rinaldo d'Este did live within seventy years of the event!

But then it is really absurd to raise, as did the Poet's contemporaries, such questions. His censors were quite right in saying that the poem observes neither historical accuracy nor true local colour. It does not. A certain panoply of real persons and places notwithstanding, the reader finds himself still in the "faerie land" of chivalric romance, land of glamour and magic, where fair ladies wander forlorn and valiant knights are ever at combat. Tasso's scene remains, in effect, Ariosto's, and will be Spenser's.

The focus of Tasso's plot is the wrath of Rinaldo, as that of Homer's is the wrath of Achilles; only, whereas the Greek hero, affronted by Agamemnon, sulks in his tent, the Italian hero, affronted by Godfrey, deserts the camp. In each case, victory is delayed, even put in jeopardy. But for Rinaldo, love, not wrath, is the deeper cause of his continued defection; and from this maleficent love hangs, virtually, the tale.

It is—by the poet's chronology—the sixth year of the Crusade. The Christians are building engines for the final assault upon the beleaguered city. The infidel king is worried. Indeed, the greater Infidel of Hell, Pluto himself, is worried. He assembles, and, with a mouth dripping black blood, exhorts his host of nightmare monsters—foul Harpies, Centaurs, Sphinxes, and pallid Gorgons, barking Scyllas and whistling Hydras and hissing Pythons and fire-vomiting Chimaeras and horrible Polyphemuses and Geryons. Without waiting for their Master to finish, these oddly assorted "Tartarean deities," eager to aid their own on earth,

"Go flying forth to see again the stars."

"*A riveder le stelle*"—singular connection in which to quote Dante's words on *his* issuing from Hell!

One "evil angel," craftier than the rest, seeks out Idraote, King of Damascus and a famous mage, and counsels him to send his daughter, fairest Armida, to the Christian camp—as a bait. Armida, who "under blond tresses and so delicate features" hides "hoary wit and a masculine heart," presents herself as a princess wronged by a wicked uncle, and begs for ten champions—ten will do—to right her wrongs.

Now volunteering under Godfrey is a company of "Gentle-men-Adventurers," *Avventurieri*, with also one Lady-Adventurer among them.

"Terror of Asia and lightning-bolts of Mars," these are to the "Captain" more than all the rest of his hosts together. Dudone is their leader; young Rinaldo their hero and boast.

Godfrey is overpersuaded to grant Armida's request; and the wily witch proceeds to cast her spells over this choice company. For although only the stipulated ten are assigned her by lot, she means to get more—and does. It is fair to say, however, that, witch as she is in power, she uses against the Christian knights only a woman's arts. Enough is plenty. Especially is she adept in that "*mediocrità difficile*" prescribed by Castiglione for luring on the over-timid, and checking the over-bold; so she

"On these draws rein, but those with spur doth prick,
    As unto love she sees them slow or quick."
[IV, 87]

For the moment, forced to leave camp for having slain insolent Gernando, Rinaldo escapes her wiles; but later, vengeful for his freeing her captives, she tricks him into her power, and—falls in love with him. Oversea, to the faraway Fortunate Isles, she conveys him sleeping, and there spins her web of seduction around him.

Meanwhile, disaster has fallen upon the Christians. Clorinda and Argante have burned their war-engines, and the wizard Ismeno has laid a spell upon the forest from which alone wood may be got for new ones. But at last, warned in dream that only Rinaldo can break the spell, Godfrey sends two messengers to recall him. By aid of miracle they find him, and by a miraculous mirror, in which he is made to see his own recreancy, they draw him away from the siren. In vain Armida—like Dido—protests and pleads; in vain—like Dido—raves and despairs; but then—unlike Dido—she vows death not for herself, but for the deserter. She offers herself to whomsoever shall bring her Rinaldo's head. Instead, in the last battle, it is Rinaldo who slays her champions one after the other. Then, hating and loving at once, she is about to slay herself:

> "I'll heal this wound of love with wound of dart,
> And giving death, give med'cine to my heart!"

But Rinaldo stays the stroke, promises her kingdom back, and persuades her to conversion. Her last words are of meek surrender: "Behold thy handmaid," *Ecco l'ancilla tua!* (I doubt if Tasso's ecclesiastical censor approved of this application of Mary's words.)

Alongside this central romance, but in no way connected, runs the double romance of Prince Tancredo and the two pagan damsels, Clorinda and Erminia,—the double romance and the twofold pathos. Only second to Rinaldo among the Christians is Tancredo; only second to Argante among the Saracens Clorinda. Fighting, he and she love; loving, are doomed to fight—until at last, all unwittingly, he slays her.

Beautifully her last words begin: "Friend, thou hast conquered. I pardon thee. Pardon thou also me!" But her sudden demand for baptism, however edifying, is, I think, out of character,—coming from one who up to that moment has fought so valiantly for her own faith. And one could spare the conceitful balance of Tancredo's atonement, giving

"With water life to her he slew with steel."
[XII, 68]

And then, from heaven,—with reminiscence of Dante to Beatrice,—Clorinda thanks Tancredo for her salvation. (XII, 91-2. Cf. *Par.* xxxi 79 ff.) This inversion of rôles jars. The "blessed damosel" thanking her earthly lover for *her* salvation!

But moving to the end is the tale of the "damsel errant," the dovelike Erminia, who to serve her unloving beloved Tancredo, puts on, all timorously, the plumage of the eagle, —the armour of the amazon Clorinda, her rival,—and braves, unrewarded, every peril for his sake and safety. She makes us think of Rosalind, trembling in her masculine disguise, and sometimes of dainty Perdita, and of Spenser's Pastorella.

These love-stories—together with the brief one of Olindo and Sofronia—are the "fringes" which Tasso admits he has "embroidered upon truth," and for which he asks pardon of the heavenly Muse. (I, 2.) They are the "sweet syrup" with which he has rubbed the brim of his medicinal cup, that so the reader, like a "sick child," may be deceived into drinking,

"And from deception life itself receive."
[I, 3]

It is a somewhat *different* application of Horace's maxim:

"Omne tulit punctum qui miscuit utile dulci."
[316]

There is really some logical force in the contention of Tasso's censors that the "sweet syrup" of vain and amatorious romance is so thickly spread on, and is so lusciously sweet, that it has diluted the medicinal "bitter juices" out of all efficacy.

The contention is logical, but quite irrelevant. I do not think the poet of the *Liberata* meant, or expected, to be edifying or heroic,—beyond, at any rate, a delicate *dilettantism* of virtue. He was himself subdued to the temper of the court in which and for which he wrote. In this *fin-de-siècle* society, paganism was *demodé;* piety was fashionable, and a thing of fashion. There was no question of really austere morals or deep faith. For aristocratic Catholic reactionaries the northern reformers were above everything detested as boors and bores. Even for unaristocratic Pietro Aretino Luther was *"pedantissimo."* Late Roman pagans felt much the same social and intellectual disdain for the early Christians.[1]

I should be inclined to reverse Tasso's figure, and to make romance the substance of his poem, history the seasoning,— the "bitters" of actuality giving a spice to the "syrup" of sentimental fiction. I do not think the readers of his own day, or since, cared or care much about the freeing of Jerusalem. The conquest of the holy city is merely the final *tableau,* one might say, to a grand opera. Godfrey himself is an excellent good man, but he hardly stirs the pulses. Outside the romantic "gentlemen-adventurers" the warriors of the Cross count for little. They are the chorus. For even upon common soldiers falls the shadow of the poet's lyric sensibility. At first sight of the holy city, each of the Christian army is supposed to exclaim (*as if to a lute!*):

> "Where from a thousand bloody streams, O Lord,
> Thou once didst leave o'ersprinkled here the way,

[1] Cf. Gaston Boissier, *La fin du Paganisme.*

Shall not I, at remembrance so abhorred,
Send forth two living springs of woe this day?
O frozen heart, why art not, melting, poured
Through eyes of mine—to flow in tears away?
Hard heart, why crushed and broken art not thou?
Forever must thou weep, if weep'st not now."

Even the hosts of Hell are not dread; they are merely grotesque. Their bloody-mouthed chieftain, Pluto, is—except for his eloquence—the ogre of a fairy-tale. In the thick of combat,—and the single combats are lively and carefully studied after the *duello*,—the combatants, like Rostand's Cyrano, exchange thrusts of wit as well as of sword. Homer's heroes make taunts; Tasso's epigrams. 'Tis pity, by the way, that at the very last Argante is made to commit a felon act of treachery; for on the whole, he is, in his virility and audacity, the most nearly *epic* figure.

Tasso writes at his best for ladies and of ladies. His actual audience was largely—certainly, most influentially—feminine. More than that, the men in it tended towards effeminacy; Tasso himself did. The really living characters of the poem —Sofronia, Clorinda, Erminia, Armida—are women. There is not a little that is womanish in Tancredo and Rinaldo.

Psychologically allied to this effeminacy of mood are the lusciousness and preciousness of manner. Sensuous appeal and stylistic artifice reach a point beyond which is only the decadent. This dangerpoint is now and then, perhaps, passed. *Curiosa felicitas* is too "curious" in couplets like these among many:

"Vince fortezza, anzi s'accorda, e face
Sè vergognosa, e la vergogna audace."
[II, 17]

(Courage doth conquer, rather accord uphold,
And shamefast makes itself, shamefastness bold.)

[318]

"Di natura, d'amor, de'cieli amici,
Le negligenze sue sono artifici."
[II, 18]

(To nature, love and heaven dear at heart,
Her every negligence is finest art.)

"Seguì le guerre; e in quelle e fra selve
Fera agli uomini parve, uomo alle belve."
[II, 40]

(When she to battle or through forest ran,
Wild beast to men she seemed, to wild beasts man.)

Dante anticipated, and Dryden approved such "beautiful turns on words" as

"Ahi! tanto amò la non amante amata."
[II, 28. Cf. *Inf.* v, 103]
(Ah! the belov'd unloving so he loved.)

But verbal—like other—*legerdemain* is hardly great art, heroic art. And the passages I have quoted are all from the one episode of Olindo and Sofronia, which is both heroic and romantic. But the overabundance of conceits trivializes what was meant to be heroic. On the other hand, where the situation is purely romantic,—as in the love-scenes of the Fortunate Isles,—the intricately interwoven *arabesques* of sound and sense are appropriate and exquisitely finished. Take these lines of a Siren of the "Fountain of Laughter":

"Rideva insieme, e insieme ella arrosia;
Ed era nel rossor più bello il riso,
E nel riso il rossor che le copria
Insino al mento il delicato viso."
[XV, 62]
[319]

The best even Edmund Spenser can do is to give the sense:

> "Withall she laughèd, and she blushed withall,
> That blushing to her laughter gave more grace,
> And laughter to her blushing, as did fall."

Here is the pretty idea; but where the really "beautiful turns on words," the caressing alliterative interplay of liquid l's and tripping r's—everything that makes the original a tiny masterpiece of verbal art?

But this very Boucher-like exquisiteness justifies, in principle, Tasso's critics. The *Gerusalemme Liberata* was submitted to them as epic *par excellence*, an heroic and indeed sacred poem upon one of the most significant events in Christian history. And if they adjudged Tasso's work to be neither heroic nor edifying, who can blame them? That their own ideas were pedantic and bigoted is beside the point. What they obscurely wanted was a Catholic Milton. And what an antithesis to the stern, uncompromising, Puritan "trumpet-voice of England" was this brilliant, sensitive, sensuous, temperamentally pagan Italian!

Tasso himself became sincerely convinced of his critics' rightness. But least of all did he realize that, for the end sought, not the poem must be remade, but the poet reborn. He did what he could in his last years—from 1587 to 1592—to make over his poem into a correct epic by "Aristotelian" rule and ecclesiastical precept. He produced a creaking mannequin. His complacency towards the incredible *Gerusalemme Conquistata*—as he chose to call the revised poem—may no doubt be laid to an enfeebled mentality; but at all times epic —as tragedy, as evidenced by his unhappy *Torrismondo*— was alien to his genius, even to his understanding. But fortunately, in spite of him, his unspoiled work lives, and shows him at his best: a matchless storyteller,—for what else can make the *Gerusalemme Liberata* the most widely popular book in Italian literature?—creator of a few memorable *silhouettes* of fair women, exquisite word-painter of idyllic panels, poet too in whom—through all the artistry and artifice —are to be felt the "tears of things."

If one may imagine Tasso's brilliant sparkle and opulent sensuousness made ends in themselves, and unenriched by the humanity of his genius, one will have fairly defined the poetry of Giambattista Marino, famous singer of *Adonis* and *Kisses*. And this soul-less simulacrum of Tasso definitively marks the Italian Renaissance in final decadence.

XXI

MARINO

IL Cavaliere Giambattista Marino has fallen upon evil days. His countrymen have come to hold him up as the arch-example of decadent taste, of *secentismo,*—literally a *mal-de-siècle*, "seventeenth-centuryism." The late Edmund Gosse gave him an undesirable prominence in English literary history. In the well-known essay *From Shakespeare to Pope,* Gosse says in effect that John Donne begat what Dr. Johnson called "the Metaphysical School" in English poetry, and that Marino begat the *metaphysical* John Donne,—as well as other less worthy word-jugglers and conceit-mongers of the period.

Marino, indeed, hardly deserves this evil eminence. He certainly did not father Donne. It would be hard to imagine more complete opposites than the virile, deep-feeling and deep-thinking Englishman and the volatile, superficial, effeminate Neapolitan. Besides, Donne had formed his highly individual style by the early nineties. The first part of Marino's *Lira*—or collected lyrics—was not published until 1602. And it seems unlikely that any of his work would have been accessible to the English poet before then. Still, Marino did influence, if not Donne, other Jacobean and Carolinian poets, —notably Lord Herbert of Cherbury and Crashaw; and his poetic style, both languishing and corruscating, undoubtedly appealed to the period.

Marino's eminence in his own day was far from an "evil"

one. He was internationally recognized as the supreme living poet of Italy; and the prestige of Italian art and literature still held. Up to the last ten years of his life, indeed, he experienced rather violent ups and downs. Like most poets of the age, he subsisted on patronage, and passed from patron to patron according as the subsistence was good. In 1600, indeed, he left his native Naples suddenly—for the still more pressing reason of avoiding jail for a second time. And in 1611 at Turin he was jailed again,—this time for slander. More than once he suffered actual want. However, these were but spots on the ever mounting sun of his glory. Leaving Naples at thirty-one, he divided the next twenty-three years almost equally among Rome, Turin and Paris, and was the literary sensation of each capital in turn. In 1623 he returned to Italy. Turin and Rome gave him a triumph; Naples received him as a divinity. Two years later he died. On his tomb was inscribed *Poetae sui saeculi maximo*.

His literary success was indeed extraordinary. His early work *Baci*, "Kisses,"—imitated from the Basia (1539) of the Dutch humanist Secundus,—created a furore in manuscript. On publication it was translated as its author boasts, into French, Spanish, Slavonian. Austere Milton praised it. At Turin he received from Carlo Emanuele I the Cross of Sts. Maurizius and Lazzarus; at Paris—for his *Adone*—from Marie de'Medici the pension of a thousand *écus* and the title of Chevalier. The Hôtel de Rambouillet idolized him; all Italy listened to him as to an oracle.

Out of his successful experience Marino formulated a new poetics, and put it into verse. The fundamental tenet of his poetic creed is in this couplet:

"È del poeta il fin la meraviglia:
  Chi non fa stupir vada alla striglia."

> (Astonishment's the poet's aim and aid:
> Who cannot startle best had stick to trade.)

One way to "startle" is to say quite ordinary things in an altogether extraordinary manner. Thus, for instance, if we say not just *stars*, but

> "Blazing half-dimes of the celestial mint"
> (Ardenti zecchini della banca del cielo),

or

> "Translucent holes in the celestial sieve"
> (Buchi lucenti del celeste cribro),

or "luminous lambkins" (*agnelle luminose*), or when in one breath we call Love

> "A lynx light-lacking, and a blindfold Argus,
> A sucking ancient and an ancient suckling,
> A wise know-nothing, naked and full-armed," etc.

> (Lince privo di lume, argo bendato,
> Vecchio lattante e pargoletto antico,
> Ignorante erudito, ignudo armato),

we "startle," we astonish. Much of Marino's poetry is a tissue of such astonishments. After a time, however, conceit on conceit ceases to astonish, merely bores. At least the twentieth century reader is bored. Apparently the seventeenth century one was not,—which only proves once more the relativity of taste.

To this "startling," corruscating style of verbal fireworks —*meraviglia*—Marino adds the complement of what he calls *leggiadria*, "grace." In effect, his *leggiadria* is a tone of effeminate voluptuousness, a scenting of his conceits with sentimental musk.

On this double recipe he composed lyrics in many forms and moods—except of real passion. We turn his pages.

Furtive desire of a kiss—A yearning kiss—A kiss artfully asked—Jest of a kiss in request—A stolen kiss—A kiss cunningly betrayed—Dear kisses—One who hesitates to kiss—A biting kiss—Apology for a biting kiss—Sweet kisses—Looks and kisses—Affectionate and mutual kisses—Kisses sweet and loving—Bitter-sweet kisses—War of kisses: so run, with a few plain kisses left out, the titles of as many consecutive madrigals, *canzoni*, eclogues. All this is not improper. It is not virile enough to be. It is sentimental philandering, at worst mawkish, sometimes languidly pretty. We hear Shelley—faintly—in this Anacreontic echo:

> "Vita dell'alme è il Bacio
> E vita è di Natura.
> Mira mentr'io ti bacio
> Colà per la verdura:
> Non vedi come strette
> Baciano i fior l'erbette?
> Bacian l'onde le rive?
> Bacian le fronde ancor l'aura lascive?"

> (Life of the soul the Kiss is;
> Life it is of Nature.
> Whilst I kiss thee, look
> Yonder over the greening:
> Seest thou not how close
> The flowers kiss the grasses?
> Kiss their banks the ripples?
> Kiss the trembling leaves the wanton zephyrs?)

There is a real picture in this tiny idyl. Shelley's perspective is grander; his imagery more vivid:

> "See, the mountains kiss high heaven,
> And the waves clasp one another;
> No sister flower would be forgiven

> If it disdained its brother;
> And the sunlight clasps the earth,
> And the moonbeams kiss the sea . . ."

Still, these gorgeous lines present an argument, not a visible picture. We cannot *see* sunlight and moonbeams both at once.

In general, Marino's lyrics express an emotional impressionism pure and simple. But a moral lesson—so the author says—underlies the epic *Adone*. To make sure that Marie de'Medici, to whom he dedicates the work, may not miss the moral, he states it briefly:

> "So, of the veil that here my spindle weaves
> In tender verses, fabulous and vain,
> Let gathered be this sense, which not deceives:
> *Immoderate pleasure terminates in pain.*"

It would hardly seem a lesson so recondite as to need forty-five thousand lines for its demonstration,—unless indeed the linkèd sweetness all too long drawn out be itself part of the proof.

The plot is an odd mixture. Venus, enamoured of young Adonis, wins by Cupid's aid his love. But, pursued by implacably jealous Mars, Adonis is forced to flee from Cyprus; and though after many adventures he returns, and is crowned as consort of the goddess, he soon—by Mars's contrivance— is fatally wounded by a wild boar. (One is inclined to applaud the boar.)

By coincidence, this last long narrative poem of the Italian Renaissance is spun out by methods quite like those used in the first significant one of the Italian revival. I mean the *Stanze* of Poliziano. As it happens, that poem also told of the victory of Venus and Cupid over a heart-free youth. If Poliziano had filled his design on the scale begun, he might well have approached the length of the *Adone*. In the fragment finished, from the slender thread of narrative is hung panel after panel, word-painted, of scenes mythological, pastoral, legendary, historical, allegorical out of classical antiquity. So is it in the *Adone;* only, since the design *is* filled out, the number of panels is many times multiplied. The decadent taste of the time is appealed to by an endless variety of effeminately sensual pictures, varnished over with a style of conceits and of syrupy sweetness—*meraviglia* and *leggiadria*. Of course, this is very different from the classic refinement and restraint of Poliziano's *Stanze;* and yet even Poliziano has his conceits, is occasionally "precious." Behind him and Marino both is the common vice of *Quattrocento* humanism,—overstress upon form, upon decoration. At the end, art is sunk in the artificial. A *precious* style does not mean a style of great value. "Beauty-treatments" rarely produce beauty. There is at least *some* justice in moral Ruskin's verdict: "All the Renaissance principles of art tended . . . to the setting of Beauty above Truth, and seeking for it always at the expense of truth. And the proper punishment of such pursuit—the punishment which all the laws of the universe rendered inevitable—was, that those who thus pursued beauty should wholly lose sight of beauty . . . The age banished beauty, so far as human effort could succeed in doing so, from the face of the earth, and the form of man. To powder the hair, to patch the cheek, to hoop the body, to buckle the foot, were all part and parcel of the same system which reduced streets to brick walls, and pictures to brown stains. One desert of ugliness was extended before the eyes of mankind; and their pursuit of the beautiful, so recklessly continued, received unexpected consummation in high-heeled shoes and periwigs,—Gower Street and Gaspar Poussin."

This highly Ruskinesque tirade applies of course beyond

the art and age of Marino. Still, it applies to these also,—except that for the prevailing ugliness there were other and more definite factors at work than merely "the setting of Beauty above Truth." Indeed, the causes of decadence in Italy at the turning of the century—from the *Cinquecento* into the *Seicento*—are all too obvious. There counted, no doubt, "faulty principles of art,"—that humanistic concern so much less with what is said than with how it is said; but against sane and sound genius this overstress might work some harm, but not much. Poliziano, for seeking beauty for its own sake, did not lose it. Nor did Tasso,—for all his acceptance of "Renaissance principles of art,"—while he remained sane and sound. The trouble with Marino's generation in Italy is not that it would, necessarily, have silenced a poetic genius, had there been one, but that it exalted a Marino as one, not knowing the difference.

It may be said that Italian taste was false because Italian life was false. Certainly, since the mid-sixteenth century the plight of Italy had been growing worse. Spanish viceroys, abetted by a selfish and servile nobility, oppressed and squeezed a cynically subservient middle class, an abject and brutalized populace. To the wrongs of misgovernment were added the ravages of constant petty wars, famines, pestilences. Religious intolerance with its terrible weapon, the Holy Inquisition, crushed independent thinking and free inquiry. Scholasticism was revived. Fifty-two new religious orders were established. In the field of taste and art, pedantry organized into Academies ruled as despotically and stupidly. The social life of the upper class was heavy with pompous ceremonial and intricate etiquette. Such social conscience as there was pivoted upon the "point of honour"—stupidest of the many stupid conventions of mankind,—and enforced its decrees by the duel or perhaps by the hired *bravo*. Is it surprising that such a vitiated society should approve the distorted pomposity of the baroque in art, and Marino's tricked-up smartness and sensual languors in poetry?

The explanation seems plausible, and has been made. But there is a difficulty. Marino—and the baroque—were esteemed, if not as highly, outside of Italy. Moreover, independently, France developed her own *préciosité*, England her *Euphuism*, Spain her *Gongorismo*, while Germany gave birth to Johann Fischart, whose translation of Rabelais, if it' created no school, incorporated every verbal artifice, conceit and stylistic affectation ever devised by man. Yet none of these countries were vitiated or enervated as was Italy. It was in the full prosperity of the French Monarchy that Molière, certainly no fettered genius, ridiculed *les précieuses ridicules* of the Hôtel de Rambouillet, which had idolized and aped Marino,—ridiculed also *les femmes savantes* with their travesty of Marino in Trissotin, pet of the drawing-room.

Now I venture to think that Molière points us to an influence at least significantly contributory towards this international disease of literary "preciousness" in which the Renaissance everywhere seemed to end its days. I mean the influence, increasingly pronounced, of women,—or rather of fine ladies of formal courts and faddish coteries. Marino, Lyly, Gongora, De Scudéry and all their likes were the product of these preciously learned ladies,—as was Cyrano turned love-poet of his Roxane.

Over four generations of high-born girls in Italy had been intensively trained in the humanities,—virtually, for them, in *belles lettres*. But to the varied disciplines which go to make the modern educated woman and woman of the world these "Roxanes" of the courts of Italy, and of Europe generally, had no access. Apart from the almost purely literary character of their studies, they did not—except as reigning princesses or by private intrigue—participate in public affairs, naturally not in business, nor in the numerous administrative and executive activities of women of today. Socially, their lives were very largely a round of forms and formalities. Their minds and tastes were inbred, sensitized to the forms and formalities of literature also, but without response to its intellectual content. And they dominated polite letters, imaginative literature. John Lyly spoke, I think, for all "courtly makers," in prose or verse, when he declared he would rather his *Euphues* "should lie closed on a lady's table than open on a scholar's desk." I am inclined therefore to think that if, in the decline of the Renaissance, polite letters became everywhere more exaggeratedly "precious," it was at least in considerable part because *les précieuses* appealed to became more *ridicules*. And perhaps the climax of this literary effeminacy was reached, also in Italy, a century later in the simpering inanities of the "Arcadians."

This hypothesis finds support in the fact that in these same decadent times of the early seventeenth century in Italy, but removed from feminine influence, appeared the virile writings of a Galileo, a Boccalini, a Sarpi. These intrepid men certainly did not "set Beauty above Truth," nor "seek for it at the expense of truth." And at least one of them, Galileo, achieved rarest beauty of style. To fix the attention upon them, and not upon the effeminate Marino and his courtly kind, is to see in the turning of the new century not an old order wasting away in disease and impotence, but a new order springing in rich vitality. And yet all three connect themselves with the best in the Renaissance. Galileo carried through to epoch-making completion the principles enounced by Leonardo da Vinci that experiment is "mother of all certainty," and that "no human investigation can be called science if it does not pass through mathematical demonstrations." [1] And one recalls Dante also declaring

"experiment
Proved source of all the rivers of your arts."
[*Par.* ii, 94-5]

Malignant bigotry could humiliate and persecute the aged Galileo, but could not annul the truths he had already spoken or written,—truths the "infallible" Church now humbly accepts. More fortunate in the powerful protection of his native Venice, Paolo Sarpi joined in spirit with Dante in denouncing the temporal claims of the Papacy, and in defending the sovereignty in civil affairs of the State. And at last in our own days Dante and Sarpi would seem to be justified by the present Pope himself. With the patriot Machiavelli of the final chapter of the *Prince*, Traiano Boccalini may be said to ally himself, inveighing, under transparent allegories, against the Spanish tyranny, and crying shame upon his cowed and effete countrymen.

Unhappily, not for generations, not really until the second half of the eighteenth century, were such proudly independent moods again to produce in Italy any greatly imaginative literature. The genius of the Italian Renaissance continued indeed active, but in other lands. As Greece the Romans, so Italy conquered her conquerors in the things of the spirit. All Europe listened, and learned; and having learned, achieved for each nation a Renaissance after the Italian model. Italy, "slave" though she might be in her own house, remained nevertheless *donna di provincie*, "mistress of the provinces"—of the mind.

Proper sequel to the Renaissance in Italy is the Renaissance in the nations of Europe.

---

[1] I am indebted for these citations to Vittorio Rossi's admirable *Storia della letteratura italiana*, ed. Milan, 1930, III, 52.

APPENDIX

Sonnet of Guido Orlandi to Guido Cavalcanti:

"Tell me, where is Love born and of what sire?
Is't substance, quality, or remembrance, pray?
What is its natural place, where it holds sway?
Fancy of eye is it, or heart's desire?
From what derives its temper or its ire?
How is it felt as flame that wastes away?
Also I ask, upon what does it prey?
How, when, and over whom has it empire?
What sort of thing, I say, is Love? has't feature?
Wears it its own shape, or some counterfeit?
And is it life, this Love, or is it death?
Who serves it, should know somewhat of its nature:
Wherefore I ask you, Guido, touching it;
You're in its service seasoned, rumor saith."

Ode of Love

by

Guido Cavalcanti

I

A Lady entreats me; wherefore I will tell
Of a quality too frequently malign,
Yet so divine that men have called it Love:
Thus may the truth whatever doubt dispel.
Adept I ask unto this task of mine,
For my design, I fear me, is above

His wit that is at heart of base degree.
For me proof philosophic is defined,
Else disinclined I feel me to recite
Where Love has place; created by what might;
And what its virtue is; and potency;
Verity essential; motions of what kind;
Its name assigned as Love for what delight;
And if it may be manifest to sight.

II

In that part where the memory resides
It makes appearance; as transparence shows
Through which light flows, so Love its form acquires,
From shadow cast by Mars, the which abides.
Created hence; nature of sense bestows
Its name, and pose of soul, and heart's desire.
It comes from visible form, which, apprehended,
Ascended into passive intellect,
There, as affect, maintains its tenancy.
Never it works in that part injury.
And since from finite kind 'tis not descended,
Unended is its radiant effect.
Nor wears aspect of joy but reverie,
For may not enter there affinity.

III

It is not virtue, but from that proceeds
Which is perfection, in complexion withal
Not rational, but feeling, I attest.
The judgment Love against well-being leads,
For ravishments intelligence enthrall.
Discernment small it has where vice is guest.
Often there follows from its puissance death,
If wrath o'ermuch the faculty dismay

[334]

Which of the way adversative is ward:
Not that with nature Love hath disaccord;
But when to perfect good lies not its path,
Who saith that life is his is led astray,
Lacking the stay which makes him his own lord.
Nor less avails Love though it be ignored.

IV

Its essence is whenas the passionate will
Beyond the measure of natural pleasure goes;
Then with repose forever is unblest.
Still fickle, smiles in tears it can fulfill,
And on the face leave pallid trace of woes.
Brief are its throes. Yet chiefly manifest
Thou shalt observe it in the nobly wise.
To sighs the new-given quality invites;
Through it man sights an ever-shifting aim,
Till in him wrath is kindled, darting flame.
Conceive it none save one its puissance tries.
Complies it never though it still incites;
And no delights one seeketh in its name,
Neither great wisdom, sooth—or small—to frame.

V

A glance Love draws from like-attempered heart
Which seeming right to all delight implies.
In secret guise Love comes not, so declared.
Indeed not scornful beauty is the dart.
For that way led desire through dread is wise,
But merit lies with spirit that is snared.
And not to sight is Love made manifest,
For by its test o'ertaken man falls white;
And, hears one right that form is seen by none,
Then least by him that is by Love undone.

Of color of being Love is dispossessed.
At rest in shadow space it cancels light.
Without false sleight saith a faith-worthy one,
That from it only is the guerdon won.

VI

Ode, thou mayst go thy ways, unfaltering,
Where pleases thee: I have thee so adorned
That never scorned shall be thy reasoning
By such as bring to thee intelligence:
To bide with others maks't thou no pretence.

Ode of Love
By Girolamo Benivieni

Stanza I

Love, from whose hands suspended hang the reins
Unto my heart, who in his high empire
Scorns not to feed the fire
By him enkindled in me long ago,
Would move my tongue, my faculties inspire
To tell what my enamoured breast retains
Of him; but courage wanes;
My tongue to utter such high things is slow,
Balks at the burden, nor excuse can show;
And yet my message it must needs impart,
Strength against greater strength availing nought.
Since Love has promised to my sluggish thought
Those wings wherewith he entered first my breast,
Therein on high to nest,
And thence, methinks, now never to take flight;
So in the guiding light
Of his live glory I may still disclose
What of him privily my spirit knows.

[336]

APPENDIX

Stanza II

I tell how Love from its celestial source
In Primal Good flows to the world of sense;
When it had birth; and whence;
How moves the heavens, refines the soul, gives laws
To all; in men's hearts taking residence,
With what arms keen and ready in resource,
It is the gracious force
Which mortal minds from earth to heaven draws;
How it may light, warm, burn; and what the cause
One love may earthward bend, one heavenward bear,
A third sustain midway 'twixt earth and heaven.
My feeble rhymes, and ye lame and uneven
Verses, for you may there be some to care,
So that to worthier prayer
Of kindled heart Apollo may incline;
Too heavy for neck of mine
The yoke: O Love, on my weak wings now plight
The promised pinions, and the blind way light!

Stanza III

When from true heaven deflected, radiance flows
To mind angelic from the highest sun,
And on that first-born one
Pours light and form through living leaves defined,—
This, that its first good longs to look upon
By natural desire which for that glows,
To that, reflected, owes
Power to express the wealth in itself shrined.
Then is the first desire which turns the mind
To the living sun of uncreated light
More wondrously inflamed and set on fire.
That heat, that glow, that flaming of desire,
Which, in the mind obscure by heavenly light

Kindled, now makes so bright
The mind angelic, is the first and true
Love, the devotion due
Born then of want and wealth when of the skies
She was conceived whom Cyprus glorifies.

Stanza IV

This Love, for that he on the amorous breast
Of the fair Cyprian at the first has lain,
To follow still is fain
The starry splendour of her fairest face.
Hence our first stirrings of desire attain
Through him an object newly manifest;
And sharing his high quest,
The way to highest good we too retrace.
By him the fire through which his living grace
Distils, in us is lit; in flames whereof
The heart consuming dies, yet dying lives.
Through him pours the live fountain, whence derives
What heaven then shaping here below does move.
Diffused is through this Love
That light in us which leads us to the skies.
Through him within us rise
Splendours reflected from the sun supernal
Until our souls are lit with love eternal.

Stanza V

As from first good the eternal intelligence
Is, lives, conceives, so conceives, moves, creates
The soul; where germinates
Each living ray shed from the breast divine,
Till from the soul's meek brooding emanates
That which endowed with motion then and sense,
Through the soul's influence,

[338]

Lives, feels, fulfilling each innate design.
And from that soul, as the heavenly from God's shrine,
Is earthly Venus born, whose beauty lights
The skies, inhabits earth, is nature's veil.
The heavenly, who from the sun is mirrored pale
Within his shade whose musing she incites,
As she receives her lights
Ev'n from the living sun that in her glows,
So she her light bestows
On the earthly; and while sacred love is hers,
To her base sister love profane defers.

Stanza VI

Whenas full-formed first from the countenance blest
Down hither to descend the soul departs,
It from the highest parts
That lodge the sun to man's heart takes its way;
Wherein applying with consummate arts
Virtue whereof 'tis from its star possessed,
And bearing in its breast
Models ertswhile celestial,—well as may
Avail its tools, it builds of human clay
Its house, moulding such matter into form
As thwarts now less now more its high designs.
And sometimes will the sun that therein shines
Stamp on another heart the imprinted form;
Which, meetly matched, will warm
That soul; and lodging there will erelong blaze
Far fairer in the rays
Of that soul's virtue: whence is it decreed
That loving hearts on a sweet error feed.

Stanza VII

On a sweet error the heart feeds, its dear
One deeming that which of itself was born;

May this then readorn
With light divine whereof it is possessed—
A rare, high gift!—and still thus upward borne,
May grade by grade to the uncreated sphere
Return, whence fashioned were
All beauties in the loved one manifest.
One sun enkindles from that countenance blest
Through three refulgent glasses every grace
That mind and soul and body here adorns.
Thus first the eyes, next through these whence sojourns
Its other handmaid, does the heart embrace
That fairness, though less base,
Not full expressed; until from many fairs
The heart from matter tears,
Is shaped a type, wherein what nature rends
In all asunder, into one image blends.

Stanza VIII

Thus by this type love heart and soul delights;
On this, as on their offspring, still they smile;
Where long-sought truth the while
Is as a sun-ray under water seen.
For in that imaged fairness glimmers still,
Though darkly, something sacred that invites
The gentle heart to heights
Where a more perfect beauty sits serene.
There not the shadow that on earth has been
Sole witness of true good, the heart shall find,
But clear light and the true sun's image true.
If gentle heart those sacred signs pursue,
It finds that image planted in the mind;
Thence soars to more refined
And pure light circumfused about that sun
By whose eternal, one

[340]

Glory illumined, loving, are made fair
The mind, the soul, the world, and all things there.

Stanza IX

O song of mine, I feel Love drawing rein
On the rash ardours that my spirit move
Beyond the path appointed to aspire:
He applies the curb; he checks the vain desire.
And now, chaste ears to all that speak of love
Turn thou; and if there prove
One with thy love informed and garmented,
Before him do not spread
Thy garner's frondage only, but its fruit;
The first alone vouchsafe to other suit.

INDEX

INDEX

INDEX